P9-DWX-550

1,000 Beautiful House Plants

and How to Grow Them

1,000
BEAUTIFUL
HOUSE PLANTS
and How to Grow Them

New, Enlarged Edition

JACK KRAMER

Harry N. Abrams, Inc., *Publishers*, New York

Designer: Gerald Pryor
Drawings by Michael Valdez

Library of Congress Cataloging in Publication Data

Kramer, Jack, 1927–
    1,000 beautiful house plants and how to grow them.

    Bibliography: p. 231
    Includes index.
    1. House plants.   2. Indoor gardening.   I. Title.
II. Title: One thousand beautiful house plants and how
to grow them.
SB419.K72   1982   635.9′65   81-10899
ISBN 0-8109-1427-1   AACR2

Copyright © 1969, 1982 by Jack Kramer
Published in 1982 by Harry N. Abrams, Incorporated, New York
All rights reserved. No part of the contents of this book may be
reproduced without the written permission of the publishers.

Printed and bound in the United States of America

Frontispiece: Aphelandra species. (Photograph by C/D Luckhart)

Contents

Preface

In 1969, when *1000 Beautiful House Plants and How to Grow Them* was first published, few guides to growing house plants were in print. In the ensuing years, almost every major publisher issued a house-plant book, so enormous was the demand for information as the greening of the American home began and intensified. During the past twelve years I have continued to grow house plants by the dozens and learned much in doing so.

Included in this new revised and updated edition is everything I know about house plants. My failures and successes with orchids, bromeliads, gesneriads, palms, ferns, cactuses, succulents, and many other kinds of plants—all is recorded. In this book you will find old favorites, popular standbys, and new discoveries. The choice is vast—here are more than a thousand plants to enrich your life and the information you need on how to grow them.

I wish sincerely to thank Andrew R. Addkison, Ben Botelli, Eldon Dannhausen, Mrs. Gold, Seaborn del Dios Ranch, Mrs. Hyacinth Smith, Carol and Red Spediacci, and Don Worth—who generously allowed us to photograph their plant rooms and personal collections of plants.

Under glass or plastic you can grow almost anything, and this greenhouse accommodates a host of plants. The display of lush ferns around the pool is particularly appealing.
(Photograph by Matthew Barr)

1 ATTRACTIVE WAYS WITH PLANTS

One plant on a window sill is attractive, but a group of them—an indoor garden—makes a picture. And when many are gathered together it is easy to water and care for each one. The garden can be part of a room or it can fill a sun porch, a bay window, or—increasingly often today—a plant room.

Under glass you can grow almost any type of plant. A lean-to (attached) greenhouse brimming with colorful or cool-looking plants will add value to your property, and in kitchen or bedroom the window unit is a cheerful plus. Living plants bring charm and freshness to any area.

Before you purchase plants and equipment, decide where the growing area will be and consider what environmental conditions you are going to be working with. Certainly choose plants for their beauty, but also bear in mind their needs. Some plants require warmth, others coolness; some grow in sun, others thrive in semishade; all need light to some degree.

GARDENS UNDER GLASS—YOUR GREENHOUSE

Years ago, only the very wealthy could afford greenhouses, but now there is a greenhouse for everyone's pocketbook. Having a place for plants makes you a gardener all year round, rather than just during those few months when outdoor weather is good. Under plastic or glass, on a roof or underground, a greenhouse full of colorful flowers and sprouting seeds fills your soul with warmth even when it is gray and cold outside. It provides a pleasant retreat from the busy world: you can sneak into your glass Eden at any time and find a totally new world. Of course a greenhouse will save you money, too, because there you can start plants from cuttings, grow herbs and vegetables, and start seeds— rather than buy seedlings in flats—to get a head start on spring.

A greenhouse can be accommodated on any property, no matter how limited the outdoor space. The greenhouse you design and build yourself, or buy prefabricated, can be small or large, sophisticated or simple in design. Prefabricated greenhouses are fine, and they are available in many sizes and styles, but building your own greenhouse has three advantages: you can adapt your structure to the exact dimensions of the available space; you can use your imagination to devise the design that will work best for you; and you can use both old and new materials. Moreover, you can save a great deal of money by doing it yourself.

This aluminum commercial greenhouse is home for many orchids and bromeliads. (Photograph by Matsumoto)

Prefabricated greenhouses are delivered knocked-down (KD), so if you opt for one you must put it together as well as supply the foundation (generally a costly undertaking). A homemade greenhouse is inexpensive or at least relatively inexpensive. For example, some excellent places for plants cost less than $50 to build—some distinctive and lovely hand-hewn ones no more than $500.

Types of Greenhouses

The greenhouse has changed greatly during the past decade and is no longer necessarily a simple glass structure. It may be built partially underground or have solar additions (panels) to conserve heat, or it may be a domed structure. If space is at a premium, you can install a window greenhouse— these are fine additions for many homes.

In addition to new structural designs there are now new techniques for growing

plants: artificial-light growing has gained thousands of followers in the past ten years, and growing plants without soil (hydroponics) is becoming popular too.

Your greenhouse can be either attached to or separate from the house, depending on what you want to use it for. If you like to display your plants, the attached unit is better: then the greenery is part of the house, and you have increased the space of your total living area. The attached unit may be adjacent to the living room, offering a pleasant view; off the kitchen, providing a cheerful note on dull days; off the bedroom, becoming a delightful addition to the daily living scheme; or even part of the bathroom, lending it a tropical look and dressing it up considerably.

The attached greenhouse offers easy accessibility in inclement weather and is the perfect place to enjoy morning coffee. If you choose an attached unit you can use existing heating facilities, adding a duct from the house furnace, and thus cut costs. The

In this handsome, modern garden-room atrium, beautiful
specimen plants abound. Three magnificent trees fill the scene
with foliage: on the right, a *Dracaena marginata* and *Ficus
lyrata*; on the left, a *Dizygotheca elegantissima*.
(Photograph by Hedrich Blessing)

12

disadvantage of the attached unit is that it is always visible to guests and thus must be kept neat.

The detached greenhouse is generally a more personal place, a place where you can conveniently work with plants. It is a potting shed, a place to propagate plants, a hospital for those plants not at their peak. Though it does not expand your living area, it can, on the other hand, be a retreat from the house if you want to get away for a while from the telephone or relatives. And the detached greenhouse can be more flexibly and imaginatively designed: an A-frame, a dome, a gazebo, an arched structure.

This type of greenhouse need not fit into the plan of the house (whereas the attached unit, of course, must). The detached greenhouse is a convenient workshop that can provide infinite pleasure. Two of its drawbacks are: it must have its own heating facilities and it is more difficult to get to when the weather is bad.

Window Greenhouses

When you add a window greenhouse to your home, you bring the outdoors indoors. You do not have to see a bleak prospect of gray concrete. You can provide your own natural scene, which will be beautiful all year because of the simulated summer conditions maintained there. What you can grow depends on what space is available; there is no other limitation. Orchids, bromeliads, vegetables, herbs, even a few annuals and perennials—all are possibilities. The kinds of plants feasible are not a problem—but space will be, so when planning the greenhouse take this factor into consideration.

You can build your own window greenhouse, have one built to your own design, or buy a prefabricated one. These greenhouses can be fitted to almost any window opening.

If you own your own home, you are the one who decides whether a greenhouse may be attached to a window; however, if you live in a rented apartment, you should —and usually must—secure permission from the owner before undertaking such a structural alteration. For you a greenhouse that can be disassembled (and most window greenhouses can be) is the best choice. Usually a landlord will not object, because a greenhouse enhances the appearance of any property. And today even the most unsympathetic superintendents are apt to have their own collections of greenery and therefore be receptive to the idea of tenants' having gardens.

If you do not have the time to make your own window greenhouse or are not handy with tools, get a prefabricated one. These units are sold unassembled at glass stores and plant shops. Before you purchase, ask if the unit can be installed from the inside, and always determine ahead of time whether you must remove the window frame or if you can leave it in place. A few models on the market are designed to fit into a frameless opening.

Perhaps the most logical place for the window greenhouse is the kitchen, because people spend a good deal of time there and a lovely green scene boosts the spirits early in the morning. And watering plants in the kitchen is convenient. If your kitchen, like so

Overleaf:
This sunroom garden was built by the author some years ago. Orchids and bromeliads predominate.
(Photograph by Joyce Wilson)

many today, has only one window, then the flow of fresh air will be blocked by a window greenhouse. If this is not objectionable, then the kitchen will probably be your first choice.

For more information on greenhouses, see my book *Your Homemade Greenhouse* (New York: Cornerstone Library, 1975).

Garden Rooms and Sun Porches

The conservatory, garden room, or sunroom of the nineteenth century was built expressly to house and display plants. So pleasant and attractive were these "plant rooms" that they are finding a place in the blueprints for many modern houses and filling many a dreary or unused area in older homes. Whether on the sun porch of an old house or

A fine garden can be accommodated in a bay window: this space contains handsome plants of many different species.
(Photograph by Jerry Bagger)

Simple but beautiful is this window garden, where ferns predominate. The curving, graceful fronds echo the gay floral-print wallpaper. Here, plants create a cheerful ambiance. (Photograph by Matthew Barr)

Even a few plants can make a window area most attractive. Bamboo makes the big statement here. Colorful geraniums sing at the base of the window. (Photograph by Matthew Barr)

The old-fashioned window garden is still a treat today. The modern touch is provided by white metal brackets and glass shelves, which support a profusion of wax begonias and cascades of ivy.

in the atrium of a new one, plants flourish in an atmosphere of light, adequate warmth, and humidity. The plants that will grow in these areas are innumerable. You can choose palms, ferns, begonias, camellias; you can have small trees in tubs; you can enjoy heliotropes, lantanas, and pelargoniums trained to grow like trees (so-called standards or standard plants). No special equipment is necessary, and locating the garden in one place makes it easy to care for.

Many popular house plants come from the tropics, but this does not mean they must be lapped in warmth; in fact, the majority prefer cool (but never freezing) nights. An unheated room is a great place for an indoor garden. I have a pantry with a south window, and here cool-temperature-loving orchids grow lavishly. It is, in fact, a small conservatory, a pleasant retreat off the kitchen. Don't overlook the possibilities of unheated but enclosed porches or storerooms for plants.

Plants in groups create an attractive setting without any special accessories. These handsome foliage plants in simple pots make an elegant accent at a patio door. (Photograph by Matthew Barr)

Seated in a comfortable chair, the owner of this window garden can enjoy hanging plants and beauty at leisure. (Photograph by Matthew Barr)

Artificial light does wonders for plants. This homemade unit with commercial canopy and lamps furnishes light for gesneriads. Note their healthy growth.
(Photograph by Matthew Barr)

ARTIFICIAL-LIGHT GARDENING

If there is not enough window space or if light is poor, closets, attics, and basements can be made into gardens by means of artificial light. African-violet enthusiasts were among the first to discover this, and they have turned many a cellar into a lovely indoor garden.

Electrical-supply stores carry the appropriate fixtures. Plastic trays to hold the plants can be purchased in various sizes and colors, or a tinsmith can bend galvanized tin to specifications. If you want to purchase a commercial unit, you can buy a table or a floor model from one of the mail-order specialty houses listed at the end of this book.

Table models come with adjustable light canopies; floor models consist of movable carts fitted with shelves, under which fluorescent tubes are mounted. Most prefabricated units are equipped with either two or four fluorescent tubes. Some models will accommodate incandescent bulbs along with the tubes.

Like a rainbow, the visible spectrum is composed of colors ranging from red to violet. Plants require blue, red, and far-red light waves in order to grow normally. Blue light enables them to manufacture carbohydrates. Red light controls their assimilation of these and also affects photoperiodism, plants' response to the relative lengths of day and night. Far-red light is one of the colors that influence plant growth. It has an elongating effect on stems and increases leaf size; it can also inhibit seed germination. Quite possibly, yellow light also plays a part in the growth of plants. Although we still do not understand all the ways light affects plants, we do know that the best sources of artificial light for indoor gardening are fluorescent and incandescent lamps.

Standard fluorescent lamps—cool-white, warm-white, daylight, and natural-white—emit red and blue waves. Cool-white has the best balance of red and blue for plant growth but sheds no far-red light. Most fluorescent lights are designed to produce high levels of red and blue but have little if any far-red. However, Sylvania's Wide-Spectrum tube does emit far-red light and a little more of the yellow-green part of the spectrum (therefore, it does not cast the purple glow usually associated with growth tubes).

If it is possible to install them, choose the eight-foot-long fluorescent tubes, which have 72–75 wattage. You can also purchase four-foot tube lengths (40 watts each), but because fluorescent tubes decline in efficiency two inches from each end, one eight-foot tube is more economical than two shorter ones. Anyone who can do simple arithmetic can accurately determine the requirements in light intensity of the plants in his own particular growing area. One easy formula that works well in most artificial-light gardens is: a minimum of 20 watts of illumination per square foot of growing area. All the plants listed below will respond well under these growing conditions, with their tops eight to ten inches from the lights.

Plants are classified as long-day, short-day, and day-neutral, but it is really the period of darkness that the plant pigment called phytochrome measures. Species vary in their phytochrome sensitivity. Long-day plants like begonias come into bloom when nights are short. If temperatures suit them, and given adequate light for the manufacture of food, day-neutral plants will bloom uninfluenced by amounts of dark and light. Short-day plants flower after experiencing long periods of darkness. A long night is so vital to some plants that light from a street lamp twenty-five feet away will inhibit their bud formation. Among these are Christmas begonias, Christmas cactuses, chrysanthemums, gardenias, morning glories, and poinsettias, none of which is a good plant for the beginner in artificial-light gardening to experiment with.

A plant's photoperiodic requirements can be determined by increasing or decreasing the half-day (twelve-hour) period of light. Most house plants are long-day (short-night) photoperiodic, and therefore require a night of less than twelve hours. For these plants, the photoperiod that will produce the best growing and blooming response for the least output is fourteen hours of light and ten hours of darkness, provided that the plants receive light of sufficient intensity to permit them to manufacture sufficient carbohydrates.

Proper temperature is also a factor in success with artificial lights. Having grown orchids in natural light, I know that cymbidiums and many coelogynes will not bloom when evening temperatures reach 65°F.; they need a cooler night—55°F., or less. However, light intensity influences response to temperatures. My cymbidiums in an

Artificial-light units can be purchased. This simple, inexpensive
arrangement provides light for almost a dozen plants.
(Photograph by Floralite Co.)

indoor environment of 52°F. bloomed freely; given more light, my outdoor cymbidiums
experienced 42°F. night temperatures and matched them in flowers. Light intensity,
light duration, and night temperature work together in influencing how plants bloom
and grow. With orchids, each kind is apparently individual in its needs.

In general, until you have gained experience with plants under lights, you will be
wise to grow only those that will thrive in temperatures comfortable to you, provided
there is about a ten-degree drop at night. This is easy to manage if your heating unit is
controlled by a thermostat: you can simply set the device lower at night before you go to
bed.

Because plants grown under artificial light never experience cloudy days, smog, or air pollution, they manufacture the sugars vital to their growth at a high, steady rate. Gray winter weeks do not keep them almost dormant, as such weather does your window plants. To keep plants well-nourished under an accelerated rate of photosynthesis, you must provide them with sufficient water and with a fertilizer somewhat weak in solution more frequently than recommended. Foliage on plants under lights is often damaged when cold water is used; a tepid temperature is best.

Here are some plants easy to grow successfully under artificial light:

Abutilon	Coleus	Hoya
Anthurium	Crassula	Kalanchoe
Aphelandra	Dieffenbachia	Lantana
Begonia	Dracaena	Maranta
Beloperone	Euphorbia	Palms
Browallia	Ferns	Pelargonium
Cactuses	Ficus	Peperomia
Caladium	Fittonia	Philodendron
Camellia	Gesneriads, especially	Rosa, particularly the
Campanula	African violets	miniature varieties
Ceropegia	Gynura	Tradescantia

Gardening under artificial light is itself the subject for a book; however, the cultural directions given in Chapter Eight apply whether you are growing plants under natural or artificial light. Follow them, and you may also want to refer to the many fine books on artificial-light gardening in your public library. You can also get a wealth of information and a good magazine if you join the Indoor Light Gardening Society of America, Inc. As of this writing, the membership secretary is Mr. Robert D. Morrison, 5305 Southwest Hamilton Street, Portland, OR 97221. Consult a horticultural society or botanical garden for the address of your local chapter.

LOBBIES AND OFFICES

Offices and lobbies in public buildings are often bleak-looking. To make them attractive, and to soften the sometimes severe lines of brick, marble, stone, and glass, interior designers have wisely learned to rely on nature. Built-in planters are now a familiar aspect of public architecture, and lush green foliage plants—and flowering ones, too—make clients and visitors feel welcome. Bromeliads and ferns are perhaps America's favorite office plants, although dieffenbachias, rubber trees, and philodendrons are close runners-up in popularity. Because bromeliads fare so well in lobbies, they have been dubbed "institutional plants."

To make plants thrive as long as possible in the office environment, proper planting is important. A rich, porous soil and adequate drainage arrangements are vital, as is regular care. Designers planning multiple-plant arrangements should select compatible types. Shade-tolerant philodendrons, ficuses, and schefferas live happily and look handsome together; dracaenas and podocarpuses make another nice association because they flourish in the same environment of bright, indirect light and ordinary house temperatures, and because their very different foliages make a striking effect together. The fine sculptural qualities of the phormium species make these plants distinguished

Research on growing plants under artificial light continues.
Here students observe a typical large-scale chamber where
many plants are being grown under lamps.
(Photograph courtesy GTE Sylvania Inc.)

This built-in planter, with a stalwart schefflera keynoting the
arrangement, would grace any public lobby. The plants' health
is assured by the skylight above and artificial light as well.
(Photograph by Max Eckert)

guests in any large area. Flowering chrysanthemums, cyclamens, and lilies offer bright seasonal color and can be replaced by other budding plants offered in season by florists and nurseries.

Container plants in offices and showrooms have indeed become commonplace —for many striking species, such as the Queensland umbrella tree (*Schefflera actinophylla*), which look as though they could flourish only in certain lush and exotic environments, actually prove hardy and adaptable in the most aseptic-looking, everyday surroundings of tile and linoleum. Whether ordered from a rental service or home-grown by an employer or employee, plants are an indispensable, tasteful, spirit-lifting decoration for places of business, and there are kinds for shade, for sun, and for every gradation in between. The three finest office specimens I have seen were a Benjamin fig (a somewhat delicate tree) thriving beside a vice president's desk, a camellia tree blooming in a New York showroom, and a standard rose ablaze with color in a doctor's waiting room.

All growing things need care, and those in institutions are no exception, for they must always be on display. Although we might not expect living plants to thrive in public buildings, in fact, they often grow superlatively well there because they receive topnotch care—better than many plants grown in the home.

Some fine foliage plants for offices are not green. This handsome philodendron—'Multicolor'—has some attractive golden leaves. (Photograph by C/D Luckhart)

2 *POTS, PLANTERS, AND BASKETS*

POTS: CLAY AND PLASTIC

Selecting containers for plants is a pleasure. Although many of the decorative ceramic jardinieres and urns on the market are attractive, you will probably choose only a few as accents, and perhaps a pedestal urn or decorative pot to complement an interior setting. For the majority of plants, I prefer ordinary clay pots. They look nice and are inexpensive; moreover, plants thrive in them because they are porous and therefore do not retain excess water, which causes root rot.

Standard clay pots, which range in diameter from two to twenty-four inches, are suitable for most plants. (Pots are always measured according to their diameter, not their depth.) A clay pot is the best choice for begonias, for many orchids, and in general for plants with scant root systems. Large Italian-style clay pots with rounded edges are most attractive, especially for camellias and citrus trees. To set off bulbs or a desert plant like an agave or echeveria, the new shallow, three-legged clay pots are excellent.

Plastic pots (choose the rigid kind) have the advantage of being lightweight, easy to handle, easy to clean, and almost unbreakable. Furthermore, algae will not grow on them, but they do retain water longer than clay pots. They come square and round, deep and shallow, with or without the conventional band at the top, and in size to twenty inches in diameter.

It is a good idea to buy saucers of the proper size along with pots. Some clay saucers now have a protective coating; they are preferable to the unglazed kinds, which do not prevent water from seeping through to stain tabletops or other surfaces.

TUBS AND PLANTERS

Square-sided or tapered tubs of redwood are fine for large plants. The wood lasts for years and needs no preservative. Tubs and porcelain containers are attractive for plants of delicate appearance; jardinieres put specimen plants on display. Glazed ceramic tubs, although handsome, usually have no drainage holes. I do not recommend them for direct planting, for gauging the exact amount of water a plant needs is tricky, and overwatering subjects the plant to the danger of root rot. I prefer to slip a potted plant on a saucer into a ceramic tub rather than run the risks of undrained, soggy soil.

A large tub with a big plant in it is heavy. Buy a dolly and put it under such a tub;

If you think all clay pots look alike, think again. There
is an infinite array of shapes and styles to choose from.
(Photograph by Matthew Barr)

then you can move it about easily as its needs or your decorative instincts indicate.

Built-in planters can be a pleasure or a pain, depending on their size and placement. If they are too large they will require more plants than you can afford or have time to care for. Committees for the beautification of churches and public buildings have sometimes discovered this to their sorrow and have had to board up all or some of their expensive new planters. As a room divider, a planter can indeed be attractive, but without overhead light few of the plants will survive—let alone flourish—for more than a month or so. In such a situation, periodic replacement of plant material will be necessary. Floor-to-ceiling windows offer a fine location for planters. Set or built in at floor level, they will break the monotony of a solid window wall and will also serve as a guardrail in front of the glass. Planters at each side of an entrance welcome guests, and, if there is a skylight there, exotic ferns and palms will thrive in them, set off by colorful flowering specimens in season—chrysanthemums, poinsettias, and lilies, perhaps.

Planters made of wood require galvanized metal insert pans. If you live near a sheet-metal shop, you can have pans made to your specifications. Remember to ask for a turned lip: sharp edges are a hazard. You can also insert purchased plastic liners in your planters.

You can grow plants in a soil-filled planter or, if you prefer, you can leave your plants in pots and place them on a layer of stones in the receptacle. If you plant directly,

Jardinieres also come in many sizes, shapes, and materials.
Here is a handsome assortment of decorative containers for plants.
(Photograph courtesy Architectural Pottery)

Glazed containers for plants can be most attractive.
The shiny glaze complements glossy leaves.
(Photograph by Joyce Wilson)

This handsome decorative pot holds a crassula, an attractive succulent. The handful of smooth stones scattered on the soil makes a pleasing accent.

Want something different? Slip an ordinary clay pot into a decorative basket—it looks fine.
(Photograph by Matthew Barr)

add charcoal bits to the soil in the planter to keep it sweet, and water your plants with the greatest care: let the soil get almost dry before each watering, for, without bottom drainage, the soil in planters can easily become a soggy mess.

HANGING BASKETS

Plants in containers suspended near windows or below skylights add color to bare walls, and their leaves and blossoms are close to eye level, where they can be fully appreciated. If your growing space is limited to windows, increase it by taking to the air.

Nurseries and florists carry a variety of hanging containers of wood, wire, clay, and plastic. Some have clip-on or built-in saucers so that no drip pans need be placed on the floor before the plants are watered.

In this colorful small window garden, cyclamens and cinerarias predominate. (Photograph by Matthew Barr)

Window greenhouses can be added to almost any room, and almost any plant can be grown in them. Here, hydrangeas and azaleas are colorful. Orchids also grow abundantly. (Photograph by Jerry Bagger)

Palms in the living room are always a handsome sight.
(Photograph by Matthew Barr)

Dish gardens can contain many different kinds of
plants. Here, sempervivums and other succulents
create a colorful tapestry.
(Photograph by Joyce Wilson)

Colorful African violets decorate a hearth.
(Photograph by Joyce Wilson)

A fine display of plants makes this garden
room an indoor jungle.
(Photograph by Matthew Barr)

It is easy to grow plants in baskets because the conditions are exceptionally beneficial: roots remain healthy as the air circulates around them; good drainage is assured; soil does not become stagnant.

Redwood baskets are good for many plants—especially so for fuchsias, ferns, and begonias—for they retain the moisture that keeps roots cool. These containers last for years. Open-wire baskets are inexpensive and in them achimenes, campanulas, and columneas become cascades of summer color. The downy foliage of ivy-leaved

Specially designed pots like this three-tiered container are still another means of enriching your plant decor.
(Photograph by Matthew Barr)

In this garden-room greenhouse, begonias steal the show.
(Photograph by C/D Luckhart)

pelargoniums or episcias is a lovely sight in a clay basket. Plastic containers are useful in situations where rapid loss of moisture poses a problem.

Most baskets come with wires, chains, or ropes for hanging. But you must supply hooks that will adequately support the weight of a basket of plants and moist soil. Use heavy-duty eyebolts, screw eyes, or clothesline hooks, and if your walls and ceilings are plaster or wallboard, be sure to use the expansion bolts especially made for hanging heavy objects.

Before planting in a slatted redwood or open-wire basket, line the container with sphagnum moss (for sale at any nursery or garden-supply center). Press it firmly against the sides. Then fill in with soil suited to the species you are growing and group plants according to their needs. A haworthia, which likes to be rather dry, will not succeed in a basket that must be kept moist enough for ferns; shade-loving orchids suffer in the sunlight that pleases campanulas and abutilons. For attractive baskets, place an accent plant in the center and surround it with such trailers as episcias and achimenes.

Hanging containers for plants come in dozens of designs, but the old-fashioned, moss-lined wire basket (left) is still tops.
(Photograph by Matthew Barr)

39

This plastic hanging container, clean and simple in appearance, does not steal the show from a rhipsalis in bloom—and it has its own water saucer.
(Photograph by Matthew Barr)

The soil in open-wire baskets dries out quickly, and in summer plants need water once a day, sometimes twice, though much less often the rest of the year.

Suspend your baskets at a convenient height so that you can water them in place with a long-beaked watering can.

Here are some plants that flourish in hanging baskets:

Abutilon, trailing varieties	Browallia	Episcia
Achimenes	Campanula	Ferns
Aeschynanthus	Chlorophytum	Kohleria, trailing
Asparagus (asparagus fern)	Columnea; trailing and	varieties
Begonia	climbing varieties	Sedum

3 *YOUR THRIVING HOUSE PLANTS*

Generally speaking, house plants are of two kinds: those that require cool growing conditions and those that revel in warmth. But every plant needs light and will not grow or even live without it. Some plants thrive at a sunny east or south window, others grow best in one with a bright western exposure, and many foliage plants make lovely greenery in north light. Select your plants accordingly. Wherever you place them, turn them regularly so that growth will be even, not one-sided, as they reach toward the source of light. African-violet enthusiasts advise a quarter-turn every day!

For many plants, humidity (air moisture) of 30 to 40 percent is adequate, and almost all living quarters provide this much. For species requiring more, humidity can be increased in ways that are discussed later in this chapter. Fresh air is also essential to plant health, even in very cold weather. Some plants need special care; others grow almost, but never entirely, untended.

WHERE TO FIND INDOOR PLANTS

Although indoor plants are more readily available now than ever before, they are still not stocked by every garden-supply store or nursery. In large cities you will usually find them in shops devoted specifically to indoor plants, and prices are generally reasonable. Nurseries have more outdoor plants than indoor ones, and their selection includes both outdoor plants that you can bring indoors and the usual assortment of indoor greenery. In any case, if you can look at the plant you want to buy, do so. It makes much more sense to choose a plant you can see at first hand rather than one from a picture in a catalog.

Because of limited space, some florists do not carry a large selection of very big plants. But if you know what you want, they generally can find it for you. Moreover, florists, like nurserymen, have reputations that they want to maintain, so if you get a sickly plant, they will usually do their utmost to help you cure it and, in some cases, will replace it with another.

If you do not live in a place where there is a plant shop or a florist, you will have to buy from one of the many mail-order suppliers located throughout the country. Most of them issue catalogs with plant descriptions, sizes, and prices. Most mail-order suppliers are reputable and will guarantee their plants' safe arrival. Shipment service is generally excellent, and if you specify "air-freight collect," as I do, you can have a tree

Even a single plant can provide that special accent. Here a
rhapis palm highlights an entry hall. The artificial light above
the plant keeps it healthy. For decorative purposes the soil has
been covered with white sand.
(Photograph by Max Eckert)

from Florida the next day. You can pick up your purchase at the airport if you have a station wagon or truck available, or you can arrange for delivery service, which will cost extra. Some mail-order suppliers specialize in certain kinds of plants. For example, Alberts & Merkel of Boynton Beach, Florida, are noted for their exotic plants, as is Oak Hill Nursery in Dundee, Illinois (see page 223 for a list of suppliers).

Whether you buy from a local source or from a mail-order house, always insist that a plant be left in its container rather than sent "bare-root" (without a pot). A plant suffers considerable shock when it is uprooted. Even though the weight of the tin can or tub adds to the freight cost, the extra expense will be well worth it.

Most wholesalers will not sell retail. This is understandable when you consider that their customers are florists or nurseries that offer personal service to individual customers throughout the year. If you try to save money by bypassing local dealers, you will put yourself and the wholesale growers in an embarrassing position. Buy from retail outlets: you won't regret it.

How to Select a Good Plant

To get the most for your money, shop for your plant as you would for a coat, a car, or a camera. Compare costs and, above all, compare the quality of plants when you buy locally. Avoid any plant in caked soil, a condition that indicates the plant may have been around awhile and become weak. Examine the leaves, especially underneath, for insects: ragged, brown edges and holes are always suspect. The presence of insects does not necessarily mean the plant will die, but why pay for diseased plants? Look at the stems, too: they should be firm and resilient rather than flabby and limp. Touch the stems: you can sometimes determine the health of a plant this way.

Avoid any plant whose roots are coming out of its container's drainage holes: the plant is potbound, and it will take twice as long to recover from repotting than another specimen in better shape.

Most reputable nurseries tag their plants, but if your new acquisition is not identified, ask for its botanical name. If you don't know what it is, you won't be able to consult a gardening book, should problems develop.

Getting Your Plants Off to a Healthy Start

As with a baby, there are certain things you must do for the new plant you bring home to get it growing right. Most people forget that in the greenhouse where the plant spent its youth, conditions were ideal. In a human environment, the conditions you give a plant may not be optimum. (This does not mean the plant will suffer long-term damage; it does mean it will take some time for the plant to adjust to the new conditions.) If you want to keep your plant as long as possible, you should do certain things when you get it home.

Do not put it in bright sun, which might kill it in a short time. Place it in a somewhat shady place for a few days before exposing it to bright light. Temperature is not very important. Generally, most homes are somewhat cool in the evening, which is what a plant needs.

Do not immediately repot the plant. A period of acclimatization is necessary to lessen the shock of transplanting. Let it grow in the original container, no matter how ugly, for a few weeks, after which you can replant it in any decorative container you choose.

Clean all the foliage with a damp cloth when you bring your new plant home. This is a tedious job, but it can save you lots of time later. Washing the leaves will eliminate insect eggs and the residue from insecticide spray and will remove dust and soot so the plant can breathe (which it does through its leaves).

Immediately trim off any decayed leaves and stems, even ones that simply look unhealthy. This is not harmful to the plant and will reduce the danger of having other leaves turn brown at the edges. Often brown-edged leaves indicate nothing harmful at all, but sometimes an invisible fungus is at work, so it is best to be safe.

So far we have mentioned only *don'ts*, but there is one very important thing you must *do*: water the plant thoroughly, and when it has soaked up all the water, water it again. This simple process eliminates from the soil any toxic salts that may have accumu-

This healthy *Dracaena marginata* is placed in front of a decorative screen, and the effect is eye-catching. (Photograph by Molly Adams)

lated during the accelerated feeding program most plants are subjected to by professional growers. Watering will also flush out hidden insects. It is not easy to give the soil a really good soaking indoors, so do it outdoors, on your porch or in the yard, when the plant arrives. (Apartment dwellers can soak their plants for a few hours in the bathtub.)

Soils

Good potting soil is essential. One part garden loam, to one part sand, to one part leaf mold is the mixture I use for most plants. For cactuses and other succulents, and some euphorbias, I use more sand (almost half the mixture). I give peat moss to the acid-loving azaleas and camellias, and also to the anthuriums and tuberous begonias, which like moist roots. Peat moss is vegetable matter in an arrested state of decomposition. It is free of fungi and rich in carbon. It has a spongelike structure that absorbs and retains ten to twenty times its weight in water. It prevents soil from caking and helps to aerate it. Orchids and bromeliads need osmunda fiber (the chopped stalks of ferns) or fir bark, ground or chopped and steamed, as a potting medium. Both can be obtained in small sacks at nurseries.

Commercial packaged soil, usually rather "light," is good for some plants, particularly African violets and begonias, but, if much is needed, it is expensive. A better soil mixture can usually be bought by the bushel from a nursery or florist's greenhouse. This will be the same soil used there. It has been sterilized and contains all the necessary ingredients. You can use it as is or alter it according to the needs of your plants. If it is not porous enough, you can add more sand; if it feels thin, put in more leaf mold or other humus.

Growing mediums that contain no soil have been developed by Cornell University, and they are called peatlite. To make one peck, combine and mix well:

4 quarts (dry measure) vermiculite (#2 Terralite)
4 quarts (dry measure) shredded peat moss (German or Canadian)
1 level tablespoon ground limestone
1 level tablespoon 5-10-15 fertilizer

Before sowing seeds or transplanting seedlings, moisten the peatlite mix well. If you are repotting established plants, the moistening can be done after the repotting.

I have found peatlite excellent for seedlings and, because it is lightweight, it is advantageous for big plants in tubs. If you use it, be sure to give a supplemental feeding of a water-soluble fertilizer every other watering throughout the growing season. Potting procedure with the peatlite mix is the same as with standard soils.

In general, garden soil contains weeds, seeds, insect grubs, and bacteria that can cause disease in plants. Sterilized soil contains none of these hazards. If you cannot buy treated soil, you can sterilize your own at home. It is a messy, smelly procedure but it can be done. Run dry soil through a fine sieve into a pan of water; don't pack it. Put the pan on the stove and turn up the heat until the water boils; then simmer for a few minutes. Drain and turn the soil into a clean baking dish and let it dry out. Alternatively, you can bake moistened soil in your oven in a roasting pan for two hours at 200°F. Boiled or baked, let the soil cool for twenty-four hours before you use it.

Certain plants prefer a more acid soil, certain others a more alkaline one. Chemists have prepared a scale that measures acidity and alkalinity of soils according to their hydrogen ion concentration, or pH value. The scale is divided into fourteen parts;

The author's living room relies on plants for its charm. The tall specimen behind the table lamp is a *Ficus roxburghii*—always a good choice for indoor beauty. The louvered doors allow air to circulate around the plants yet screen them from the hot California sun.
(Photograph by Clark Photo/Graphic)

7.0 indicates neutrality (alkalinity and acidity in balance). Numbers above 7.0 indicate increasing alkalinity, numbers below 7.0 indicate increasing acidity. An inexpensive soil-test kit (available through garden suppliers) will enable you to determine the exact alkalinity or acidity of your soil, should you need to know. To maintain the proper balance for acid-loving plants, add peat moss or cottonseed meal to the soil. Alternatively, you can water with a diluted acid fertilizer like Miracid or, about twice a month, with a vinegar solution (one-half teaspoon vinegar to one quart water). To make soil more alkaline, add lime.

Healthy plants look that way—lush and robust.
This beautiful philodendron is a case in point.
(Photograph by Matthew Barr)

Here are the pH preferences of some plants:

4.5-6.0	6.0-8.0
Araucaria	African violet
Azalea	Asparagus (asparagus fern)
Cactuses	Begonia
Camellia	Oxalis
Coffea	Palm
Dieffenbachia	Pelargonium
Ferns	
Gardenia	
Hippeastrum	
Hydrangea	
Philodendron	

POTTING AND REPOTTING

Potting refers to the first planting of a seedling or a cutting in a container; repotting refers to the transfer of an established plant from one pot to another, usually a larger one. To ensure good growth, pot your plants properly.

Select a container neither too large nor too small in relation to the size of the specimen. Be sure the container is clean. New clay pots should be soaked overnight in water or they will draw too much moisture from the soil of new plants. Reused pots should be well scrubbed with steel-wool soap pads and hot water to remove any algae or salts that have accumulated. In regions where the water is full of chemicals, the accumulated salts on rims are so difficult to remove that it is necessary to discard the pots.

Fit a curved piece or two of broken crockery over the drainage hole at the bottom of the pot. Over the shards, spread some perlite or porous stones with a few pieces of charcoal (charcoal will keep the soil sweet). Then, holding the plant with one hand in the center of the pot, with roots hanging down and stem base about an inch below the rim, fill in and around the plant with fresh soil. Firm the soil around the stem with your thumbs. To settle the soil and eliminate air spaces around the roots, tap the base of the pot on a table a few times. After it is established, a properly potted plant can be lifted by the stem without being loosened.

Water newly potted plants thoroughly; then for a few days keep them in a light place—not a sunny one. Once accustomed to brightness, they can be moved. Label all plants: it's nice to know what you are growing.

When roots push through the drainage hole or appear on the surface, it is time to give the plant more room and also to replenish the soil. An exact schedule for repotting can't be given; watch each plant carefully. If leaves fade, lower leaves drop off, or new leaves appear small, it is probably time for fresh soil. If you fertilize regularly, thus replacing soil nutrients, plants thrive in the same pot longer than if they are not fed.

A separate place for plants makes this kitchen inviting— and the place was well chosen. The plants receive plenty of light and fresh air in their window setting. (Photograph courtesy Kentile Corp.)

It is easy to repot plants in pots up to eight or ten inches in diameter. Hold your hand over the soil (it should be slightly moist), keeping the main stem between your fingers. Invert the pot and rap the rim sharply against the edge of a shelf or table. Rap the base also. The whole root ball will then drop easily into your hand. Lay larger pots on their side and gently tap all around with a rubber or wooden mallet until the plant can be slipped out. If the root ball is covered with a network of roots, the plant needs a larger pot. Choose one an inch larger in diameter or, in extreme cases, two inches larger. Specimens in very large containers (more than fourteen inches across) or in built-in planters are best left undisturbed as long as possible. To recondition them, dig out three or four inches of surface soil and replace it with a fresh mixture. This process is called "top-dressing."

Sometimes examination of a poor specimen will reveal a partially rotted root system or roots too underdeveloped for the pot in which the plant struggles to survive. Then a smaller pot is needed: reestablished in a smaller pot, a somewhat sickly plant may make a surprisingly quick recovery. Whenever you shift a plant to a smaller or larger pot, crumble away as much old soil as possible and replenish with fresh.

Sometimes it is absolutely necessary to reduce the size of an enormous plant that has outgrown the space you can allow it. This can be done with a strong heart and a sharp kitchen knife. Slice off the root system three or four inches at the base and two to three inches around the sides. Repot the plant in a smaller, more manageable container. Water well with a soluble fertilizer and keep feeding the plant to promote root growth. The best time for this drastic treatment is in summer, with two months of agreeable outdoor living ahead. By September, the plant will usually have made a full recovery. This procedure has worked for me with asparagus ferns and gardenias.

WATERING AND FEEDING

How and when to water depends on the type of plant, the type of pot, and where you live. No plant should be allowed to become completely dry (even during semi-dormancy), and none should be kept in soggy soil. If the soil is too dry, roots become dehydrated and plant growth stops. Continuously wet soil becomes sour, and roots rot.

Soils that contain a great deal of organic matter—leaf mold, peat moss, or humus—are apt to become sour as a result of repeated waterings. Charcoal granules help to sweeten the soil and prevent this condition.

Some plants prefer soil that is always moist; others grow best in soil that is allowed to approach dryness between waterings. Cactuses and some other succulents may be permitted to become almost completely dry.

Edema (oedema) is a condition that occurs when plants absorb water rapidly but lose moisture slowly from their leaves. Extra water backs up and cells burst. Leaves develop water-soaked spots that become reddish brown. On cloudy days when the soil is warm and moist and the air is cool and moist, edema gets started. Avoid overwatering plants, especially pelargoniums, and let the soil stay on the dry side in cloudy damp weather. To stop the progress of edema, raise heat, lower humidity, and space out plants; don't mist the foliage. Allow the soil to get quite dry before watering. Generally, plants recover from edema, though not quickly.

When you water, do it thoroughly. Water should pour through the drainage hole: the complete root system needs moisture. If only the soil at the top gets wet, then the whole mixture usually turns sour, and plant growth is retarded.

Water at room temperature is best. If possible, water in the morning so the soil can dry out before evening. Lingering moisture and cool nights are an invitation to fungus diseases.

Soaking in a pail of water or at the sink is good for most plants and necessary for large ones with heavy roots, which too often are not thoroughly moistened when top-watered. Set the pot in water up to the rim for an hour or more, and by capillary attraction the soil will become moist throughout. Do not remove the pot until the top soil feels damp. Azaleas, camellias, hydrangeas, philodendrons, rubber plants, and ferns thrive on an occasional soaking. Of course, this treatment works only for plants in porous pots.

After repeated waterings and feedings, chemical salts may build up in soil. These salts must be flushed out, or they set up a roadblock so that roots cannot get nutrients.

Overleaf:
Plants make this room, and the room was designed for plants. Note the handsome brick floor, which can't be hurt by mud or water, and the amount of wall and ceiling space devoted to glass.
(Photograph by Max Eckert; Chris Christiansen, Designer)

Occasionally put your plants under a strong stream of water—several times—to wash out accumulated salts.

Most plants, though not all, benefit from feeding (bromeliads, many orchids, and clerodendrums do not need it). Commercial fertilizers contain some nitrogen, an element that stimulates foliage growth, too much of which can retard the development of flower buds. Fertilizers also contain phosphorus, to promote root and stem development and to stimulate bloom, and potash (potassium), which promotes health, stabilizes growth, and intensifies color. The proportionate amounts of these nutrients are marked on each package or bottle of chemical fertilizer in this order: nitrogen, phosphorus, potash. There are many generally and specifically applicable formulas; I prefer 10-10-5 for most house plants.

New plants and ailing plants do not require feeding. Plants in fresh soil find adequate nutrients there; ailing plants are not capable of absorbing nutrients. After they flower, allow plants to rest for a few weeks; water them only occasionally and do not feed them. A safe rule is to fertilize only plants that are in active growth.

Foliar feeding (applying fertilizer in a water solution to the leaves) is often recommended. However, hairy-leaved plants, such as African violets and some begonias, object to lingering moisture on their leaves, especially when it is not at room temperature. I have obtained best results by applying commercial soluble fertilizer to the soil.

There are dozens of plant foods on the market. Contents and recommendations are marked on the containers. Do follow the manufacturer's directions.

Heat and Humidity

Plants that like cool temperatures, such as campanulas and hoyas, grow best at 50°F. to 60°F. at night, with a ten to fifteen degree rise in temperature during the day. Plants that like warmth, such as anthuriums, require temperatures of 65°F. to 70°F. at night, 75°F. to 80°F. during the day. With few exceptions, plants fall into one of these groups. In other words, average home temperatures suit most plants.

In winter, it is necessary to protect plants from extreme cold. On bitter nights, put cardboard or newspapers between plants and windows to mitigate the chill of the glass.

Although an automatic humidifier is now part of many heating systems, older apartment houses and homes do not have this advantage. Humidity—the amount of moisture in the air—should be kept at a level healthful for both people and plants. A humidity gauge (hygrometer) will register the amount of humidity in the atmosphere. The humidity range in most homes (30 to 40 percent) suits most plants; a few—clivias and philodendrons, for example—will grow in low-humidity environments of 30 percent or less; others—rechsteinerias and gloxinias—require humidity of 40 to 50 percent.

It is important to keep enough water in the air as artificial or natural heat increases: the hotter it is, the faster the air dries out. Because plants take up water through their roots and release it through their leaves, they give off moisture faster when the surrounding air is dry than when it is damp. If they lose water more quickly than they can replace it, their foliage becomes thin and brown around the edges. When summer heat is at its peak, between eleven o'clock in the morning and one o'clock in the afternoon, spray your plants lightly with water. In winter when artificial heat is high, between six and eight in the evening, you should also put more moisture in the air. Turn on your room humidifier, or mist pots and soil surfaces—but not foliage. At night, wet foliage is an invitation to disease. Keep plants away from hot radiators and blasts of hot air.

For years an inexpensive window-cleaning-fluid bottle was part of my essential equipment. But commercial sprayers designed for misting plants now give better results than my old-fashioned gadget. Sold under various trade names, the hand-operated fogmaker has a washable plastic body and comes in 16- or 32-ounce sizes. It dispenses a fine mist that is beneficial to almost all plants, cleansing the foliage and, for a brief time anyway, increasing the humidity.

In addition to misting, you can set plants on wet gravel in a large metal or plastic tray, perhaps three inches deep. This will furnish a plentiful amount of additional humidity. Plants can also be placed on pebble-filled saucers kept continually moist. Best of all, purchase an inexpensive space humidifier with a small motor. These machines break water up into minute particles and diffuse it through the atmosphere.

If the proper temperature and light are also provided, strong growth and firm leaves will result from adequate humidity. Spindly growth and limp leaves usually indicate that a plant is suffering from too little moisture in the air. Give sickly plants that you suspect are in need of damper air an easy first-aid treatment. Draw a plastic bag, perforated in a few places, over the plant. Prop it up if necessary on sticks. Secure the bag around the pot rim with a rubber band. Improved health is often evident in a week: leaves stop falling and buds begin to form and open. The bag can be removed for days at a time if the plant is to go on display. My ailing brunfelsias, gardenias, and ferns have responded well to the bag treatment.

Fresh Air and Air Conditioning

Plants grown in rooms with good air circulation do better than plants in a stuffy atmosphere. It is a good idea to let outside air into rooms where plants are growing. When artificial heat is used indoors, the air around your house plants is drier than it is outside, and ventilation helps maintain desirable humidity. If it is impossible to open windows where your plants are growing, see to it that there is adequate ventilation in an adjoining room. But always avoid admitting air in cold drafts that blow directly on the plants.

Air conditioning is a boon to people in climates where summers are hot. It is interesting that many plants also resent torrid weather—ferns and rhizomatous begonias, for example. I have seen bromeliads and palms enjoying excellent health in public

These robust plants are in peak health: their foliage
glistens and they have a well-groomed look.
(Photograph by Matthew Barr)

buildings with central air conditioning, despite the low humidity. However, as with
wintry blasts, cold streams of air from wall or window air conditioners are harmful to
plants directly in their path. Drafts have a desiccating effect, causing leaves to wilt or
turn yellow and fall.

SEASONAL CARE

One all-important determinant of plant growth, indoors and out, is the weather. As

This lovely epiphyllum enjoys the summer on a patio,
where its flowers provide an exciting scene.
(Photograph by Matthew Barr)

seasons change, so do plant requirements. In spring, new growth begins. Give plants more water then and start a light feeding program. Repot, prune, and trim. February and March are the busiest months for the indoor gardener, particularly if a fresh green look for spring window gardens and plenty of summer color are wanted. Be sure that plants are ready for the warming trend. New soil with adequate nutrients starts them off right. Adequate humidity and regular watering keep them healthy.

In summer most plants grow rapidly, even indoors. Some, like columneas and fuchsias, need plenty of moisture at the roots. Water them at least once and, if necessary, twice a day. Feed plants that are in active growth. Protect them from the noonday sun, which now may be too strong for them. Usually a window screen suffices, but in the South a thin curtain may be required.

Watch out for pests, and provide good ventilation and adequate humidity. Avoid a stuffy atmosphere. On very hot days, mist plants several times to reduce heat.

Fall brings changing weather—some days hot, some cool—a crucial time for house plants. Water them with care, each according to its need. Many of them— fuchsias, hedychiums, oleanders—have achieved their annual growth by wintertime, when they enter a semidormant state. Stop feeding these plants: never try to force them to sprout fresh leaves. Let the soil become somewhat dry, but not so dry as to become caked.

When You're Away

Years ago, what to do with plants at vacation time was a problem. There are now many new devices you can buy to water your plants while you are away. You can purchase wick-fed flowerpots. Here, moisture flows up continuously to plant roots from a saucer via a glass-fiber wick. Wicks are also available for converting ordinary containers with drainage holes into self-watering pots. The Floramatic waterer, a glass vial filled with water and inserted in the pot soil, will automatically dispense water to a plant. If these devices are not available in your local stores, simply water your plants thoroughly, place them, without their saucers, in plastic bags, seal the bags tight, and set them away from the window in light but not in sun. It is important to keep the plastic from crushing the plants, so prop the bags on stakes inserted into the soil. You can also place pots on a brick in a bowl of water (the water should cover the brick). But if you are going to be away for more than ten days or two weeks, ask your local greenhouse to board the plants for you, or get a plant-sitter to air and water your plants.

House Plants Outdoors

A summer outdoors is beneficial for almost all house plants. It helps them to store up vigor so they will be at their best later indoors. Given warmth, natural light, and rain, they grow rapidly and prosper. Move them out to porch or patio when the weather is warm and unchangeable—late in May or in June, depending on climate—and bring them indoors soon after Labor Day.

Some plants, mainly such hairy- or soft-leaved species as African violets, gloxinias, ruellias, and hirsute begonias, are better left inside. They do not respond well to increased humidity and periods of high heat. Drying winds and lingering moisture or dew on their foliage almost always cause trouble. Big vines, such as bougainvilleas and passifloras, are also better not moved. Outside they grow too vigorously in warm weather: I have occasionally had to hack away half of one of these plants because I could not otherwise disentangle it from an outdoor post or wall.

House plants are decorative outdoors. Philodendrons, grape ivy, English ivy, vining pelargoniums, and fuchsias look most attractive in hanging baskets suspended from a porch or pergola beam. They also make a graceful addition to a veranda when they are set on brackets fastened to the house wall. Screened and shaded porches become green gardens with ferns and large foliage plants that have been indoors all year, and these are refreshed by a summer outside in a protected situation. Baskets of sun-loving pelargoniums and lantanas hanging at the side of an entrance, and pots of carissas, prayer plants, jasmine, and zonal pelargoniums are a welcome sight grouped beside a flight of wide steps.

Assemble the majority of your plants in some protected place outdoors, perhaps under a large shrub or an open-branched tree where wind and rain will not harm them yet the sun will find them. Stake large plants so they will not tip over on windy days. Keep them all in pots: the growing season in most climates is too short to make it sensible to put them in the ground, and when you must dig them up in the fall, their roots will surely be damaged and they will suffer a setback just when you want them to be at their peak indoors. You can, however, sink the pots in earth up to the rim.

Light is intense outdoors, and even sun-loving plants can be scorched by a sudden move from house to garden. In fact, only pelargoniums and a few other plants, after gradual conditioning, can endure full sun all summer long. I find the best location for vacationing house plants is along the east or west wall of my house. Having them in one area makes it easier for me to care for them, too.

Give house plants outdoors in summer routine garden care. Water and spray the foliage lightly with a hose every day except in wet weather. On hot, dry days they may need to be soaked and sprayed twice. In periods of high humidity, mildew may appear. Dusting with sulfur is one deterrent, but never dust on a day when you expect the temperature to rise above 80°F., or the foliage will be burned. Phaltan and Zineb are also good mildew controls.

When Plants Rest

A plant is a living organism and, as people sleep to regain energy, plants rest during some part of the year, growing more slowly or not at all and, in the case of flowering kinds, ceasing to send out buds. This period of dormancy is vital. Many of the plants we grow indoors—orchids, fuchsias, and hypocyrtas—come from climates with sharply defined seasons of rain and drought. Though far removed from their habitat, their cycles of growth remain the same, and we must respect them if we are to be successful in cultivating them.

Many plants rest a little after flowering unless, like clerodendrums and pentas, they make their heavy foliage growth then. Summer-flowering plants, such as achimenes and epiphyllums, become somewhat dormant in winter. Hardy bulbs, of course, become completely dormant and should be left entirely dry for several months; tender bulbs, such as amaryllises, freesias, and zantedeschias, also become fully dormant. But some plants, given good culture, bloom continuously; the African violet is one of these. Most pelargoniums never stop making new growth and buds, though a few species go fully dormant in summer. Ruellias do not die down, but after a long period of fall-to-early-summer bloom, they stop growing and set not a single flower until about October.

Usually plants plainly indicate their need for rest. You will see signs of declining vigor. After checking for a pest or disease, encourage them to slow down: stop fertilizing and, with a few exceptions (eranthemums, for example), gradually reduce the amount of water the plants receive.

4 *PLANTS FOR SPECIAL PLACES*

Terrariums and Dish Gardens

Small, choice displays of plant material have great charm—perhaps because they give such a wonderfully close-up view of nature, perhaps because we find an almost childlike pleasure in creating landscapes in miniature. Any container will do for a dish garden. Terrariums, which function as self-contained mini-worlds, must be of clear glass or plastic and have an airtight top. An unused fish tank with a transparent cover is an excellent choice. Large glass bottles with stoppers make unusual and attractive terrariums, but they are more difficult to work with, as you can't insert your hand inside and must use tongs or other tools to tend to the plants.

There are hundreds of miniature varieties of flowering-plant species to choose from for your dish garden or terrarium—African violets, begonias, pelargoniums, orchids, and roses—as well as many tiny foliage beauties like the English ivy 'Star.' Most appealing is the minute *Sinningia pusilla*, the miniature gloxinia, with inch-long, lavender flowers.

Terrariums make excellent houses for plants. They need not always be simple glass rectangles: this charming pyramidal design was executed by the author. Small ferns and grasses live inside.
(Photograph by Matthew Barr)

Terrariums

Before planting a sizable terrarium, make a rough sketch of the interior scene you want to create. Then clean and polish the container thoroughly inside and out, put in soil, and mound it into hills and valleys. Include a few stones, and select one of the tiny ground covers—the artillery plant (*Pilea microphylla*), baby's tears (*Helxine soleiroli*), or moneywort (*Lysimachia nummularia*). Since every terrarium is a humid and somewhat dark place, it is wise to choose plants that enjoy dampness and reduced light. Keep large plants at the back or in the center of the landscape, put smaller ones closer to the glass. Choose kinds that are naturally small or that grow slowly, and don't fertilize them; you want the plants to stay in proportion to the container. Lift the top of the container briefly once a day to let fresh air circulate inside.

Keep these glass gardens out of sun but in bright light. The moisture that accumulates on the sides of the glass will drip down to freshen the plants. It may not be necessary to water your diminutive garden for weeks or even months.

Planting a bottle garden takes patience and a steady hand. First, clean and polish the inside and outside of the glass. Be sure to scrub off any film or residue on the inside wall of the bottle with a lintless cloth fastened to a bent wire. Through a

Another hand-crafted terrarium—this one with colored glass and a domelike top. Small plants of almost any type can be grown in it. (Photograph by Matthew Barr; design by Lee)

Don't forget the glass dome when planning a terrarium—
this Victorian clock cover makes a handsome scene.
(Photograph by the author)

funnel, pour in tiny broken pieces of clay pots for drainage and then, still using the funnel, fill the container about one-third full with soil.

With the wire or a clean stick, make holes for roots. Now you are ready to plant. Remove the plants from their pots, wash the soil from their roots, and insert them in the prepared holes with the bent wire or kitchen tongs. Press earth firmly around the roots and mist the plants lightly.

Dish Gardens

A pottery bowl, a bonsai pot, a clay saucer, or even a baking tin makes an attractive setting for a dish garden. You can create a complex landscape there with trees, shrubs, and grass or display a collection of interesting plants quite simply. Your miniature garden can be the product of your imagination or a small duplicate of some

large, outdoor garden. The atmosphere may be formal, informal, Oriental, tropical, or contemporary. Unusual rocks and figurines among the plants may appeal to you, but even a single plant and a few well-chosen stones can be effective.

Proper scale—a pleasing size-relationship between rocks and plants, and between them and the container—is all-important. One plant out of proportion can spoil the whole effect. Start with a stone, a piece of fencing, a figure, or a plant you wish to keynote and then design around it.

Two popular types of dish gardens are the Oriental arrangement, with dwarf palms and small azaleas, and the desert scene, with cactuses and other succulents. I have also seen tropical rain forests and beach scenes ingeniously created. At local nurseries and in mail-order catalogs, you can locate fascinating plants to stimulate your imagination and keep your fingers busy.

Select a container two to three inches deep and in keeping with your motif. If you plan to create an elaborate landscape, a container of Oriental design may be your best choice. A teacup or sherbet dish is good for a simple arrangement with, say, one plant and a few well-chosen stones. To simulate trees, choose plants with single stems; for shrubs, pick branching kinds.

It is essential to group together only plants that thrive under the same conditions. In a dry, sandy soil and full sun, aloes, crassulas, echeverias, haworthias, and peperomias will flourish happily together. Dwarf ferns, certain gesneriads, and azaleas, which need semishade and rich, evenly moist soil, make fine companions in a dish garden.

Water plants in dish gardens less often than ordinary house plants, for the "dish" has no drainage outlet. Don't fertilize them: as with plants in terrariums, you don't want the greenery to outgrow the container.

Bonsai

The art of bonsai—growing dwarfed potted plants—is truly delightful and requires skill. Traditional Japanese bonsai plants—native hardy shrubs and trees—are expensive and difficult to obtain. However, there are many inexpensive plants that adapt to the bonsai type of culture. For example, some of the Kurume azaleas have lovely sculptural growth and can be pruned drastically without harm. They are a wealth of color in bloom. Flowering quince does well as a bonsai specimen and is always a spectacle in spring. Small spruce, juniper, pine, and hemlock have endearing qualities when properly pruned and potted in a suitable container. Even miniature fibrous-rooted begonias and ficus species can make striking bonsai pictures, and so can *Malpighia coccigera* and *Carissa grandiflora nana compacta* with its lush green leaves. Do not be afraid to try the unusual; if you find that a plant is not suitable for bonsai culture, you can repot it for window growing.

Look for species with interesting trunks or stems and well-placed lower branches. Select varieties with small leaves, which will be in keeping with short limbs and a

Succulents like *Huernia primulina* make fascinating special subjects for the sunny window garden. (Photograph by C/D Luckhart)

65

Bonsai is disciplined beauty. The branches of this exquisitely trained flowering fruit tree echo the linear pattern on the ceramic container. (Photograph courtesy Bob Behme)

small trunk or stem. Form and scale must be maintained in the bonsai plant. The composition formed by the plant and its small container is of critical importance. Bonsai plants are art in miniature; every leaf and twig must be perfect in shape and perfectly balanced.

Ordinary potting soil can be used, but I find a soil on the "poor" side, with some clay and sand in it, to be better for most dwarf plants than a commercial potting mixture.

Before potting or repotting, prune the roots of the plant to discourage normal growth. The idea is to keep the plant small, so do not feed it. Train branches into interesting shapes with wire and prune them regularly and drastically to keep them in proportion and to achieve pleasing and handsome growth patterns.

While pruning and shaping are important, good environmental conditions are necessary too. Use bonsai only as temporary decoration indoors. Most species need an airy, nonwindy situation outside. Some shade is necessary during the heat of the day, and soil must be kept consistently moist during the growing season (even in winter, the soil should be damp to the touch). During extremely cold winters, the bonsai garden will need some protection: a deep cold frame or an unheated but not freezing room.

If you want to try growing a bonsai plant, remember that the container makes an important contribution to the total effect. Pottery containers—unglazed inside, glazed or unglazed outside—in earth colors are generally preferred. The color of the container should complement the color of the plant. For example, a red maple looks best in a brown or gray dish, a green pine in a brown container. An upright plant looks best in a round or square container, and spreading plants are handsome in shallow dishes. A heavy-trunked tree needs a pot that is as deep as it is wide, and plants that are very gnarled—with growth on a horizontal plane—are stunning in rectangular or oval pots. Authentic, decorative bonsai containers are available, but they are generally expensive and not easy to find. Whatever container you use, remember that there must always be a pleasing relationship between the size and shape of the plant and the size and shape of the container it grows in.

STANDARDS

Standards—plants grown to resemble trees, with a single stem and lush crown of foliage—are not only for garden and terrace. They can also be enjoyed indoors. Acacias, chrysanthemums, citruses, fuchsias, pelargoniums, heliotropes, lantanas, oleanders, and roses are some of the many plants that lend themselves to this kind of training. Select a suitable container. Standards are always on display, so perhaps use a decorative tub for direct planting or an attractive jardiniere to hold the actual growing-pot. Select a handsome flowering or foliage specimen. Fuchsias and oleanders are excellent, should you want colorful flowers; acacias and citruses have particularly attractive foliage.

You can train a plant into a standard right from a cutting, but it does take patience, care, and time to nurture a small piece of tip growth to tall maturity—usually four years for a pelargonium. It is easier and quicker to start with a well-rooted plant from a nursery. Firmly stake your standard, and give it good culture, considering its requirements for light, temperature, humidity, water, and food. Remove all side shoots as soon as they form. In summer, enjoy your standard outdoors, where it will benefit from natural air currents and rain. Most admired are my azalea and chrysanthemum standards that have been outdoors in summer and moved into the house for fall and winter decoration. I doubt that you can grow a standard at a window, but most certainly you will succeed if you have a plant room or an enclosed porch. Try one: a well-grown standard is a delight.

Here are some plants that make excellent flowering standards:

Azaleas
'Alaska'—large, double, pure white flowers
'Constance'—single, cerise-pink flowers
'George Tabor'—single, delicate pink flowers

Begonias (Angel-wing)
'Corallina de Lucerna'—rosy pink flowers
'Ellen Dee'—orange flowers
'Orange Rubra'—orange flowers
'Thurstoni'—cerise flowers

Fuchsias
'Amy Lye'—single, white flowers tinged with pink
'Beauty'—double, scarlet and rosy magenta flowers
'Flying Cloud'—double, creamy white flowers with a touch of pink
'San Mateo'—double, pink and dark violet flowers
'Stream Liner'—single to semidouble, crimson flowers

Pelargoniums
'Lavender Ricard'—double, lavender-rose, white-centered flowers
'Masure's Beauty'—double, rosy red flowers
'Orange Ricard'—double, orange-to-scarlet flowers
'Will Rogers'—single, vivid purple-crimson flowers

In this greenhouse, tuberous begonias bloom profusely. Some rex begonias and other flowering plants extend the panorama of color.
(Photograph by C/D Luckhart)

Overleaf:
Handsome begonias in bloom
set this greenhouse ablaze.
(Photograph by C/D Luckhart)

The plants in this Chicago green-house are thoughtfully—even sculp-turally—displayed.
(Photograph by Matsumoto)

A windowsill of plants enjoy-ing sunlight and fresh air.
(Photograph by Matsumoto)

This rooftop greenhouse in
Chicago brings country plea-
sures to an apartment dweller.
(Photograph by Keeler)

This second-story greenhouse—a glass haven for plants of all kinds—gives an additional dimension to the view from the garden below.
(Photograph by Matsumoto)

Trays of gesneriads under artificial light.

This handsome garden room is
resplendent with plants.
(Photograph by the author)

5 BULBS FOR COLOR—
WINTER INTO SPRING

The beauty of the hardy bulb is not only in its flowers: bulbs are easy to grow. With a minimum of effort, several dozen bulbs, and some soil, you can have color indoors from late November until April. Tulips and hyacinths make any winter morning a promise of the spring that is to come. Planting bulbs in late fall is like burying treasure for the new year. When they burst into bloom some rainy February morning, you'll know what I mean.

A bulb already holds within its dull-looking exterior the makings of roots, leaves, and flowers. If you give it reasonable care, you are assured of colorful bloom.

FORCING HARDY BULBS IN POTS

Tulips, Hyacinths, and Daffodils

Forcing is a way of handling bulbs so that they will bloom indoors well before their natural outdoor flowering season. Tulips, Dutch hyacinths (*Hyacinthus orientalis*), and daffodils are perhaps the most commonly forced large bulbs. You can plant them in soil you purchase in bags, or you can make your own mixture by combining half a pail of coarse sand with one pail of rich soil, adding a little lime and enough bonemeal to fill a five-inch pot.

I prefer to plant in bulb pans, which are not so deep as ordinary pots but are deep enough to accommodate the roots of most bulbs. A pan five inches in diameter is large enough for one daffodil or one hyacinth bulb. An eight-inch bulb pan is large enough for several tulips. The soil beneath a bulb should be loose, to encourage rooting; the soil on top should be firm, to keep the developing roots from lifting up the bulb. The neck of a planted bulb should be slightly above the soil line. After potting your bulbs, moisten the soil well.

Bulbs are forced in three stages. First, they need a period of cool rooting, either indoors in a dark and cold but not freezing (40°F. to 50°F.) cellar, closet, or garage, or outdoors in a cold-frame trench or basement window-well. Second, they require brief exposure to moderate warmth (60°F. to 65°F.) and some light, but no sun. During the third and final stage, they are moved to a not-too-warm (about 70°F.), bright window where they can perfect their flowers.

For indoor rooting, I put my pots in an unheated pantry where the temperature

There are hundreds of bulbous plants. Not all are winter-
or spring-flowering— the hanging tuberous begonia may
be the most popular summer- blooming kind.
(Photograph by Vetterle and Reinelt)

remains between 45°F. and 50°F. during the late fall months. The shelves there are airy, and there is no light. (If light is a problem, put burlap or set boxes or pots over your bulbs.) I keep the bulbs just moist: the soil must not be either soggy or dry during this important rooting time.

To root bulbs outdoors, prepare a trench deep and wide enough to accommodate the largest pot. The bottom of the pots should be about a foot below the soil surface. Place well-watered pots of bulbs in the trench and, to keep the new leaves clean, cover the soil in the pots with two to three inches of sand. Then spill soil in between and over the pots to ground level. To prevent freezing, spread over all a thick layer of oak leaves, salt hay, or evergreen boughs. A cold frame with a hinged top is easier to deal with than a trench, but be sure it is in a well-drained place. Cover the sunken pots inside the frame with straw or a similar material.

Bring the pots into light for the second stage of forcing as soon as they are filled with roots—in six to nine weeks, depending on the type. They are ready to move if roots are making their way down through the drainage holes in the bottom of the pots. Before exposing them to the moderate warmth of this second stage, give the bulbs a day

A very charming arrangement featuring forced scillas (*Scilla sibirica*)
and grape hyacinths (*Muscari botryoides*)—both fine,
small bulbous plants.

or two of temperatures around 50°F. Water the bulbs as you do other house plants. Don't fertilize them: the embryo flower has already been formed.

Before bringing the plants into the third stage of growth, be sure that tulip stems are up about four inches, that the stalks of Dutch hyacinths are showing pale color, and that the buds of daffodils are well up and vigorous-looking.

If you want to keep bulbs for next year's outdoor garden, move the pots into the sun after the blooms have faded, and continue to water the soil until the leaves wither naturally. Allow the pots to rest in a dry, cool place, and then, after frost, plant the bulbs permanently in the garden. If you don't have a garden, discard them, for it is not possible to force them again. But after one or two years outdoors, forced bulbs will recover and bloom there as well as new ones.

You will find the following types excellent for forcing:

Early tulips
'Brilliant Star'
'Crown Imperial'
'Scarlet Cardinal'

Early hyacinths
'Bismarck'
'Delight'
'Dr. Lieber'

Late tulips
'Fantasy'
'Rising Sun'
'Scarlet Admiral'

Late hyacinths
'King of Blues'
'Marconi'

Small Bulbs

The small hardy bulbs—crocuses, grape hyacinths (*Muscari*), and scillas—can also be brought into early bloom indoors. They are treated much the same way as the larger bulbs.

There are many crocus species. Perhaps the most popular is the lavender-blue or purple *Crocus sieberi*, but you might also try one of the fine whites—*Crocus biflorus* 'White Lady'—or the orange *Crocus aureus*. 'Venus Vanguard,' a rosy violet variety, stays in bloom from Christmas until late January if planted not later than October 15.

The grape hyacinth is of dwarf habit and produces blue, violet, or pure white flowers that are sweetly scented. *Muscari botryoides album* is a good white for forcing, and *Muscari armeniacum cantab* is an excellent blue.

Scillas are dwarf and compact and bear white or blue flowers. The best for indoors is *Scilla siberica*, a blue-flowered type; if you prefer white, try *Scilla siberica alba*.

Plant the small bulbs as soon as they become available in fall. Put ten or twelve in a container six or eight inches in diameter in the same soil you use for larger bulbs, and water them. Place the pots in larger containers filled with sphaghnum moss or peat moss to keep them cool. After a period of dark rooting at 40°F. to 50°F., during which you must keep the pots moist, bring them in for forcing. When leaves are up, move the pots to an airy place at 60°F. until the buds are almost open. Then place the pots at your coolest window, out of the sun.

FORCING HARDY BULBS IN WATER

Some bulbs, such as Dutch hyacinths, French Roman hyacinths, and *tazetta* narcissuses, grow as well in water as in soil, and there are advantages to this procedure. It's easier to handle bulbs without soil, and forcing can take place entirely indoors, at temperatures of about 45°F. to 60°F.

Hyacinths

Start Dutch hyacinths at any time between December 1 and February 15. Dust off any soil from the bulbs and remove any loose skin, which might cause rot. Fill a hyacinth glass (available at florists) with water up to the neck and place a bulb in the top section. Keep the water supply up to the base of the bulb, but don't fill the neck, or the bulb may decay.

Put the glass in a dark, airy place at 40°F. to 45°F. Add water from time to time to keep it at the proper level. Wait until the bulb has good root growth and foliage and the flower spike is in evidence: six to eight weeks are required. The leaves should become not less than four inches long before the glass is moved to a bright but not too warm room to bloom.

These are good Dutch hyacinths to force:

'Grand Maître'—single blue spike
'L'Innocence'—single white spike
'Pink Pearl'—single rosy spike

Here is a schedule for some Dutch hyacinths I forced:

December 15: bulbs planted
February 8: bulbs brought into light
February 10: bulbs showed color
February 11: first floret opened
February 13: bulbs came into full bloom

French Roman hyacinths are smaller, often more charming than the Dutch type. The flowers—white, blue, or pink—last longer and they, too, have a delightful

Potted jonquils (*Narcissus*) make a handsome spring
indoor accent and are easy to grow.
(Photograph by Burpee Seeds)

perfume. Set these bulbs in a bowl or similar container on a bed of pearl chips (available
at pet stores that sell aquarium equipment), stones, or vermiculite. Fill bedding material
in between the bulbs to hold them firmly upright. Six or seven bulbs will fit into an
eight-inch container. Add water until it touches the base of the bulbs and maintain the
water at this level until the forcing process is over. Keep them in a dark, airy place at
50°F. to 55°F. until the bulbs are well rooted (this takes six to eight weeks). Then move
them into the light (not sun) and grow them in a cool place until the buds show. Then
move them to a warmer spot in your house for bloom.

A handsome display of beautiful *Scilla campanulata*,
potted in fall and brought to bloom in winter.

Start these dependable kinds early in the fall:

'Rosalie'—pink flowers, for Christmas
'Snow Princess'—white flowers, for mid-January
'Vanguard'—pink flowers, for Christmas

Wait until January to start others. Some will be in bloom by March.

Narcissuses

There are many kinds of narcissuses but probably the easiest ones to force are the *tazetta* or *polyanthus* varieties. *Tazetta* flowers are fragrant and appealing in color: orange-and-yellow, all-yellow, or all-white (the familiar 'Paperwhites'). Narcissus bulbs bloom readily when planted in a bowl of pebbles and water. Select a bowl about three inches deep, and wide enough to hold at least three bulbs. Fill the bowl half full with pebbles and set the bulbs in place with one-half inch of space between them. Add more pebbles to cover all but a third of each bulb. Pour water into the bowl until it just touches the base of the bulbs; add more occasionally as required to maintain this level.

Now set the container in a cool place (50°F. to 55°F. is perfect) for about three weeks, until roots are formed. Then move the dish to a bright window, where the bulbs will bloom. The time to start 'Paperwhites' for Thanksgiving is October 15; for Christmas, November 15. Plantings made at intervals of ten days will give a succession of bloom through winter and spring. Discard the bulbs after they flower. The orange-and-white 'Chinese Sacred Lily' and golden 'Soleil d'Or' are slower than the 'Paperwhites' and better held for February and March flowers.

A new plant from a single leaf—why not? African violets can easily be started from leaves. Plant the stems in a sterile medium and place a glass jar over the pot to ensure adequate humidity. (Photograph by the author)

6 *INCREASING YOUR SUPPLY*

Plants are generous with offspring. In fact, sometimes I hardly know what to do with all my divisions, cuttings, and seedlings. Seeing your own plants grow brings satisfaction, and, as with your children, you like your own best. You do not have to be a botanist to propagate plants. It is an easy procedure, and there are many ways of going about it.

STEM AND LEAF CUTTINGS

The best time to make stem cuttings is usually spring or summer, when plants are growing actively. Select sturdy shoots. Cut off a four-to-six-inch piece of stem with several pairs of leaves just above another pair on the mother plant. Trim off the cutting squarely just below the lowest pair of leaves and remove these leaves. Remove any flowers on the cutting as well. You can root cuttings of some plants (rhizomatous begonias, philodendrons, and syngoniums, for example) in a jar of water on a window sill. Others—the majority of cuttings—should be planted in vermiculite, sand, or other

light growing medium, moistened, and placed in a warm, humid atmosphere. A breadbox, baking dish, plastic container, casserole—any container with a transparent cover—makes a good propagating case. You can also use bulb pans with glass jars over them or sealed plastic bags propped up so as not to crush the cuttings. Before planting, you can dip the base of the cuttings in hormone powder to stimulate root growth. Then insert them, one-third to one-half their length, in the propagating mixture. Grow cuttings warm, 70°F. to 80°F., and place them in light rather than in sun. Keep the growing medium moist. Lift the cover of the propagating container for an hour or so a day to allow some ventilation.

STEM CUTTINGS

1. Cut at base.

2. Insert in sand.

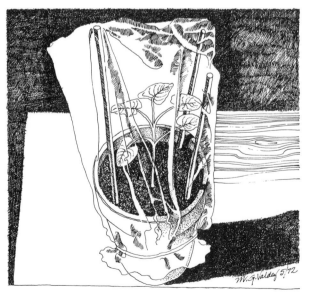

3. Cover with plastic bag.

Many plants—rex begonias, African violets, sedums, kalanchoes, and others—can also be propagated from leaf cuttings. Select a firm, healthy, mature leaf. Make a few small cuts across the main veins on the underside of the leaf with a sterilized knife or razor blade (run the instrument through a match flame). Lay the leaf on moist vermiculite in a propagating container. To ensure contact between leaf and growing medium, weight the leaf with pebbles. Plantlets form at the slit veins and draw nourishment from the mother leaf. When the plants are large enough to handle easily, put each in a two- or three-inch pot. You can also simply plant a single leaf as though it were a stem cutting (see the photograph on page 85).

Certain large foliage plants, such as alocasias, dieffenbachias, and philodendrons, can be propagated by a process called cane cutting. Sever a four- to eight-inch piece of mature stem (or cane). Coat both ends with sulfur, lay it in a rooting medium such as sand, cover the cane lightly, and press it firmly in place. New plants will form from dormant eyes all along the cane.

STOLONS AND OFFSETS

Many plants produce stolons or runners. If you want to propagate a plant of this type—a chlorophytum, episcia, or neomarica, for example—cut three-inch-long sections of these plant-producing stems and handle them like other cuttings. Roots will develop and plants will be ready for potting in soil in four weeks to four months, depending on the type. Bromeliads, agaves, gesneriads, and many orchids develop offsets or suckers at the base of the mature plant. When these offsets are two to four inches long, cut them off with a sterile knife and root them as you do cuttings.

ROOT, BULB, AND ROOTSTOCK DIVISION

Plants that make root clumps or multiple crowns—African violets, clivias, some orchids, and some ferns—can be propagated by division. Pull such plants apart into two or three sections, making sure that each section has some roots. If plants are massive, as chlorophytums can be, or woody, as is, for example, the fiddle-leaved fig, divide them with a clean, sharp knife, preferably sterilized. Cut back the foliage of your divided plants to encourage new growth, and plant the divisions in pots two to four inches larger than the rootball or crown.

Bulbous plants, such as amaryllises, eucharises, and haemanthuses, increase themselves by producing smaller bulbs: these can be separated from the mother bulb and potted up to make new plants. Sometimes when you are not watching, one of the smaller bulbs that develops within the mother bulb starts to grow on its own—this is called an offset bulb.

With dahlias and other tuberous plants, clumps of fleshy roots develop— all joined to one stem. To propagate these rootstocks, divide the stem into sections—each

POTTING OFFSETS AND STOLONS

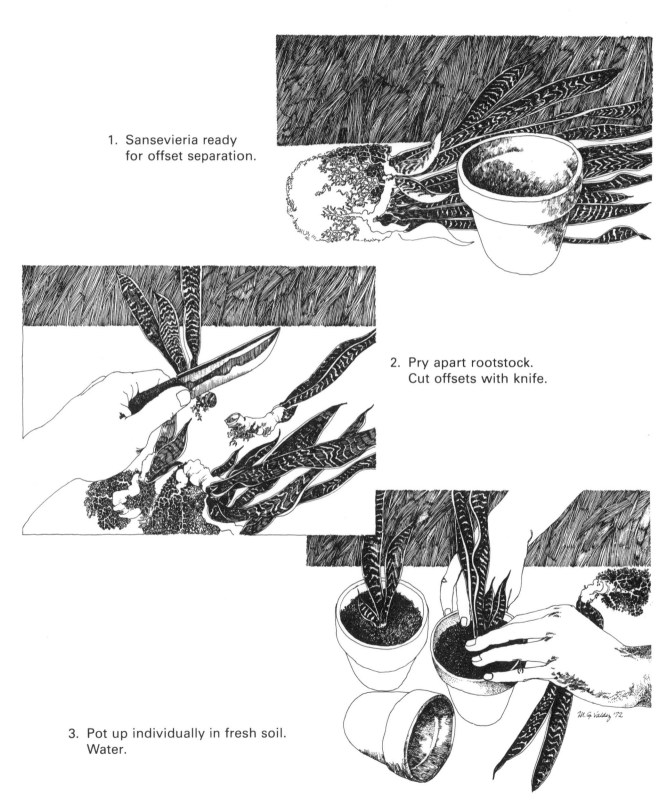

1. Sansevieria ready
   for offset separation.

2. Pry apart rootstock.
   Cut offsets with knife.

3. Pot up individually in fresh soil.
   Water.

Two plants can easily be made from one by pulling apart clumps of roots. This spathiphyllum has just been divided, and each part will go into a separate pot. (Photograph by the author)

Here cuttings are being dipped in rooting hormone before planting. (Photograph by USDA)

with an "eye" and attached to a root. Tuberous begonias, on the other hand, never really multiply; rather, the original bulb grows larger. In time this bulb can be cut into sections, each with an eye or bud, and the sections can be individually potted.

AIR LAYERING

Plants with large leaves and woody stems (dieffenbachias, ficuses, and philodendrons) are often difficult to reproduce from cuttings and can instead be propagated by air layering. On a healthy, sturdy stem near the top of a plant either remove a strip of bark about one-inch wide directly below a leaf node or cut a notch about half way through the stem. Then wrap a big clump of moist osmunda or sphagnum moss around the strip or notch and cover it with a piece of plastic wrap secured at top and bottom with string (the ball must be moisture-proof or growth will not start).

Air layering takes time. It may be six to nine months before roots form. When you can see them poking through the moss ball, sever the new plant just below the ball of roots. Then pot it, moss and all.

Air layering is a common method of propagating woody plants like this dieffenbachia. Make a notch midway up the trunk or up a branch, wrap osmunda around it, and cover the bandage with plastic wrap. When roots begin to show, sever the stem just below the new roots and pot the new plant. (Photograph by Matthew Barr)

AIR LAYERING

1. Notch one-inch band around stem. Do not cut through stem. Discard bark.

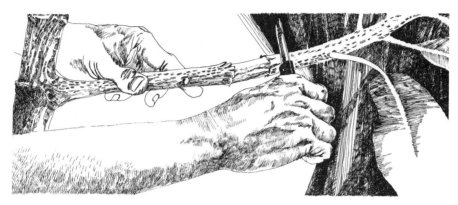

2. Cover entire notch with ball of osmunda.

3. Cover osmunda with plastic sheet and tie both ends.

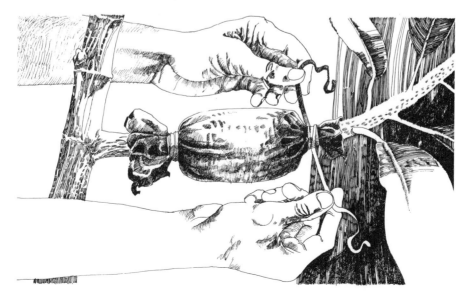

1. Cut back leaves to one-third.

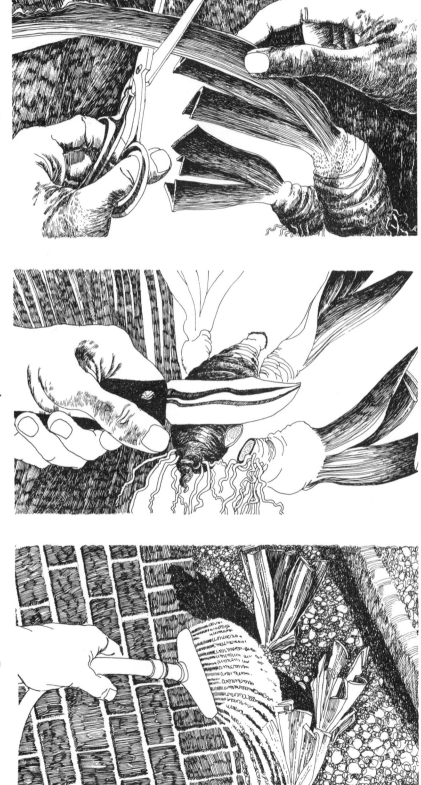

2. Divide rootstock with sharp knife.

3. Cover roots with soil. Firm them down. Water.

It is easy to start plants from seed. Simply choose a sterile
potting medium and scatter seed on top. Water lightly.
(Photograph by the author)

SEED AND SPORE PROPAGATION

Calceolarias, cobaeas, asparagus ferns, and many other plants are readily increased from
seed. Growing from seed is a fascinating and simple way of getting many plants for little
money. Sow seeds sparingly and evenly in a scrupulously clean plastic pot or pan filled
with vermiculite, sand, or other light growing medium kept between 70°F. and 75°F.
Bottom heat hastens germination. Soil-heating cables, available at house-plant supply
stores, are helpful, or you can set the container of seeds on top of an electric refrigerator,
where it is warm. Cover the seeds lightly with vermiculite. Moisten the soil (gently!) with
warm water. Then cover the container with plastic wrap to seal in the moisture. Label
each planting. Be sure the rooting mixture stays moderately moist: never allow it to get
soggy or to dry out. Remove the cover of the container for a few minutes several times a
day. Place it in the shade until you see signs of growth, then move it to bright light.
Keep it out of the sun.

Begonia seeds—and many other kinds, too—are as fine as powder. Don't cover
them with vermiculite. Sow them as thinly as possible on top of the growing medium
and press them in place. Mixing them with sand before sowing makes even distribution
easier to achieve. Larger seeds, like those of coleus and impatiens, should be covered to a
depth about twice their size.

As soon as leaves sprout, feed seedlings with diluted plant food. Pot them individually before they get crowded. Place the pots in a bright, warm spot for a few weeks before moving them to more permanent quarters in the indoor garden.

Ferns are propagated, not from seed, but from spores. These look like small dark spots on the underside of mature fronds. When ripe, they are dark brown and can easily be detached (rub them off with your fingertip). Mature fronds do not grow directly from spores, however. Spores first develop little heart-shaped green plants called prothallia; later, fronds are produced.

After detaching spores, sow them in flats or three-inch trays filled with sand and soil. Dust the spores across the surface and then cover the container with plastic to provide adequate humidity. Keep the growing medium moist, never wet. Remove the plastic for a few hours a day if condensation occurs. When true fronds have sprouted, the tiny plants can be put into individual pots of soil.

7 HOUSE-PLANT CLINIC

Maintaining good culture and nipping trouble in the bud are the best ways of keeping pests and diseases from killing your plants. Keep them well groomed. Pick off dead leaves and faded flowers. Mist the foliage at least once a week with clear, tepid water. This cleansing removes insect eggs and spider mites and, in general, prevents plagues and pests. It also helps to develop healthy, shiny leaves. (Plain water is always preferable to leaf-shining preparations, which clog leaf pores.) Plants too large to move easily to a place where you can conveniently spray them can be freshened by wiping their leaves with a damp cloth.

Is It Poor Culture?

Discolored or falling leaves and premature bud drop are not necessarily caused by insects or disease: sometimes the decline of a plant is the result of improper culture. It may be that repotting to improve drainage, adopting a different method of watering, increasing or decreasing humidity, or simply admitting fresh air regularly into the house will bring plants back to health. If your plants exhibit the following symptoms, check their environment for the cause of the ailment before you spray or dust. The specific cultural requirements of most house plants are described in Chapter Eight.

Symptoms	Causes
Brown or yellow leaves	Too high heat; or too low humidity; or not enough fresh air; or soil too dry or too wet.
Yellow or white rings on leaves (especially common in African violets)	Watering with cold water. Use tepid water or water at room temperature.
Leaf drop	Rapid and extreme changes of temperature; or watering with cold water; or too low humidity.
Pale leaves, weak growth	Too little light; or too high heat; or too much plant food, particularly if your brand is high in nitrogen.
Slow growth	Sour, poorly drained soil; or cramped roots; or plant may be *naturally* in a somewhat inactive period.

Swelling and corky ridges on leaves (especially common in ivy-leaved pelargoniums)	Soil too wet. Do not water on dark or humid days, and water less often in general.
Bud drop	The plant was grown too hot or too cold, or shocked by a draft or an abrupt move from greenhouse to home; more likely, too low humidity.
Collapse	Extreme cold or heat; root rot (poor drainage).
Dry, crumbling leaves (especially common in English ivy)	Too high heat; too low humidity. Check also for spider mites.

You may think this schlumbergera has been attacked by insects, but not so: this is a case of neglect—no water—and the plant has succumbed. (Photograph by the author)

The venerable ladybug eats aphids and other plant pests. Here one climbs to a dinner. Natural preventatives are an excellent way of protecting plants, and ladybugs can be purchased from suppliers. (Photograph by Joyce Wilson)

If It's a Pest or Disease

Almost inevitably, your indoor plants—even with the best culture—will at some time suffer an insect attack. Less likely, though possibly, they may contract a disease. It is a good policy to schedule a spraying with an all-purpose natural pesticide, such as one with a rotenone or pyrethrum base, once a month—and always before you bring plants inside in fall. Another good preventative measure is to isolate any plant that looks limp or sickly, or isn't growing well. It is also wise to give newcomers a trial period by themselves before admitting them to your indoor garden. Do give each plant enough room so that air can circulate around it: crowding is always unhealthy.

If one of your plants experiences a light insect attack, first try to eliminate the pests with a vigorous spray of clear or soapy water, followed by a clear rinse. Spider mites and aphids can often be eliminated completely by this treatment. Applying a solution of one tablespoon alcohol and one quart of soapy water to foliage will do the job, too. Dip small plants (first cover the soil with aluminum foil), wash medium-sized ones by hand, and spray large specimens. Rinse them thoroughly afterwards. To exterminate mealy bugs, try washing the plant with a solution of equal parts water and

Mealy bugs have started to invade this grape ivy. There
is still time to stop them with a natural preventative.
(Photograph by the author)

alcohol and then with soap and water, and finally rinsing with clear water. Or go over an
infested plant with a cotton swab dipped in alcohol. Scales can often be scrubbed
off—never to return—with a stiff brush dipped in soapy water.

    There are other simple but effective home remedies that I usually resort to before
reaching for an insecticide. Potatoes cut in half and laid on the soil will lure snails and
slugs to the surface, where you can destroy them. Occasionally, moist, humusy soil will
harbor springtails, minute insects. Hot water (90°F.) poured over the soil will chase
them out, but first place a saucer beneath the pot to trap them.

    If an insect invasion is heavy, you had better apply a chemical insecticide. Some
come in powder form for dusting; others are liquids to be diluted with water for
spraying. Avoid strong preparations concocted for outdoor use. Try to select either a
good all-purpose indoor brand or one designed to attack a specific problem: a miticide

Here is a close-up of mealy bugs in action. This plant
is beyond recovery and should be discarded.
(Photograph by the author)

won't cure diseases, and the spray that kills mealy bugs won't clean up scales. Know
what you are fighting before you do battle. If problems persist, try different preparations: each one has a unique chemistry that works effectively in one situation, less so in
another. After spraying, allow the preparation to dry, then rinse the leaves with clean
water.

Dunking an infested plant in a pail of solution is the surest way to eliminate
severe infestations and plagues. Cover the top of the pot with a piece of aluminum foil,
invert the plant, and douse it in the solution several times. Let it drip dry out of the sun,
then rinse it with clear water. Though it is more trouble than in-place spraying, dunking
usually brings about the quickest clean-up.

If you have only a few plants, keep on hand an all-purpose pesticide spray can.
These push-button cans tend to be expensive, but they are certainly a convenience. Read

the label to be sure what you are buying. Always spray the whole plant—the stems and the tops and undersides of the leaves. Don't spray at close range: the recommended distance is twelve to fourteen inches away from the plant.

Systemic insecticides, which you apply to the soil, are proving a boon to indoor gardeners. One application will protect most flowering and foliage plants (but not ferns and palms) from most types of sucking and chewing insects for six to eight weeks. Systemics come in granular form. Spread them over the soil and then water the plant thoroughly. The insecticide is drawn up through the roots of the plant into the sap stream, making it toxic to insects.

Whatever products you select, be sure to follow the manufacturer's directions. When plants are tended to carefully, trouble rarely occurs. Most important is not to grow plants in an atmosphere that is too warm—always an invitation to spider mites—or too stuffy. Let in some fresh air—indirect, of course, in very cold weather—every day. A hot, close atmosphere can spell disaster.

Should your indoor garden be visited by pests or disease, the following chart will help you to pinpoint the problem and take the proper action.

Symptoms	Causes	Controls
White, cottony clusters in stem and leaf axils; undersized foliage; spindly growth	Mealy bugs	First try washing the plant thoroughly with soapy water and then rinsing with clear water; or you can kill bugs by touching them with a cotton swab dipped in alcohol. If bugs persist, apply a malathion spray. You may also apply a systemic insecticide to the soil. Destroy the plant if the infestation is very heavy.
Deformed, streaked or silvery leaves with dark specks	Thrips (almost invisible yellow, brown, or black sucking insects)	First try washing the plant thoroughly with soapy water and then rinsing with clear water. If pests persist, apply a malathion spray.
Green, black, red, or pink insects on new growth or under leaves; sticky, shiny leaves, often cupped; sooty mold on leaves and stems; stunted growth	Aphids	First try washing the plant thoroughly with soapy water and then rinsing with clear water. If pests persist, apply a malathion or nicotine spray. You may also apply a systemic insecticide to the soil.

Stunted growth; crowns bunched; leaves cupped up or down; buds blackened	Cyclamen mites or broad mites	Destroy plant. To prevent infestations, spray with Dimite or Kalthane every two to four weeks; pot plants in sterilized soil.
Fine webs in leaf and stem axils and underneath leaves; leaves mottled and crumbly, turning gray or brown	Spider mites (microscopic)	Try vigorously spraying plant with soapy water from above and below to break webs. If pests persist, spray with Dimite or Aramite. Destroy plant if mites persist.
When plant is touched, small white insects fly up; sooty deposits on leaves and stems; leaves stippled or yellowing	White flies	Apply a malathion spray.
Clusters of little brown, gray, or white lumps under leaves; loss of vigor	Scales (insects with hard or soft shells)	First try picking the bugs off by hand or scrubbing the plant thoroughly with a soft brush dipped in soapy water and then rinsing with clear water. If the pests persist, apply a malathion or nicotine spray. (Do not confuse the seed cases on the underside of fern fronds with scales.)
Gray, or watery green, or yellow leaves; crown rotting	Bacterial blight	Spray with Captan or Fermate.
Holes in leaves	Slugs or snails	Pick slugs or snails off at night. Remove plant debris from pot. Apply Bug-Getta around and near pot.
Flowers, leaves, and stalks spotted or circled	Virus disease	It is best to destroy the infected plant, though spraying every three days with Zineb *may* check the disease.

Coated white leaves	Mildew	Spray with Karathane or Phaltan, or dust with Zineb or sulfur (never use sulfur on a day that will be hotter than 80°F.).
Gray mold on flowers and leaves	Botrytis blight	Get rid of badly infected plants. If blight is not serious, try applying Ferbam or Zineb; cut out and destroy diseased sections; water less often, avoid crowding.

Root nematodes, tiny eelworms, suck juice from roots and leaves and cause knots or swellings on the roots. Although there are chemical preparations that kill young nematodes (VC-13 is one), they are extremely poisonous and best not used at home. I usually discard any plants attacked by nematodes.

8 *DICTIONARY OF MORE THAN ONE THOUSAND HOUSE PLANTS*

I have used *Hortus* as my chief authority on botanical nomenclature and consulted Alfred B. Graf's *Tropica* for additional information. However, I have chosen to use popular spellings and older botanical names for plants so listed in the majority of important suppliers' catalogs.

The name of the genus to which a group of plants belongs appears at the head of each entry. Often this Latin name is the only one by which these plants are called. Common names for the entire genus (when they exist), the family of plants to which the whole genus belongs, and the temperature range in which these plants thrive are given, in that order, opposite the genus name. Popular and attractive species, varieties, and hybrids are listed, with their own common names, at the end of each entry.

An asterisk preceding a plant name indicates that it is a smaller-than-average type. Since specialists have defined the categories "dwarf" and "miniature" quite specifically, I like to call these diminutive plants, none of which grows taller than about fourteen inches, "windowsill size." Be sure to look into these lilliputian gems that are so well suited to the limited space in the apartment or house.

In addition to entries on individual plants, articles will be found on the following plant groups: Bromeliads, Cactuses, Ferns, Gesneriads, Orchids, and Palms.

ABUTILON   **flowering maple**
Malvaceae
45°–65°F.

Vigorous, freely flowering shrubs to 36 inches, with large, bell-shaped, paper-thin flowers that are orange, yellow, red, or white—abutilons put on a colorful display from May to August. The foliage is handsome: pure or variegated green. Grow the bushy kinds in pots, the trailers in hanging baskets. Give them full sun, moderate amounts of fertilizer, and lots of water. Plants tend to get leggy, so pinch back young shoots to force lush growth. Keep them somewhat potbound to encourage bloom. Start new plants from cuttings or from seed in spring.

A. hybridum—bushy growth, spotted leaves, flowers of various colors: orange ('Apricot'), yellow ('Golden Fleece'), orange-and-red ('Souvenir de Bonn').

A. megapotamicum variegatum—trailing growth, green-and-yellow leaves, red-and-yellow flowers.

A. striatum—trailing growth, orange flowers.

A. striatum thompsonii—trailing growth, variegated leaves, yellow flowers.

ACACIA

kangaroo thorn, wattle
Leguminosae
45°–55°F.

Somewhat thorny plants, acacias can grow to 48 inches indoors in suitably large pots. Plants have flattened leaf stalks instead of leaves and, usually in spring, bear clusters of lovely yellow flowers. These plants require a rich, freely draining soil kept consistently moist all year. Do not overwater them. Give them bright light and grow them cool (55°F.). After flowering, let your plants rest a few months; prune them back to 6 to 10 inches. Grow new plants from stem cuttings in spring. Acacias are nice, unusual, treelike plants.

A. *armata pendula*—bright green foliage, clusters of yellow flowers.
A. *decurrens*—beautiful silver-blue foliage, bright yellow flowers in winter.
A. *pubescens*—silver-gray foliage, yellow flowers.

ACALYPHA

Euphorbiaceae
65°–75°F.

Showy strings of red or greenish white flowers spring from acalyphas' leaf axils throughout the year. The foliage is green or copper-colored. Provide a sunny window and keep soil consistently moist, humidity around 50 percent. Feed plants while they are actively growing. For a good show, put several plants in one container. Propagate acalyphas from cuttings in fall.

A. *godseffiana*—to 20 inches; bright green, yellow-edged leaves; greenish white flowers.
A. *hispida*—to 30 inches, hairy green leaves, bright red flowers. Called chenille plant.
A. *macrophylla*—to 30 inches, bronze-and-copper leaves, red flowers.
A. *wilkesiana macafeana*—to 30 inches, coppery leaves. Grown for its foliage. Called copperleaf.

ACANTHUS

Grecian urn plant
Acanthaceae
50°–70°F.

Decorative plants to 36 inches, acanthuses make effective accents and require little attention. Leaves are ornamental, lush, and green; the showy summer flowers are white, lilac, or rose-colored. Give them bright light and keep soil wet during growth. Thirty to fifty percent humidity is best for them. Let plants die down after flowering and keep soil barely moist. Propagate acanthuses from seed or by division of rhizomes in early spring. These are excellent plants for patio tubs.

A. *mollis*—broad glossy green leaves, thrusting heads of rose-colored or white flowers.
A. *montanus*—narrow dark green leaves with spines, rose-colored flowers.

ACHIMENES

rainbow flower
Gesneriaceae
60°–70°F.

These plants offer the best possible summer display. With glossy, cut-leaf foliage and flowers in all colors of the rainbow except green, they are indispensable for window gardens, on sunny terraces, and in hanging baskets. Some are compact, to 16 inches; others upright, from 16 to 20 inches; and many are basket plants, with up to 28-inch-long flowering stems. Start fifteen to twenty rhizomes in an 8-inch bulb pan at any time from January on. When growth is a few inches high, move each plant to a 5-inch pot. Bloom will appear in six to eight weeks and continue for four months in sun. Keep soil consistently moist: if it dries out while plants are in growth or bloom, they may become dormant. When flowers fade, store pots indoors in a dim, cool place. In early spring, divide and repot the rhizomes. You can also grow plants from seed in spring.

A. *antirrhina*—upright growth to 20 inches, scarlet-and-yellow flowers.
A. 'Charm'—compact growth to 16 inches, pink flowers.
A. *flava*—golden yellow blooms. A basket plant.
A. 'François Cardinaux'—to 20 inches, lavender-and-white flowers.
A. *grandiflora*—to 26 inches, purple flowers with white throats.
A. 'Master Ingram'—to 20 inches, orange-and-red flowers.

A. pedunculata—to 28 inches, fiery orange flowers.

A. 'Purity'—to 16 inches, lovely soft-white flowers.

A. 'Purple King'—to 16 inches, floriferous. Popular.

A. 'Vivid'—to 18 inches, orange-and-magenta flowers. A dazzling basket plant.

ACINETA
Orchidaceae
55°–75°F.

These splendid epiphytic orchids bear a profusion of yellow, red-spotted flowers on 24-inch, pendent stems. Leaves are broad, a pleasing green. Give them morning sun and pot them in large-grade fir bark in slatted redwood baskets; keep the bark moist, never wet. Mist leaves frequently after they mature. Flower spikes develop at the base of the bulbs. Don't let water lodge in young buds or they will rot. Obtain new plants from specialists.

A. densa—2-inch flowers in spring.

A. superba—3-inch flowers in summer.

ACORUS
miniature flagplant
Araceae
40°–60°F.

Tufted plants to about 10 inches with iris-like leaves, acoruses are fine for a north window. I have never seen them bloom indoors. Generally they are used as base plantings for such specimen plants as dracaenas or podocarpuses. They are favorites of the Chinese and Japanese, who use them for bonsai. Keep soil moist: these are marsh-growers. To obtain more plants, divide rhizomes in spring or fall.

A. gramineus pusillus—flat, waxy, dark green leaves.

A. gramineus variegatus—green-and-white, leathery leaves.

ADIANTUM
maidenhair fern
Polypodiaceae
55°–70°F.

Delicate, lacy fronds and wiry black stems make these fast-growing, decorative ferns de-

sirable, even though they do need a little pampering. Protect them from strong sun in summer and from excessive heat. Keep soil consistently moist and provide 40 to 60 percent humidity. Mist foliage at least once a week and occasionally stand plants in a pail of water until all roots are moistened. Frond tips are delicate and if they drag on sills they turn brown. If possible, place pots on pedestals (inverted pots will do) or grow plants in baskets. Propagate them by division of roots.

A. bellum—to 12 inches, fluffy fronds. Easier to grow than most.

A. cuneatum—to 20 inches. Popular, elegant, and graceful.

A. hispidulum—to 12 inches, forked leaves.

A. microphylla—to 24 inches; beautiful, tiny, lacy fronds. Perhaps the prettiest in the genus.

A. 'Sea Foam'—to 24 inches. Very handsome and lush.

A. tenerum wrightii—to 20 inches; pale pinkish green fronds maturing to a lush, deep green.

ADROMISCHUS
Crassulaceae
60°–75°F.

Miniature succulents from Cape Province in South Africa with thick, beautifully formed and colored leaves, these plants rarely bloom indoors. Adromischuses are easy to grow in a sunny window. Keep soil somewhat dry: these are desert plants. Propagate them from offsets.

A. clavifolius—to 6 inches; clusters of fat, club-shaped, silver-green leaves.

A. cooperii—to 12 inches, small leaves dotted with red.

A. cristatus—to 10 inches, crested leaves, red stems.

A. maculatus—to 10 inches; thick, chocolate-brown foliage.

AECHMEA
living vase plant
Bromeliaceae
60°–75°F.

Requiring almost no care, these small, medium, or large epiphytic plants are usually vase-shaped, with brilliantly colored leaves— variegated, some appearing lacquered. The flower spike is usually long, the small flowers hidden in the bracts. Many bear white, red, or blue berries that last for several months. Give them bright light and pot them in fir bark or osmunda. Do not fertilize them. Keep the "vase" formed by the leaves filled with water. Most species bloom in spring or summer, a few in winter. When flowers fade, suckers appear at the base of the plants. Cut these shoots off when they are 2 to 4 inches high, and pot them separately.

A. calyculata—to 20 inches, flower head of vivid yellow in mid-spring.

A. fasciata—to 24 inches, tufted blue-and-pink flower head in spring.

A. 'Maginali'—to 30 inches; an outstanding hybrid with pendent red flowers, usually in winter, followed by blue-black berries.

A. pubescens—to 20 inches (often less), wheat-colored flower head in fall, followed by white berries.

A. racinae—to 14 inches; red, black, and yellow flowers at Christmastime.

A. ramosa—to 40 inches; pyramidal head of yellow flowers with red bracts in summer.

A. weilbachii—to 20 inches, lavender flowers with red bracts, usually in winter.

AEONIUM
Crassulaceae
55°–70°F.

Aeoniums are striking succulent plants from 10 to 36 inches across. Some have rosettes of leaves that hug the soil, others rosettes that perch on stem ends. Give them bright light rather than sun, and keep plants in active growth almost dry. In winter give only enough water for leaves to stay firm. Add extra sand to the basic soil mix. Plants die after flowering in spring and summer, but offsets are usually produced first.

A. arboreum—to 36 inches, thick stem topped with a rosette of green leaves, yellow flowers.

A. arboreum atropurpureum—to 36 inches, coppery red leaves, golden-yellow flowers.

A. decorum—to 30 inches, coppery red leaves, white flowers.

A. domesticum—shrubby growth to 20 inches, hairy foliage, yellow flowers.

A. haworthii—shrubby growth to 18 inches, blue-green leaves edged with red, pale yellow flowers.

A. nobile—to 24 inches, olive-green leaves, scarlet flowers.

A. 'Schwartzkopf'—to 24 inches, greenish black leaves, yellow flowers. A highly prized, dazzling hybrid.

A. tabulaeforme—to 20 inches; open rosette of small, fresh green leaves; yellow flowers. My favorite.

AERIDES
Orchidaceae
55°–75°F.

These lovely, freely flowering epiphytic orchids are valued for their pretty flowers and sweet fragrance. Most species have dark green, leathery, strap-shaped leaves. Waxy flowers, which last for three weeks, are borne in pendent racemes, sometimes 20 inches long. The usual flower color is pale pink, though white also occurs. Place them at your sunniest window, and pot them in medium-grade fir bark. Mist them frequently and give them ample moisture all year: 40 to 60 percent humidity. Most kinds are summer-flowering. Buy seedlings from specialists.

A. affine—to 20 inches, dark-rose-colored flowers with purple spots.

A. crassifolium—to 14 inches, amethyst-purple flowers, generally spotted.

A. falcatum—to 14 inches; white-and-rose-colored flowers, usually spotted.

A. maculosum—to 20 inches, light-rose-colored flowers with purple spots.

A. odoratum—to 24 inches, large, fragrant white flowers stained with magenta. Popular.

AESCHYNANTHUS
(TRICHOSPORUM)
lipstick vine
Gesneriaceae
60°–75°F.

These are not the easiest plants to bring into bloom but they are beautiful when they do. They are trailing epiphytes, some over 36 inches, with glossy, dark green leaves and a wealth of tubular flowers, usually orange or red. Most kinds bloom in summer. Don't make the mistake of keeping them in hot sun: they prefer a somewhat shaded position. During active growth they require plenty of water. Give plants warmth, and spray them frequently to keep humidity high—between 50 and 70 percent. Propagate by air layering or from cuttings.

A. hildebrandia—pendent to 30 inches, handsome velvety green leaves, globular scarlet flowers.

A. lobbianus—brilliant red flowers clustered at the tips of branches.

A. longiflorus—masses of red flowers. Robust.

A. marmoratus—green flowers with brown spots.

A. obconicus—pendent to 40 inches; short-tubed, bright red flowers; lovely, thick, glossy, dark green leaves. A winner—and it blooms in winter!

A. pulcher—red-and-yellow flowers.

A. speciosus—spectacular orange-red flowers.

AFRICAN VIOLET. See SAINTPAULIA and GESNERIADS.

AGAPANTHUS
lily-of-the-Nile
Liliaceae
50°–70°F.

These are handsome large or dwarf tub plants with fleshy green leaves. In mid-to-late spring, erect spikes crowned with great spheres of white or dazzling blue blooms appear. Give these lilies a bright window and keep them potbound. Water them freely until flowering ends, then maintain them somewhat dry through late summer. In winter, foliage dies down naturally and plants can be stored in a basement or garage at 40°F. to 50°F., during which time you should water them about once a month. Try dwarfs indoors, others on the patio. It is best to grow plants undisturbed in the same container for several years. Grow new plants from seed or by division of roots when repotting in spring.

A. africanus—to 36 inches, large umbels of blue flowers. The most popular species.

A. 'Dwarf White'—to 24 inches.

A. inapertus—to 18 inches, compact flower heads of deep blue.

A. orientalis—to 48 inches, blue flowers.

※A. 'Peter Pan'—to 12 inches, dark blue flowers.

AGAVE
century plant
Amaryllidaceae
55°–75°F.

These succulent plants produce 10-inch to 60-inch rosettes of stiff leaves in shades of blue, gray, green, banded white, or yellow. Despite their name, they do not require a century to bloom but begin to flower after ten years. Greenish flowers are carried in a terminal cluster at the end of a long stalk. Don't expect flowers from plants indoors, however. Agaves are slow-growing and adjust to almost any conditions. They prefer sun or bright light. Provide sandy soil, water them once a week, and let them grow in the same pot for years. The very large varieties are landscape specimens requiring much space; smaller types are bold and dramatic pot plants for porch or window. Start new ones from offsets.

A. americana marginata—trunkless, to 60 inches; green leaves edged with yellow.

A. attenuata—trunk to 36 inches, soft gray-green rosettes.

A. medio-picta—trunkless, to 60 inches, central yellow stripes on green leaves.

A. miradorensis—trunkless, to 36 inches; sword-shaped green leaves. Called dwarf century plant.

※A. victoriae-reginae—trunkless, to 10 inches; narrow olive-green leaves penciled white. A compact globe of great beauty.

AGLAONEMA
Chinese evergreen
Araceae
60°–75°F.

Tough to beat, these plants from tropical forests will thrive under conditions that would kill most house plants. Most species have dark green leaves; some have leaves marked with silver or white. Flowers are white. Give them bright light or semishade and constant moisture at the roots, or grow them in a vase of water. They are easy to propagate: cut stems into 3-inch pieces, place them in moist sand, and barely cover. Only potbound plants will bloom, but bloom they do—luxuriantly—in late summer and early fall.

A. commutatum—to 24 inches; silver-marked, dark green leaves.

A. commutatum 'Pseudo-bracteatum' (generally classed as a hybrid)—to 24 inches, green leaves splashed with yellow.

A. modestum—to 24 inches; waxy dark green leaves. Popular.

**A. pictum*—to 12 inches; dark green, velvety leaves spotted silver.

A. roebelinii—to 36 inches, blue-green leaves. Very robust.

A. simplex—to 36 inches, dark green leaves. This Chinese evergreen grows like a weed in a jar of water.

A. treubii—to 24 inches, lance-shaped, blue-green leaves marked with silver.

ALBUCA
Liliaceae
45°–60°F.

Albucas are South African bulbous plants that grow to 48 inches, with basal leaves and, in spring and summer, erect racemes of flowers that resemble scillas. Plant four bulbs close together in a 6-inch pot for a good display. Provide a sandy soil, full sun, and plenty of water in spring and moderate moisture in summer. After plants bloom, let foliage ripen; then store pots dry in a shady place until fall. Offsets grow from mature bulbs, and they may be broken off and potted individually.

A. crinifolia—to 36 inches; 2-inch, waxy white flowers with a green midrib.

A. major—to 34 inches, lovely pale yellow flowers.

A. nelsonii—to 42 inches, white flowers.

ALGERIAN IVY. See HEDERA.

ALLAMANDA
Apocynaceae
55°–65°F.

These are mostly evergreen climbers with tubular green leaves and waxy flowers that appear in spring and summer. Give them full sun and plenty of water during growth. They need 30 to 50 percent humidity. In winter keep soil barely moist. Prune them back in spring to keep them in bounds. Propagate them from cuttings. Large species do well on a sun porch; small ones are fine for window gardens.

A. cathartica hendersonii—a giant, to 7 feet, golden yellow flowers.

A. neriifolia—a shrub, to 36 inches, golden yellow flowers.

A. violacea—a climber, to 48 inches, startling red-purple flowers.

ALLIUM
flowering onion
Liliaceae
50°–70°F.

Handsome bulbous plants with green, strap-shaped leaves and lovely umbels of rose, lilac, or white flowers, these onions offer a great deal for little care and bloom well indoors. Pot them in sandy soil and place them at a bright window. Give them plenty of water. Propagate them from offset bulbs. Dramatic as cut flowers, they last for days in a vase of water. When they finally fade, spray them with gold or silver paint (from the florist) for a unique decoration.

A. neapolitanum—to 30 inches, slender leaves, large starry white flowers.

A. schoenoprasum—to 30 inches, round heads of rose-purple flowers.

A. triquetrum—to 18 inches, large white flowers.

ALLOPHYTON
(TETRANEMA)
Mexican foxglove
Scrophulariaceae
50°–70°F.

The Mexican foxglove is a charming plant with long, leathery, dark green leaves and fragrant, tubular flowers that appear in spring and summer. Place these plants in a sunny window and keep soil consistently moist. They are stubborn to force into bloom. Propagate plants from seed in spring.

A. mexicanum—to 20 inches, small lavender flowers. This plant is often overlooked, but it is a beauty.

A. mexicanum 'Alba'—white flowers.

Aeonium 'Schwartzkopf.' (Photograph by C/D Luckhart)

Anguloa clowesii. (Photograph by C/D Luckhart)

Anthurium species. (Photograph by C/D Luckhart)

Aphelandra species. (Photograph by C/D Luckhart)　　　　　*Astrophytum asterias*. (Photograph by C/D Luckhart)

Beloperone guttata 'Yellow Queen.
(Photograph by C/D Luckhart)

Billbergia brasiliense. (Photograph by C/D Luckhart)

Cattleya hybrid. (Photograph by C/D Luckhart)

ALOCASIA

Araceae
65°–75°F.

These dramatic exotics have showy velvety green foliage veined with copper, gray, silver or red. The heart-shaped leaves are held high on thin stems. From tropical Asia, these plants prefer a shaded location. Add peat moss to a basic soil mixture and keep soil moist. Feed plants monthly with diluted fertilizer. Make sure drainage is perfect. Although these plants require more care and higher humidity—to 80 percent—than most indoor subjects, a well-grown specimen is a beautiful sight. Grow new plants from cane cuttings.

A. amazonica—bushy growth to 20 inches; white-veined, scalloped leaves.

A. chantrieri—bushy growth to 20 inches; dark green leaves, gray veins. Handsome.

A. cuprea—compact growth to 15 inches; shiny purple-green leaves.

A. lowii grandis—to 24 inches; metallic brownish green leaves.

A. lowii veitchii—to 24 inches; smaller, marbled, arrow-shaped, brownish green leaves.

A. watsoniana—to 28 inches, corrugated blue-green leaves with silver veins. Described as "queen of alocasias."

A. zebrina—to 18 inches, green leaves with brown bands resembling a zebra's.

ALOE

Liliaceae
55°–75°F.

These succulents are grown for their handsome rosettes of all-green or spotted green leaves. Although they have soft, pulpy foliage, they are nevertheless often confused with agaves, which have tough, fibrous leaves. Plants are of three types: small—for windows and dish gardens; medium-sized—for plant rooms; giant—for tubs outdoors. Give them sun and a sandy, well-drained soil. Keep them barely moist: overwatering will prove fatal. Aloes produce spectacular orange, red, or yellow tubular blooms in fall or winter, though rarely indoors. Grow new plants from offsets.

A. arborescens—to 10 feet across; thick blue-green leaves. Called candelabra aloe.

A. aristata—green-gray rosette to 6 inches across, dotted with white and tipped with white marginal teeth. Called lace aloe.

A. brevifolia—gray-green rosette to 4 inches across. Occasionally one will bear a tall spike of red flowers for me in late fall.

A. ciliaris—to 6 inches across; soft, green-white, toothed leaves with sprawling growth and pencil-like stems.

A. globosa—to 7 inches across, gray-green leaves. Called crocodile aloe.

A. nobilis—to about 24 inches, bright green leaves edged with yellow. Called gold-spined aloe.

A. variegata—to 12 inches across; a rosette of three-cornered, dark rich-green leaves, marbled and margined with white. Called partridge-breast aloe.

ALPINIA

ginger
Zingiberaceae
50°–70°F.

Alpinias are good ornamental plants from the South Seas and New Guinea. They need shade from summer sun and ample moisture (50 percent humidity). Propagate your plants by division of the rhizomes.

A. purpurata—to 36 inches, dense clusters of red bracts emerging from the center of the leafy stem.

A. sanderae—to 16 inches, pale green leaves edged with white. Grown for its foliage.

ALTERNANTHERA

Amaranthaceae
55°–75°F.

Decorative foliage plants, your alternantheras will produce white flowers, too. Grow them at a south window, keep soil on the dry side, and provide 50 percent humidity. They are charming for a windowsill. Propagate them from cuttings.

A. ramosissima—to 12 inches; broad-pointed, metallic wine-red leaves.

A. versicolor—to 3 inches, copper or red leaves.

ALUMINUM PLANT. See PILEA.

AMARYLLIS. See HIPPEASTRUM.

AMAZON LILY. See EUCHARIS.

ANANAS
pineapple
Bromeliaceae
50°–70°F.

Ananas are spiny-leaved plants with handsome foliage that is usually striped green, cream, and pink, but some species may be plain green. Pink, red, and white bracts on tall spikes are dramatic and appear in summer. Give these plants sandy soil or equal parts soil and osmunda, bright light, and moderate moisture. Large species are excellent as tub plants; smaller ones are fine for pot-growing. Wipe leaves with a damp cloth to bring out their beauty. New plants may be grown from offsets.

A. comosus—rosette of dark green leaves to 36 inches across. The pineapple of commerce.

A. comosus variegatus—spectacular rosette of yellow-green-and-pink leaves to 36 inches across.

A. nanus—rosette of fresh green leaves to 15 inches. Available in fruit at florist shops.

ANGEL LILY. See CRINUM.

ANGEL'S TRUMPET. See DATURA.

ANGRAECUM
comet orchid
Orchidaceae
55°–75°F.

Large and small epiphytes with leathery leaves, angraecums bear blossoms with a long spur, sometimes to 12 inches. Not demanding as to temperature or humidity, these plants thrive with little care. Pot them in large-grade fir bark, place them in a bright spot, and keep them moderately moist. Propagate them from offsets.

A. compactum—to 3 inches, 4-inch flowers in winter.

A. eburneum—to 36 inches, alternating rows of flowers in winter.

A. falcatum—to 6 inches, fragrant flowers in late fall or early winter.

A. veitchii—to 24 inches, star-shaped flowers from January on.

ANGULOA
tulip orchid
Orchidaceae
55°–75°F.

These exquisitely beautiful orchids from Colombia look more like large tulips than orchids. Plants have large, thin leaves up to 30 inches long. Flowers are produced from the base of the plant in summer or fall. The blooms may be pure yellow or almost red (pinkish brown). These plants require a shady place. Pot them in medium-grade fir bark. Water them through the year. Do not feed them. Keep them out of drafts and provide ample ventilation. New plants should be purchased from suppliers.

A. clowesii—to 30 inches; large apple-green leaves; pure yellow flowers. A joy to see.

A. ruckerii—to 30 inches; light green, paper-thin foliage; pinkish brown (almost red), waxy flowers.

ANSELLIA
spider orchid
Orchidaceae
50°–70°F.

You cannot find a better orchid than *A. africana*. Freely flowering and easy to grow, this epiphyte has crowns of bright green leaves. Thriving specimens, which may grow to 48 inches, bear up to a hundred red-and-yellow flowers on branching stems. Keep them in sun with plenty of water. Pot them in large-grade fir bark and maintain 40 to 60 percent humidity. You can increase your supply by division of plants (and young ones do bloom), but it is best to buy mature specimens.

A. africana (also sold as *A. gigantea* and *A. nilotica*).

ANTHURIUM
flamingo flower
Araceae
65°–80°F.

From Central and South American jungles, these plants bear brilliantly colored, shiny bracts called spathes with yellow "tails," on which grow the plants' minute, true flowers. Anthuriums make superb indoor decoration. They need a potting mix of half standard soil and half fine-grade fir bark to ensure perfect drainage. Grow them in a shaded location and keep soil moist. Unless you can give them warmth and 80 percent humidity, better not try them. They require time and patience but are worth every effort. Obtain more plants from seed.

A. *andraeanum*—to 16 inches; green leaves; red, white, coral, or pink spathes.

A. *bakeri*—to 15 inches, green leaves, brilliant red spathes.

*A. *crystallinum*—to 14 inches. Perhaps the most handsome type, with velvety green, silver-veined leaves; insignificant spathes.

A. *forgetti*—to 16 inches. Similar to A. *crystallinum* but with oval, not heart-shaped, leaves.

A. *scandens*—climbing, to 36 inches; dark green leaves.

A. *scherzerianum*—to 16 inches; green leaves; red, yellow, pink, or white spathes. The most familiar type, a favorite for arrangements.

A. *warocqueanum*—to 30 inches; long, velvety leaves with pale green veins; spathe green with very long "tail." Outstanding.

APHELANDRA
Acanthaceae
55°–75°F.

These plants have long-lasting terminal clusters of orange or yellow, spring or summer flowers and gray-green or dark green leaves attractively veined with white. Supply a rich, porous soil and pots that look slightly small for the plants. They grow rapidly in sun and need plenty of water while active—less at other times. They tend to get leggy in winter, so it is best to start new ones annually from cuttings.

A. *aurantiaca roezlii*—to 16 inches, vivid orange-red flowers.

*A. *chamissoniana*—to 14 inches, cheerful yellow bracts. Popular. Called zebra plant.

A. *squarrosa louisae*—compact growth to 20 inches; shiny, corrugated leaves; shaded yellow bracts.

APOROCACTUS
rattail cactus
Cactaceae
55°–75°F.

In this small genus with only a few species one group of plants stands out and is grown often. Rattail cactuses have long, pendent, slender stems and bear showy rose-pink flowers in late spring, followed by red berries. Epiphytic plants, they grow well in a mixture of equal parts soil and fir bark. Allow them almost to dry out between waterings. Give them as much sun as possible. Propagate them from cuttings in summer.

A. *flagelliformis*—unusual and worth the space.

APOROPHYLLUM
Cactaceae
55°–75°F.

These are hybrids of the Aporocactus and Epiphyllum genera of the cactus family—lovely plants, with long green stems and handsome red flowers throughout the year. These plants like a well-drained potting mix: half soil and half fir bark is fine. Keep them in bright light, for sun can harm plants. Water them freely all year except in winter, when soil may be somewhat dry. Propagate aporophyllums from cuttings in summer.

A. 'Starfire.'

APOSTLE PLANT. See NEOMARICA.

ARABIAN COFFEE PLANT. See COFFEA.

ARABIAN JASMINE. See JASMINUM.

ARALIA. See DIZYGOTHECA, POLYSCIAS.

ARAUCARIA
Norfolk Island pine
Araucariaceae
50°–70°F.

One species of this genus of handsome trees is a splendid pot plant. With its lovely, long needles, *Araucaria excelsa* looks like a miniature Christmas tree. It is easily grown in north or bright light and requires only consistently moist soil

It is easy to see why Norfolk Island pines (*Araucaria excelsa*) are often used for Christmas trees in small apartments. (Photograph by Merry Gardens)

and deep watering in a pail once a week. An elegant evergreen, it will be with you for years. Araucarias are slow-growing (to 48 inches) and best kept potbound. Propagate new plants from seed or by air layering.

A. excelsa.

ARDISIA
coralberry
Myrsinaceae
50°–60°F.

Here is a colorful fruit plant for Christmas, often available at supermarkets then. The leaves on this appealing little tree look like holly. The fragrant white flowers of mid-winter or early spring are followed by coral-red or white berries that often persist along with a cloud of new bloom. Plants need bright light, and sand should be added to any standard potting mixture. Keep soil just moist, but occasionally give plants a deep soaking in a pail of water. Mist foliage frequently, and watch out for scales. Propagate this one from cuttings or seed.

A. crenulata (or *A. crispa*)—to 30 inches, glossy green leaves, red berries.
A. japonica—to 18 inches, white berries. Not so colorful but still nice.

ARIOCARPUS
living rock plant
Cactaceae
55°–75°F.

This cactus is an almost spineless, globular, desert type, with leaflike "foliage" arranged in a spiral and the greater part of the plant below the ground. Lovely, large pink, white, or lavender flowers crown the top of these plants in summer. Grow them in sandy soil in sun with scant water. Keep them in a 3-inch or 4-inch pot, or use them in a dish garden. Propagate ariocarpuses from offsets.

A. furfuraceus (or *A. retusus*)—to 8 inches, pink flowers. Called seven stars.
A. mcdowellii—to 8 inches, lavender flowers.

ARISTOLOCHIA
calico flower
Aristolochiaceae
55°–75°F.

Here is an unusual vine—growing to 15 feet and producing flamboyant, spotted flowers—for tubs on terraces or in sun rooms. Leaves are heart-shaped, large, and light green. It grows rapidly in spring and summer and needs plenty of room. Flowers, more curious than pretty, form on hanging shoots, so don't cut these off. Give plants full sun and copious watering in summer. Let them rest with little water, but not entirely dry, in winter. Obtain new plants from seed.

A. elegans—a slender, woody climber; yellow-green-and-brown flowers.
A. grandiflora—yellow-green flowers with spurs, veined and spotted purple.

ARROWHEAD. See SYNGONIUM.

ARROWROOT. See MARANTA.

ARTHROPODIUM

Liliaceae
50°–70°F.

One species of the lily family, *A. cirrhatum*, grows to 36 inches with light green, grassy leaves and clusters of starry white flowers in February and March. Give these plants sun and plenty of water during active growth and bloom. Decrease moisture after they flower but never let soil dry out completely. Propagate this plant by division.

A. cirrhatum.

ARTILLERY PLANT. See PILEA.

ASCOCENTRUM

carnival orchid
Orchidaceae
55°–75°F.

Their gay colors—orange, red, cerise—have earned these small epiphytes their common name. A well-grown plant bears about forty 1-inch blooms in early spring. The strap-shaped foliage is leathery. Plant them in medium-grade fir bark in 5-inch pots. Give them full sun and copious watering during growth (not so much at other times) and 50 percent humidity. They are charmers for the window. Buy new plants from specialists.

A. ampullaceum—to 20 inches, dainty cerise flowers.
A. curvifolium—to 14 inches, red flowers.
A. miniatum—to 10 inches, orange flowers.

ASPARAGUS

asparagus fern
Liliaceae
55°–75°F.

These plants, which arch or twine depending on training, are desirable wherever there is space for them. Some species reach 60 inches—becoming a mass of lovely, feathery foliage with tiny whitish or pinkish, sometimes fragrant flowers, followed by red or purple berries. The plants are attractive throughout the year, and, best of all, easily grown, even in north light. Give them plenty of water and, about once a month, a bucket-soaking. They are handsome

in baskets—or set them on a pedestal or table to keep the delicate foliage tips from touching a hard surface and bruising. Divide root clumps or sow seed.

A. asparagoides—to 36 inches, feathery and ferny. Used by florists in arrangements.
A. crispus—to 36 inches; a billowy cloud of tiny rich-green leaves (needle-like); lovely white flowers, followed by red berries.
A. plumosus—to 36 inches, horizontal needle growth.
A. sprengerii—to 60 inches; light green, needle-like foliage. An exceptionally good house plant. Called emerald feather.

ASPARAGUS FERN. See ASPARAGUS.

ASPIDISTRA

cast-iron plant
Liliaceae
50°–70°F.

A. elatior, an old favorite with long leaves, survives in almost any situation. The 24-inch-long foliage is sometimes complemented by sprays of purple-brown flowers. It provides a fine green accent in an orphan north window. Keep soil consistently moist. Grow several plants to a pot for a good display. Divide root clumps carefully for new plants.

A. elatior—shiny green-black leaves.
A. elatior variegata—green-and-white striped foliage.

ASPLENIUM

Polypodiaceae
50°–70°F.

Handsome, 14-to-30-inch ferns, aspleniums add interest to the indoor garden with their fresh, shiny green, parchment-thin fronds. Add chopped osmunda to any standard potting mixture, and grow them in full light. Keep soil consistently moist and provide 50 percent humidity. Mist them often, soak the rootball occasionally, and watch out for scales (do not confuse spore cases under the leaves with scales, however). Propagate them from offsets or spores.

117

A. bulbiferum—wiry, divided fronds; black stems. Plantlets grow on the surface of the leaves and can be individually potted: hence, this variety is called mother fern.

A. nidus—wavy, light green fronds that are smooth, broad, and handsome. Called bird's-nest fern.

ASTROPHYTUM
star cactus
Cactaceae
55°–75°F.

This easy-to-grow desert genus includes some fine, spineless or almost spineless, star-shaped plants with large, yellow, reddish-centered flowers in spring. Add sand to the soil in their pots and give them full sun. Keep soil somewhat dry. Propagate them from offsets.

A. asterias—to 1 inch tall, to 3 inches across; spineless, with an eight-segment dome.
A. capricorne—to 10 inches tall; globular, with white ribs and papery spines.
A. myriostigma—to 2 inches tall; a spineless globe divided into five segments. Called bishop's-hood cactus.

AUCUBA
Cornaceae
50°–70°F.

One species of this small genus of evergreens, *Aucuba japonica*, makes a fine house plant. To 60 inches indoors, this shrub has handsomely marked leaves, insignificant flowers, and pretty red, white, or yellow berries. Give it a semi-shaded place and plenty of water. Shape young plants by pruning. This one is best for a sun room or terrace, as only young plants are small enough for windows. Grow new ones from cuttings or seed.

A. japonica picturata—leaves with yellow centers and green edges.
A. japonica variegata—shiny green leaves spotted with yellow. Called gold-dust tree.

AUSTRALIAN BRACKEN. See PTERIS and FERNS.

AZALEA
(RHODODENDRON)
Ericaceae
50°–60°F.

Azaleas make outdoor gardens blaze with color, and in the home they also make bright accents for bright windows. Usually they arrive in the house as seasonal gift plants—bushy or treelike to perhaps 20 inches—but it is not impossible to carry them along as house plants through the years. (Whether or not the one you receive is a hardy type for the permanent outdoor garden is difficult to discover: even the florist can rarely tell you.) Indoors, grow them as cool as possible. Mist the foliage frequently and keep soil consistently moist. To accomplish this, stand the pot in a deep bowl and pour in water every morning; it will be empty by night, for azaleas require a great deal of moisture. About once a week, skip the morning watering, let the soil get just a little dry, then stand the pot in a pail of water to within an inch of the rim and let it stay there until the top soil feels moist. (The pot must be porous or this treatment will not work.) If you received a well-budded plant, you can expect color for months to come. Put an in-bud plant in the sun, an in-bloom plant in a brightly lit place. After flowers fade, a slight rest is necessary, so give your plant less water until the weather is warm enough to take it outside. Repot it in a fresh soil mixture with plenty of humus and set it on a porch, or plunge the pot in a shady garden spot. Water it daily and fertilize it about once a month. To encourage bud formation for next year, leave the plant outdoors until the temperature is likely to go below 40°F. Then bring it in, admit plenty of fresh air during the first weeks indoors, and mist the foliage daily. The plant will need less water now than when in bloom and no fertilizing until November. Start weekly feedings then. Depending on the type of plant it is, budding will commence in early December or later. These varieties are my favorites:

A. 'Alaska'—double, white flowers.
A. 'Beatrice'—double, brick-red flowers.
A. 'Constance'—single, cerise-pink flowers.
A. 'Coral Bells'—double, pink flowers with darker pink centers.

A. 'Hexe'—double, red flowers.
A. 'Orange Queen'—double, pink-orange flowers.
A. 'Pink Pearl'—double, rosy salmon-colored flowers.
A. 'Purity'—double, white flowers.
A. 'Salmon Beauty'—semidouble, salmon-colored flowers.
A. 'Snow'—double, white flowers.
A. 'Sweetheart'—double, salmon-pink flowers.

AZTEC LILY. See SPREKELIA.

BABY PRIMROSE. See PRIMULA.

BABY'S TEARS. See HELXINE.

BALL CACTUS. See NOTOCACTUS, PARODIA, and CACTUSES.

BAMBOO. See BAMBUSA.

BAMBOO PALM. See CHAMAEDOREA and PALMS.

BAMBUSA
bamboo
Gramineae
50°–70°F.

Feathery and tall, these plants thrive for years in the same pot, and a well-grown specimen has exceptional beauty. They are easy to grow if given a bright, airy location and plenty of water. Divide root clumps in spring for new plants.

B. *multiplex* 'Chinese Goddess'—to 72 inches, gold-and-green leaves.
B. *nana*—to 40 inches; 3-inch, blue-green leaves. Stays small.
B. *phyllostachys aurea*—to 10 feet. Called golden bamboo.

BANANA. See MUSA.

BAYONET PLANT. See YUCCA.

BEAUCARNEA
pony plant
Lilaceae
55°–75°F.

Beaucarnea is a genus of unusual plants—more bizarre than beautiful, perhaps—with thick trunks to about 60 inches, topped by a rosette of linear, pendent green leaves. These plants need a sandy soil that drains readily, and they can be grown in the same pot for many years. Do not overwater—keep them on the dry side. Bright light is adequate. If you want something different, this is it. Buy new plants from suppliers.

B. *recurvata*.

BEEFSTEAK BEGONIA. See BEGONIA, Rhizomatous.

BEGONIA
Begoniaceae
55°–75°F.

These favorites for house decoration come in several hundred species and thousands of varieties. Few begonias require exacting care; most thrive with little attention. For convenience, they are generally divided into five groups.

Wax Begonias (B. semperflorens)

Wax begonias have the wonderful habit of blooming almost all year. Plants have glossy, dark green or mahogany-colored leaves and single, or semidouble, or double blooms in shades ranging from white to fiery red. Give them small pots and sun, and avoid overwatering them. They like to be quite dry: too much water rots their fibrous roots quickly. Prune back the tops as plants get leggy. Propagate wax begonias from cuttings or seed.

* 'Andy'—to 6 inches; grass-green leaves; single, rose-colored flowers.
* 'Apple Blossom'—to 12 inches; double, pale pink flowers.
* 'Ballet'—to 12 inches; bronze leaves; double, white flowers.
* 'Cinderella'—to 12 inches; single, pink flowers tipped red.
* 'Green Thimbleberry'—pale green leaves; double, crested, pink flowers.

* 'Jack Horner'—to 12 inches; dark green leaves; double, pink flowers.
* 'Little Gem'—to 6 inches; bronze leaves; double, pink flowers.
* 'Lucy Locket'—to 14 inches; double, pink flowers.
* 'South Pacific'—to 10 inches; double, bright orange-red flowers.

Rhizomatous Begonias

These are so called because of their gnarled and thickened root systems. Leaves are round or star-shaped, in plain or fancy patterns, their textures satiny or nubbly. Roots naturally skim the surface of the soil and should not be buried. Rhizomes are storehouses, so these begonias can endure drought if necessary. Tall stalks of flowers appear in early spring or late winter. Provide shallow pots and let soil dry out thoroughly between waterings. Some varieties take a short rest in late winter; water them sparingly through these weeks until you see signs of new growth. Propagate this kind from cuttings or seed.

* B. boweri—to 14 inches, delicate green leaves stitched in black, pink flowers. Called eyelash begonia.

This lovely hirsute begonia has handsome foliage and charming small flowers.
(Photograph by Matthew Barr)

* B. 'China Doll'—to 8 inches, light-green-to-purple leaves, pink flowers.
* B. crestabruchii—to 16 inches; heavily ruffled, yellow-green leaves with twisted edges; pink flowers. Called lettuce-leaf begonia.
* B. erythrophylla—to 14 inches; crested, round green leaves, red underneath; long-stemmed pink flowers. Called beefsteak begonia.
* B. heracleifolia—to 14 inches, star-shaped leaves, pink flowers. Called star begonia.
* B. hydrocotylifolia—to 10 inches; round, dark green leaves; pink flowers. Called pennywort begonia.
* B. imperialis 'Otto Forster'—to 14 inches, dark green leaves, white flowers.
* B. 'Maphil' (or B. 'Cleopatra')—to 20 inches; star-shaped leaves splashed with gold, brown, and chartreuse; tall spikes of pink flowers.
* B. ricinifolia—to 16 inches, large green leaves, pink flowers. Resembles the castor-oil plant.
* B. strigilosa—to 16 inches; brown-spotted green leaves on graceful stems; blush-white flowers.

Angel-wing Begonias

This group is named for its wing-shaped leaves. The roots are fibrous. Provide a constantly moist soil and morning or afternoon sun. Cascades of colorful flowers are the reward. Prune frequently to keep growth in bounds, as plants can grow inconveniently tall. Propagate by cuttings.

B. 'Alzasco'—to 36 inches, dark green leaves with silver spots, red flowers in pendent clusters.
B. coccinea—to 48 inches; bright green, shiny leaves; coral-red flowers. Constant bloom.
B. 'Elvira Swisher'—to 48 inches, large-lobed leaves laced with silver, pink flowers.
B. 'Grey Feather'—to 48 inches; shiny, arrow-like leaves; white flowers.
B. maculata—to 40 inches; silver-marked foliage; pink flowers.
B. 'Orange Rubra'—to 36 inches; clear green leaves sometimes spotted with silver; orange flowers.
B. 'Pink Rubra'—to 60 inches; pointed bright green leaves; large pink flowers.
B. 'Rubaiyat'—to 48 inches, smooth green leaves, salmon-pink flowers.

The beauty of tuberous begonias is well shown in
this photograph.
(Photograph courtesy Carl Meyer)

B. 'Velma'—to 40 inches; green, cupped leaves; red flowers.

Hirsute or Hairy-leaved Begonias

These begonias have furry foliage and whiskered flowers. The leaves are round, lobed, or tapered; the blooms—red, pink, or white—always impressive. These plants perform superbly, even in apartments; they can live with dry air if they must and they can tolerate coolness if they have to. Just be sure they get some winter sun so they will bloom. And a word of caution: keep them only moderately moist, as overwatering causes root rot. Propagate them from stem cuttings.

B. alleryi—to 30 inches, dark green leaves with white hairs, pale pink flowers.
B. drostii—to 30 inches, very hairy leaves, pink flowers.
B. prunifolia—to 30 inches, cupped leaves, white flowers.
B. scharffiana—to 30 inches; green-red, plush leaves; ivory flowers.
B. viaudii—to 36 inches; leaves green on top, red below, with fine white hairs; white flowers.

Rex Begonias

These, mostly rhizomatous, are grown for their exquisitely patterned leaves rather than their pink or white flowers, which usually appear in spring. Provide warmth (75°F. in daytime, 65°F. at night), high humidity (60 percent), and bright light but not much sun. A north window is fine. Keep soil consistently moist. Most kinds drop their leaves and become dormant in winter; don't try to force them to grow then. Water them sparingly and wait for new growth. It will appear about mid-March. Propagate plants from leaf cuttings or seed.

B. 'Autumn Glow'—to 14 inches, rose-colored leaves with silver markings.
B. 'Baby Rainbow'—to 12 inches, cupped silvery-green-and-purple leaves.
B. 'Berry's Autumn'—to 8 inches, olive-green leaves with silver spots.
B. 'Calico'—to 8 inches; crimson, green, and silver leaves.

B. 'Cardoza Gardens'—to 16 inches, large purple-silver-and-green leaves. A striking plant.
B. 'Glory of St. Albans'—to 14 inches, metallic rose-purple leaves.
B. 'Merry Christmas'—to 12 inches, multicolored leaves, predominantly red.
B. 'Peace'—to 14 inches, metallic red-and-silver leaves.
B. 'Queen of Hanover'—to 14 inches, light green leaves banded with darker green.
B. 'Red Berry'—to 14 inches, wine-red leaves.
B. 'Red Wing'—to 14 inches, wine-red leaves with silver edges.
B. 'Thrush'—to 14 inches; crimson, star-shaped leaves dotted with silver.
B. 'Winter Queen'—to 14 inches, spiral-shaped silver-purple-and-pink leaves.

Tuberous Begonias

These are summer-flowering aristocrats of the garden, growing to about 24 inches. I have never succeeded with them indoors, but I have seen them in bloom under artificial lights. If you are very fond of begonias and want some of these, you can start them indoors for early garden bloom. In March, select large tubers and plant them in a 2-inch bed of peat moss and sand in a flat or similar container. Set the tubers about 2 inches apart and ½-inch deep, hollow side up. Cover them with ¼-inch of the mix. Grow them at 60°F. to 70°F. and keep them barely moist. When sprouts are 2 inches high, plant the tubers in individual 4-inch pots of porous soil. In mid-May, transfer them to 8- or 9-inch pans, or plant them directly in the garden.

After danger of frost is over, set your plants outdoors where they will get three to four hours of sun, and hope for cool weather. Water plants heavily in clear weather, less when it is cloudy. When they are growing well, apply a fertilizer every third week. Let growth continue until leaves turn yellow in fall. Then lift the tubers from their pots, wash and dry them, and store them at 45°F. to 50°F. Keep them dry until spring.

B. 'Black Knight'—double, deep crimson flowers.

B. 'Flambeau'—lovely, double, orange-scarlet flowers.

B. 'Flamboyante'—single, scarlet flowers.

B. 'Frances Powell'—double, pink flowers.

B. 'Mandarin'—double, salmon-orange flowers.

B. 'Rosado'—deeply frilled and ruffled pink flowers.

B. 'Sweet Home'—double, red flowers.

B. 'Tasso'—semidouble, pink flowers.

Hanging-basket tuberous begonias are sometimes listed by suppliers as "pendulas" or, occasionally, as "lloydii" types. With blossoms that cascade all summer, they are among the most beautiful of all trailing plants. Give them protection from wind and sun. Keep soil moderately moist. Plant two or three medium-sized tubers to a 5-inch pot. Pinch out young shoots early in the growing season to promote growth.

B. 'Andy Lee'—brilliant red flowers.

B. 'Darlene'—pink flowers with white centers.

B. 'Pink Shower'—clear pink flowers.

B. 'Wild Rose'—dark pink flowers.

B. cheimantha and *B. hiemalis* are 20-inch-high, winter-flowering tuberous begonias grown mainly as Christmas and Easter gift plants. Cheimanthas, known as Christmas begonias, bloom from November to March. Grow them rather cool and draft-free, and keep the soil constantly moist. When the flowers fade, cut back the plants severely and grow them at 55°F. until new shoots appear. After the hiemalis types bloom, grow them cool, at about 50°F., and water them sparingly until spring. Then shake off soil around the tubers and repot them. Grow them at 65°F. and keep the soil moderately wet through the summer.

B. cheimantha
   'Gloire de Sceaux'—rose-colored flowers.
   'Lady Mac'—pink or white flowers.
   'Marjorie Gibbs'—pale pink flowers.
   'Spirit of Norway'—vibrant red flowers.
   'Tove'—rose-colored flowers.

B. hiemalis
   'Altrincham Pink'—large, double, long-lasting pink flowers.
   'Emily Clibran'—double, pink flowers. Considered one of the best.

'John C. Mensing'—abundant, double, orange flowers.

BELLFLOWER. See CAMPANULA.

BELOPERONE shrimp plant
Acanthaceae
55°–75°F.

These are most satisfactory flowering plants for a sunny window. They have paper-thin bracts with tiny white flowers and deep green leaves. Let these 36-to-48-inch plants almost dry out between waterings. Prune back leggy growth in late summer. Propagate them from cuttings.

B. guttata—coral-colored bracts. The most popular type.

B. guttata 'Red King'—cascades of red bracts.

B. guttata 'Yellow Queen'—yellow bracts, white flowers.

BENJAMIN FIG. See FICUS.

BERMUDA BUTTERCUP. See OXALIS.

BIFRENARIA *Orchidaceae*
55°–75°F.

An uncommonly beautiful genus of 20-inch, epiphytic orchids with 10-to-16-inch dark green leaves and impressive, colorful flowers in spring. Pot them in fir bark. Undemanding, these plants bloom readily if they are properly rested. After they flower, keep them almost dry and in a dim place for about two months with only an occasional misting (about once a week). Then give them bright light and plenty of water through summer. Obtain new plants from suppliers.

B. harrisoniae—large, waxy white flowers, magenta lip.

B. tyrianthina—lovely pink-and-red flowers on an erect stem.

BILLBERGIA living vase plant
Bromeliaceae
55°–75°F.

Decorative plants, mostly large, with multicolored foliage and bizarre flowers, billbergias are perfect for indoor growing. Some have gray-green, some silver-green, others purple leaves. Flowers are small, but the colorful bracts are striking—red, or pink, or purple. Pot them in fir bark or an osmunda-and-soil mix. Give them bright light and keep the "vase" formed by leaves filled with water. They are good for planters in public places. Propagate them from offsets.

B. *amoena*—to 16 inches, shiny green leaves, rose-colored bracts in spring and summer.

B. *brasiliense*—to 48 inches; tubular gray-green plant; handsome, pendent cerise flowers. Highly desirable.

*B. *morelii*—to 10 inches, green leaves, blue flowers in red bracts in summer.

B. *nutans*—to 30 inches; chartreuse, pink, and cerise flowers in winter. Called queen's tears.

B. *pyramidalis*—to 24 inches, golden green leaves, orange-pink flowers and bracts in summer.

B. *pyramidalis* 'Fantasia'—to 24 inches, robust hybrid with multicolored leaves, red bracts and red-and-blue flowers in fall.

B. *zebrina*—to 40 inches, gray-green leaves flecked with silver, cascading rose-colored bracts, usually in summer.

BIRD-OF-PARADISE. See STRELITZIA.

BIRD'S-NEST FERN. See ASPLENIUM and FERNS.

BISHOP'S-HOOD CACTUS. See ASTRO-PHYTUM and CACTUSES.

BLACK-EYED-SUSAN VINE. See THUN-BERGIA.

BLACK ORCHID. See COELOGYNE.

BLAKEA *Melastomaceae* 60°–75°F.

This genus of about fifteen species of evergreen trees and shrubs from tropical America includes a few stellar house plants that are very rewarding to grow. Leaves are usually leathery, smooth and shiny above and covered with hair underneath. Flowers are reddish pink and showy. Use equal parts peat moss and a soil that drains readily. Give plants ample heat. Water them copiously in spring and summer, not so much the rest of the year. Propagate blakeas from cuttings in sand in spring. These very fine plants are often overlooked.

B. *gracilis*—to about 60 inches indoors; oval, leathery leaves; handsome rosy pink flowers in early spring.

B. *trinervia*—to 36 inches; oval, shiny leaves; handsome rose-colored flowers in summer.

BLECHNUM tree fern *Polypodiaceae* 55°–75°F.

Seldom seen, but made to order for warm, dry houses, these tree ferns offer splendid vertical accents. Unlike most ferns, they will grow in low humidity with regular root watering and good light. Young leaves are copper-and-green, maturing to a lovely dark green. Avoid over-watering. Propagate blechnums from spores or offsets.

B. *brasiliense*—to 48 inches. Good for plant rooms or public places.

B. *gibbum*—to 40 inches. Nice tree-size fern, developing a lateral habit, with dark green fronds deeply cut and finely divided.

B. *occidentale*—to 24 inches. Fine in windows.

BLOOD LILY. See HAEMANTHUS.

BLUE ORCHID. See VANDA and ORCHIDS.

BLUE SAGE. See ERANTHEMUM.

BOSTON FERN. See NEPHROLEPIS and FERNS.

BOUGAINVILLEA paper flower *Nyctaginaceae* 60°–80°F.

Too often overlooked, bougainvilleas offer brilliant color for little effort. Some grow to 20 feet outdoors in temperate climates. Indoors, the

2-to-15-foot plants bloom a long time in summer. Some are vines, others shrubby. Plants need sun and constant moisture in summer; in winter, grow them somewhat dry. Cut them back whenever they get too large. There are some splendid varieties. Obtain new plants from seed.

B. 'Barbara Karst'—tall, bushy growth; masses of red bracts.

B. *glabra*—a strong vine, purplish pink bracts.

B. 'Harrisii'—low, bushy growth; variegated leaves; white flowers on purple bracts.

B. 'Temple Fire'—low and compact growth, red-to-cerise bracts.

BOUVARDIA

jasmine plant
Rubiaceae
55°–75°F.

This is a garden plant that does well indoors in large pots. Plants have oval leaves in groups of two or three and clusters of brightly colored, tubular, fragrant flowers from summer to late fall. Flower color is generally white, pink, or red; there are many varieties. Bouvardias need a sunny window to bloom. Plant them in a packaged soil that drains well. Water them freely in warm months but not much the rest of the year. They are easily grown and make a nice addition to the window garden. Propagate them from cuttings in spring.

B. *domesticum*.

BOWIEA

onion plant
Liliaceae
55°–75°F.

This genus of but one species from South Africa is widely grown. It is an oddity in the plant world, a large, bulbous, underground growth topped with twining stems. The onion plant needs much sun and a loose soil that drains readily. Keep soil consistently moist. Disturb it as seldom as possible—top-dress soil rather than repot the plant. Propagate this one from seed or offsets.

B. *volubilis*.

BRAKE FERN. See PTERIS and FERNS.

BRASSAIA. See SCHEFFLERA.

BRASSAVOLA

Orchidaceae
55°–75°F.

These small epiphytes, perfect for windows, have large, flamboyant white flowers, usually scented, in fall. Grow them in 4- or 5-inch pots of fir bark kept quite dry. Give them plenty of sun and humidity (at least 50 percent). Purchase new plants from specialists.

B. acaulis—to 12 inches, grasslike foliage, pure white flowers with heart-shaped lip.

B. cucullata—to 12 inches. Similar to *B. acaulis* but with greenish flowers.

B. nodosa—to 10 inches. The popular lady-of-the-night orchid, with sweet-scented white flowers. One plant perfumes an entire room.

BRAZILIAN EDELWEISS. See RECHSTEINERIA and GESNERIADS.

BROMELIA

volcano plant
Bromeliaceae
55°–75°F.

In bloom, with fiery centers of red, these large plants are awesome. Their leaves are dark green and heavily spined, so wear gloves when handling them. Pot them in equal parts osmunda-and-soil mix; give them sun and consistent moisture all year. Not demanding about humidity, they make good tub plants, well-suited to public rooms and lobbies. Grow new plants from offsets: when they have several leaves, pot the plantlets individually.

B. *balansae*—24-to-36-inch-wide rosette of stiff green leaves with hooked spines, center turning red when plant blooms; white flowers.

B. *humilis*—36-to-50-inch rosette of leaves. A beautiful giant, similar to *B. balansae*.

B. *serra*—20-to-30-inch-wide rosette of leaves. Similar to *B. balansae*.

B. *serra variegata*—36-to-50-inch-wide rosette of very spiny grayish green leaves with ivory margins, center turning fiery red when plant blooms.

BROMELIADS

Ten years ago these plants were rarely seen; today their colorful bracts and decorative foliage make interiors across the country glorious greenhouses. Often called institutional plants, they are almost care-free and can survive in shade for many months. In the home, too, they scoff at neglect and still furnish color and grace. There are small, medium, and giant species. Most kinds form rosettes of leaves; some, tubular vases of foliage. There are epiphytic and terrestrial kinds, and both succeed in osmunda or in a mixture of osmunda and potting soil. Keep the center of these plants filled with water, the potting mix barely moist. Bright sun makes their foliage glow with color. The great beauty of bromeliads lies in the bright bracts of spectacular color that remains vibrant for six months: cerise, violet, chartreuse, scarlet—even almost black! The flowers are small and hidden within the bracts. Don't feed these plants. You can throw away insecticides, too, for the leaves are too tough for insects. For descriptions of some plants in this family and their culture, see:

Aechmea
Ananas
Billbergia
Bromelia
Catopsis
Cryptanthus
Dyckia
Guzmania
Hohenbergia
Neoregelia
Nidularium
Portea
Tillandsia
Vriesea

BROUGHTONIA
Orchidaceae
55°–75°F.

This is a charming, 4-to-6-inch, epiphytic orchid with colorful cerise flowers all winter. Leaves are dark green and leathery. Grow them in 4-inch pots of osmunda or fir bark. Provide sun and water, and the plants will take care of themselves. Flowers are tiny replicas of the popular cattleya corsage orchid. Obtain seedlings from suppliers.

*B. sanguinea.

BROWALLIA
purple passion
Solanaceae
55°–75°F.

Browallia is a genus of lovely shrublike plants with glossy leaves and star-shaped blue, violet, or white flowers in summer. Put several plants in a pot for a handsome display. Somewhat difficult to get growing, browallias are worth the attempt because their flowers are very appealing. Grow browallias in a shady place: sun can harm them. Use a packaged soil that drains readily, and be sure drainage is good. Keep soil consistently moist; it should never be dry. Discard plants after flowering—they seldom flourish more than one season. Propagate them from seed in spring.

B. speciosa major—to 20 inches; handsome leaves; exquisite purple, blue, or white flowers.
B. viscosa compacta 'Sapphire'—to 12 inches, emerald-green leaves, blue flowers with white eyes.

BRUNFELSIA
yesterday-today-and-tomorrow
Solanaceae
50°–68°F.

Brunfelsia is a fine (but difficult to grow) winter-blooming plant to 36 inches. It bears pretty, fragrant purple flowers that turn white about a week after opening. Its foliage is green and bushy. Grow it in bright light and keep soil consistently moist. It likes 50 percent humidity. If you have trouble with this one, try a large pot: a 6- or 8-inch one, and keep pinching the shoots back when the plant is young. Put it in the shady garden in summer. Propagate brunfelsia from stem cuttings in spring.

B. calycina floribunda.

BURRO'S TAIL. See SEDUM.

BUTTERFLY ORCHID. See ONCIDIUM and ORCHIDS.

BUTTON FERN. See PELLAEA and FERNS.

CACTUSES

The cactus family is extensive. Although all cactuses are succulents, not all succulents are cactuses. Cactuses offer the indoor gardener an array of unusual forms and brilliant blossoms. There are small types that stay small for years—perfect for windows—larger kinds that are delightful, if you have space for them.

Most cactuses have spines or scales that reduce the evaporation of stored moisture during the long dry spells of their native lands. Many are from the desert; they rest in winter, grow in summer. This type needs porous soil and well-drained containers just big enough to hold them. Don't overpot them, and repot them only every second or third year—in fresh soil but usually in the same container, since these plants grow very slowly. In summer and spring, it's usually best to keep soil consistently moist; in fall and winter, allow it to become somewhat dry, but never bone-dry.

The orchid cactus (epiphyllum), chain or mistletoe cactus (rhipsalis), Thanksgiving or crab cactus (*Zygocactus truncatus*), Easter cactus (*Epiphylopsis gaertnerii*), Christmas cactus (*Schlumbergera bridgesii*), and certain other species are not from the desert. They are jungle plants, mostly epiphytic. They need a potting mixture that might consist of leaf mold, sand, and shredded osmunda. Be sure their containers have good drainage, and pot plants tightly. Keep them consistently moist in spring and summer, but let them almost dry out between waterings in fall and winter. Give most of them full sun then, bright light the rest of the year. Cool nights (50°F. to 55°F.) are necessary to encourage bud formation in fall; for many of them, about a month of uninterrupted twelve-hour darkness at night is also essential. Even light from a street lamp will disturb the budding cycle.

Insects rarely attack cactuses: their leaves are just too tough. For descriptions of some species and their culture, see:

Aporocactus
Aporophyllum
Ariocarpus
Astrophytum
Cephalocereus
Chamaecereus
Cleistocactus
Coryphantha
Echinocactus
Echinocereus
Echinopsis
Epiphyllum
Epiphylopsis (Rhipsalidopsis)
Ferocactus
Gymnocalycium
Heliocereus
Hylocereus
Leuchtenbergia
Lobivia
Lophophora
Mammillaria
Notocactus
Opuntia
Pereskia
Rebutia
Rhipsalis
Schlumbergera
Selenicereus
Trichocereus
Zygocactus

CALADIUM

Araceae
60°–70°F.

This is a large tribe of 20-to-30-inch plants with stunning foliage. The paper-thin, heart-shaped leaves are stained with white, pink, red, green, and many shades in between. Provide shade and warmth, and water them well while in active growth. They like to be really wet: 60 percent (or higher) humidity suits them best. The growing season is generally from April until October. In fall, when leaves die down, gradually reduce their allowance of water. When growth has completely stopped, remove the tubers from their pots, dry them out, and store them in heavy paper bags at 60°F. for two or three months. Then repot them: one tuber to each 5-inch container. Although you can buy mature plants at nurseries, it is easy and fun to start your own. They make grand summer decoration for shaded windows or terrace borders. Here are some varieties I have grown:

'Ace of Hearts'—crimson-and-mossy-green leaves.

'Ace of Spades'—leaves with red veins, red-and-white marbling, green edges.

'Ann Greer'—large red-bronze leaves with emerald-green tracery.

'Edith Mead'—dark-green-and-white leaves, red veins.

'Frieda Herple'—red-and-deep-green leaves.

'Gray Ghost'—creamy-white-and-green leaves.

'Jessie Thayer'—scarlet-and-metallic-green leaves.

'Keystone'—forest-green leaves with white spots.

'Maid of Orleans'—deep green leaves marbled in pink.

'Pink Blush'—crinkled pink-and-cream leaves.

'Pinkie'—delicate pink leaves with red veins.

'Red Chief'—scarlet leaves.

'Red Flame'—rosy purple leaves.

'Stacy'—large white-and-pink leaves.

'White Queen'—pure white leaves with crimson veins. Stunning.

CALATHEA
Marantaceae
60°–80°F.

Fine foliage plants from Brazil, calatheas are prized for their decorative green leaves marked or striped with other colors. They need bright light and plenty of water. Give them heat and high (to 80 percent) humidity. Though they are not easy to grow, they have such beautiful foliage that they are worth the extra care. Many kinds are available, and new ones are introduced frequently. Propagate them by root division at repotting time.

Calathea, podocarpus, and aglaonema (left to right): a trio of excellent indoor plants.
(Photograph by USDA)

C. *bachemiana*—to 16 inches, gray-green leaves marked with dark green.

C. *concinna*—to 20 inches; leaves with a dark green feather design over a deeper green on top, purple underneath. An outstanding plant.

C. *kegeliana*—to 24 inches; thick, leathery leaves of silver-gray with lance-shaped bands of dark green on top, gray-green underneath. A dramatic foliage plant.

*C. *leopardina*—to 12 inches, waxy green foliage with contrasting darker green bands.

C. *lietzei*—to 24 inches; light green leaves, purple underneath.

C. *makoyana*—to 48 inches, olive-green-and-pink leaves veined in silver. A fine foliage plant.

*C. *roseo-picta*—to 12 inches, dark-green-and-red leaves.

C. *vandenheckei*—to 30 inches, white-and-dark-green leaves.

C. *veitchiana*—to 48 inches; leaves with a peacock feather design in brown, chartreuse, green, and red.

C. *zebrina*—to 36 inches; dark, velvety leaves with a chartreuse background.

CALCEOLARIA

pocketbook plant
Scrophulariaceae
50°–60°F.

These funny little plants with dark green leaves and puffy, pouchy flowers are colorful annuals. When flowering is over you have to discard them, but even so they are desirable. Usually calceolarias arrive as gift plants, but if kept cool and shaded with even moisture at the roots, they will stay fresh for two to three weeks. Sow seed in April or August for new plants. Seedlings need a cool growing environment.

C. *herbeohybrida*—to 24 inches; bushy, compact ball of flowers, usually yellow or red with spots.

C. *multiflora*—to 16 inches, yellow flowers in terminal clusters.

*C. *multiflora nana*—to 10 inches. A popular dwarf often sold as a gift plant.

CALICO FLOWER. See ARISTOLOCHIA.

CALLA LILY. See ZANTEDESCHIA.

CAMELLIA

Theaceae
45°–60°F.

Don't believe these plants cannot be grown indoors. If you have a place that is brightly lit or sunny for three to four hours a day, where night temperatures are between 45°F. and 55°F. and days rarely above 65°F., you will be amazed at the flowers you can have. Some varieties bloom in winter, others in spring. For soil, use two parts garden loam, one part peat moss, and one part sand. Acidity is essential: pH 5–5.5. Give plants plenty of water (soil should never dry out), and mist foliage every day in summer and about every other day the rest of the year. Apply an acid fertilizer during active growth in spring and keep humidity about 60 percent then. Repot plants only when absolutely necessary. Indoors, watch for occasional attacks of scales or mealy bugs, but if plants are grown cool with good air circulation there is little danger of pests. To ensure bloom, put plants outdoors in summer. Bud drop or buds failing to open are rather frequent complaints: too much water in cool weather prevents buds from opening; too little water will cause buds to drop. Most camellias are tall—to about 48 inches—ideal as floor plants in front of cool windows or on sun porches or in plant rooms. You may grow new plants from seed or stem cuttings or by layering. Most nurseries carry C. *japonica* and C. *sasanqua* varieties.

C. *japonica* produces large flowers in a wide range of whites, pinks, and reds. A long season of bloom—usually five to seven months—also makes them desirable.

'Colonel Fiery'—double, crimson flowers from January on.

'Debutante'—single, crested pink flowers from October to January.

'Elegans'—peony-form, red-and-white flowers in January.

'Pink Perfection'—double, flat pink flowers from November to April.

'Purity'—double, pure white flowers from November to April.

C. sasanqua offers a profusion of small flowers from October to April. There are single, fragrant whites and also pink and cherry-red varieties.

'William S. Hastie'—a good single, crimson type, blooming from February to April.

CAMPANULA
bellflower, star-of-Bethlehem
Campanulaceae
50°–60°F.

For basket or bracket, these rewarding plants with trailing stems to 20 inches are covered with white or blue flowers from August until December. A healthy specimen has hundreds of blooms. Campanulas need fresh air and good light; shade them only in summer. Fertilize plants while they are in active growth, and let soil dry out between waterings. Usually in winter (depending upon the species), when growth slows, cut plants back to about 5 inches and keep them on the dry side and cool (55°F.). Come spring, repot them in fresh soil and increase moisture. Pick off flowers as they fade, as seed formation reduces bloom. Take cuttings for new plants.

C. elatines alba plena—double, white flowers.
C. elatines florepleno—double, blue flowers.
C. fragilis—single, pale blue flowers.
C. isophylla alba—single, snow-white flowers. The most popular variety.
C. isophylla mayii—single, larger, intense blue flowers.

CANDELABRA ALOE. See ALOE.

CAPE JASMINE. See GARDENIA.

CAPE PRIMROSE. See STREPTOCARPUS and GESNERIADS.

CAPSICUM
red pepper plant, ornamental pepper
Solanaceae
55°–65°F.

C. annum (or *C. frutescens*) is a delightful Christmas gift plant, usually with white spring flowers followed by colorful autumn fruits—some shaped like miniature peppers—that hold through Christmas. Give them full sun and a consistently moist soil, and do grow them cool, for the fruit drops in a hot room. Although this annual lasts only a season, the cheerful plants are still worthwhile, especially for the holidays. Propagate capsicums by seed in spring. There are many varieties. These I have found reliable and attractive:

'Christmas Candle'—to 24 inches; broad, spreading growth; slender, conical yellow-to-red fruit up to 3 inches long.
'Piccolo'—to 26 inches; variegated leaves, some almost white; starry lavender flowers; black-purple fruit.
'Robert Crain'—to 30 inches, conical red fruit.
'Weatherillii'—to 30 inches; large, conical yellow-to-red fruit that remains attractive a long time.

CARDINAL FLOWER. See RECHSTEINERIA and GESNERIADS.

CARISSA
natal plum
Apocynaceae
55°–65°F.

Spiny—but not thorny—vining shrubs to about 2 feet indoors, with small, glossy green leaves and scented white flowers followed by red berries, carissas make a most decorative showing through all seasons in a bracket. Plants need full sun, consistently moist soil, and frequent misting to help maintain 50 percent humidity and ensure development of flower buds. Water them sparingly when plants rest in winter. Propagate carissas from cuttings.

C. grandiflora nana compacta—to 24 inches.
C. 'Petit Point'—to 10 inches. A fine miniature, with tiny green leaves.

CARNIVAL ORCHID. See ASCOCENTRUM and ORCHIDS.

CAROLINA JASMINE. See GELSEMIUM.

CARRION FLOWER. See STAPELIA.

CARROT FERN. See DAVALLIA and FERNS.

CARYOTA
fishtail palm
Palmaceae
55°–75°F.

Thirty-six-inch palms from tropical Asia and Australia with graceful, glossy green, scalloped foliage on tall stems, caryotas are fine plants for the house. Although the zigzag leaf edges turn brown with age, the plants are most decorative, slow-growing, and easy to maintain. Give these palms bright light, and keep soil consistently moist. Grow new plants from offsets or by root division.

C. mitis—multistemmed clusters of fan-shaped green leaves.

C. plumosa—leathery, bright green fronds on a dominant trunk.

CASHMERE BOUQUET. See CLERODENDRUM.

CASSIA
senna, shower tree
Leguminosae
55°–75°F.

Upright, 36-to-50 inch plants (indoors) with yellow cascades of flowers in spring and summer, cassias are great as specimens for a patio or on the floor in front of a sunny window. Cassias flourish in ordinary potting soil. During active growth, give them plenty of water. In winter, store them like an oleander in a frost-free place with less light. New plants can be grown from cuttings.

C. corymbosa—leathery leaflets in pairs, open clusters of flowers.

C. splendida—oval leaflets, large golden flowers in racemes.

CAST-IRON PLANT. See ASPIDISTRA.

CATOPSIS
Bromeliaceae
55°–70F.

These are easy-to-grow, bottle-shaped, terrestrial bromeliads with spikes of white or yellow flowers. Pot them in equal parts soil and osmunda and place them at your sunniest window. In summer flood them with water; the rest of the year grow them somewhat dry. They like 50 to 60 percent humidity. Grow new plants from offsets.

C. berteroniana—bottle-shaped growth to 20 inches, apple-green leaves, yellow flowers.

C. floribunda—to 14 inches, dark green leaves, white-and-yellow flowers.

CATTLEYA
corsage flower
Orchidaceae
60°–75°F.

This most popular genus of orchids has many fine plants for indoor use. While cattleyas are hardly attractive out of bloom, with flowers they are dazzling. Leaves are straplike and leathery; flowers are large, to 5 inches across, in a rainbow of colors—white, pink, cerise, red. There are many varieties. Cattleyas need sun. Pot them in medium-grade fir bark. Keep plants consistently moist all year and provide high humidity (50 percent). Mist with tepid water frequently. Purchase new plants from suppliers.

C. forbesii—to 40 inches; in summer bears two to five flowers, 3 inches across, greenish yellow, lip streaked red.

C. hybrids—to 36 inches; large flowers at various times in a variety of colors—white, pink, lavender.

C. luteola—to 6 inches, pale yellow flowers in fall. A very pretty miniature.

C. skinnerii—to 36 inches; in summer bears lovely clusters of pink flowers, 3 inches across. Easy to grow, sure to please.

C. walkeriana—to 12 inches; in fall or winter bears exquisite magenta flowers, 4 inches across. Somewhat difficult, but not impossible to grow.

CELOSIA cockscomb
Amaranthaceae
55°–75°F.

Popular garden plants from Asia and Africa,
the celosias include about thirty species. Plants
have somewhat furry pale green leaves, and
their flowers resemble a cockscomb in shape—
they may be yellow or red. Plants require
warmth and standard packaged potting soil.
Keep them consistently moist and provide full
sun. No special tricks here—celosias grow by
themselves. Allow plants to die in winter. Buy
new plants each year from suppliers.

C. argentea cristata—crested flowers.
C. argentea plumosa—plumed flowers.

CENTIPEDE PLANT. See MUEHLEN-
BECKIA.

CENTURY PLANT. See AGAVE.

CEPHALOCEREUS old-man cactus
Cactaceae
55°–75°F.

Long hairs, spines, and a ribbed, barrel shape
characterize these familiar 12-to-30-inch desert
plants. Since they seem to thrive almost untended, you may want one for your indoor
garden. They need a sandy soil kept barely
moist, tight potting, and sun. Slow-growing,
they are seemingly impervious to the effects of
time. Propagate them from seed.

C. chrysacanthus—blue-ribbed stems with yellow spines, golden hairs, rosy red flowers.
C. palmeri—white hairs, purplish flowers.
C. senilis—yellow spines, long gray hairs, rosy
flowers. A curiosity.

CEROPEGIA rosary vine
Asclepiadaceae
50°–60°F.

Fascinating vines, sometimes to 72 inches, with
usually heart-shaped leaves and tiny tubular
flowers, ceropegias grow best in an airy place.
More bizarre than beautiful, they are novelties.

Give them full sun and let soil dry out between
waterings. Obtain new plants from cuttings.

C. barklyi—to 18 inches, fleshy dark green leaves,
purple-brown flowers.
C. caffrorum—to 20 inches, wiry stems,
green-and-purple flowers.
C. krainzii—to 40 inches, succulent stems,
yellow flowers.
C. naygarthii—to 36 inches, small oval leaves,
unusual cream-colored flowers spotted red.
C. sandersonii—to 20 inches, small green leaves,
twining succulent stems, white flowers
marked with purple.
C. woodii—to 20 inches; leaves on trailing,
threadlike stems; pink or purple flowers with
small tubers at the ends of the stems. Called
string-of-hearts.

CESTRUM jasmine
Solanaceae
55°–75°F.

These shrubs are grown for their scent; they
bear fragrant red or white flowers on and off
throughout the year. Foliage is bright green.
Grow them in a sunny window and keep soil
consistently moist. They like 50 percent humidity. Plants grow large: some become specimens to 72 inches. Prune plants drastically to
keep them in bounds; even small ones bloom.
Propagate cestrums from cuttings in spring.

C. nocturnum—to 72 inches; fragrant, star-
shaped white flowers opening in the evening. Called night jasmine.
C. parqui—to 36 inches, greenish white flowers. This is the best one for indoors. Called
willow-leaved jasmine.
C. purpureum—to 20 inches; continuously
blooming, handsome red flowers. Very
desirable.

CHAIN CACTUS. See RHIPSALIS and
CACTUSES.

CHAIN FERN. See WOODWARDIA and
FERNS.

CHAIN PLANT. See TRADESCANTIA.

CHAMAECEREUS   peanut cactus
Cactaceae
55°–75°F.

A desert cactus with only one species in cultivation, the chamaecereus is a handsome plant abloom in summer with lovely orange-red flowers. Stems are cylindrical and prickly with small white spines. Keep plants in bright light and choose a sandy soil that drains readily. Water them sparsely all year. Grow new plants from offsets.

C. silvestri.

CHAMAEDOREA   palm
(COLLINIA)   *Palmaceae*
55°–70°F.

Rather showy, shade-loving palms from Central America and northern South Africa with single or multiple trunks, chamaedoreas are graceful on a porch, patio, or pedestal stand. Give plants bright light and keep soil consistently moist. Provide 50 percent humidity. Grow new plants from seed.

C. cataractarum—compact, 30-inch rosette; dark green fronds.
C. elegans—to 72 inches (often less), a fast grower with dark green fronds. Called parlor palm.
C. erumpens—20-to-30-inch rosette. Called bamboo palm.
C. graminifolia—horizontal growth to 60 inches, slender light green leaflets.

CHENILLE PLANT. See ACALYPHA.

CHILEAN JASMINE. See DIPLADENIA.

CHIN CACTUS. See GYMNOCALYCIUM and CACTUSES.

CHINCHERINCHEE. See ORNITHO-GALUM.

CHINESE BANYAN. See FICUS.

CHINESE EVERGREEN. See AGLAO-NEMA.

CHINESE FAN PALM. See LIVISTONA and PALMS.

CHINESE PRIMROSE. See PRIMULA.

CHLOROPHYTUM   spider plant
Liliaceae
50°–75°F.

These are fine, 36-inch plants that can be neglected and still survive. With grassy green leaves, some on pendent stems, chlorophytums are excellent for baskets. Large pots are best, as roots quickly fill containers. Mature specimens bear tiny white flowers on tall stiff stems in winter. Don't cut these off, as leaf clusters, some of which are tiny plantlets that can be rooted, form after the flowers. Give chlorophytums bright light and let soil dry out between waterings. Their strong, ropelike roots store water, which protects the plants should you forget to tend them. Propagate them by potting the plantlets growing on the stem runners, or cut mature plants apart with a sharp knife and pot the divisions separately.

C. bichetii—green-and-white striped leaves.
C. comosum picturatum—yellow-and-green striped leaves.
C. comosum variegatum—green leaves with white margins.
C. elatum—glossy green leaves. The most popular variety.

CHRISTMAS BEGONIA. See BEGONIA, Tuberous.

CHRISTMAS CACTUS. See SCHLUM-BERGERA and CACTUSES.

CHRISTMAS FERN. See POLYSTICHUM and FERNS.

Enjoy the beauty of ferns and such vining plants as cissus in ornamental wall brackets. (Photograph by Bradbury)

CHRYSANTHEMUM
Compositae
55°–65°F.

Handsome with yellow, white, bronze, or red flowers, these are popular year-round gift plants. They grow to about 20 inches. To make flowers last for weeks, put plants in a cool place with morning or afternoon sun. Keep soil consistently moist. After flowers fade, cut back stems to 2 inches and set plants in a frost-free garage or coldframe, keeping soil barely moist until spring. Then set plants out permanently in the garden.

C. morifolium.

CINERARIA. See SENECIO.

CISSUS
(VITIS)
Vitaceae
50°–75°F.

These pretty, ambitious trailers or climbers (to 60 inches or more—unless pruned) are among the easiest vines for an indoor planter, basket, or bracket, thriving even in dark apartments. Grow them in sun or shade, and allow soil to dry out between waterings. Repot plants every year or two, as they thrive in fresh soil. Propagate plants from cuttings or by root division.

C. adenapada—climbs rapidly to 72 inches; three-lobed leaves, red and hairy. Different.

C. antarctica—climbs to 60 inches; fresh, shiny green leaves with brown veins. Called kangaroo vine.

C. capensis—climbs to 60 inches; large, feltlike leaves, a beautiful silver-green.

C. discolor—climbs to 60 inches; velvety green leaves with toothed edges, red veins, and tintings of white and pink.

C. quadrangularis—climbs to 60 inches; four-winged, fleshy, rich-green stems. Plant needs winter rest.

C. rhombifolia—climbs to 60 inches; metallic, greenish brown, veined leaves. The very familiar grape ivy.

C. striata—a miniature type with bronze-green leaves.

www.dav.org
Cincinnati, Ohio 45250-0301
P.O. Box 14301
Disabled American Veterans
DAV

Thank You!

Thank you for your generous support. These bookmarks are a gift
to you and there is no obligation
to pay for them. When you use
them, remember that your gift
helps disabled veterans.

DAV National Help
Fundraising Program

If you are, or know of a disabled
veteran who could use a helping
hand, please write to the address
listed below.

The Purpose of the DAV

To provide support, encouragement and a better life for the noble
men and women who became
disabled while upholding the world
peace and the freedom of the
United States of America.

lemon tree, lime tree, orange tree
Rutaceae
55°–70°F.

...mental trees grow up to 72 inches
...excellent in tubs. Their foliage
...d shiny, their branching habit
...them on a cold, sunny, en-
...a plant room. Water plants
...ower or fruit; at other times
...ry. Fragrant blossoms open
...hout the year. To encour-
...e the blooms with a small
...or spider mites, and mist
...cks. These trees like acid
...ar solution or an acid
...Propagate these plants

...ome, spiny lime tree.
...a lovely bonsai form.
...idwarf and spread-
...e for pots. Called
...green, oval leaves.
...t in a tub.
...tree. A good pot
...ge.

Cactaceae
55°–75°F.

In th... ...p of desert cactuses there are a few
columnar species that do well indoors. Plants
have erect ribbed stems with spines, and fine
tubular flowers. Give them full sun and choose
a sandy soil that drains readily. Give them water
only when soil feels dry, as overwatering can
harm plants. Grow new plants from offsets.

C. baumannii—stout stems to 36 inches with
spines, scarlet flowers.
C. strausii—erect, many-ribbed columns to 36
inches; red flowers. A good indoor plant.

CLERODENDRUM
glory bower
Verbenaceae
50°–65°F.

Free-flowering, these plants have long been overlooked by indoor gardeners, yet they offer a
wealth of color for little effort. Their vining
growth, 48 to 72 inches, is attractive. Their
foliage is lush green, and the spring, summer,
and sometimes even fall flowers are just grand.
Give them full sun and keep soil consistently
moist except in winter, when plants naturally
lose some leaves and need little water. Don't
try to force them into growth then. They are
decorative as pot plants or in baskets. Cuttings
root easily and bloom the first year. You can
also grow plants from seed.

C. bungei—rose-red, marvelously fragrant flowers in late summer or early fall. Called Mexican hydrangea.
C. fragrans pleniflorum—double, scented
pale-pink-and-purple flowers in early fall.
Called Cashmere bouquet.
C. nutans (or *C. wallachii*)—to 40 inches; handsome dark green leaves, white flowers.
C. speciosum—rose-pink flowers in summer.
C. thomsonae—white-and-deep crimson flowers in spring and summer.
C. ugandense—bright blue flowers from winter to spring.

CLIFF-BRAKE FERN. See PELLAEA and
FERNS.

CLIMBING FERN. See LYGODIUM.

CLIVIA
Kafir lily
Amaryllidaceae
55°–70°F.

Growing to 30 inches, these aristocrats among
pot plants make a striking picture when in bloom
in April and May. Their leaves are ornamental,
the vivid, tubular flowers exciting. These plants
bloom best when potbound, so use 5-, 6-, or
7-inch containers. Although they tolerate sun,
they bloom better in light shade. Water them
heavily during growth, not so much the rest of
the year. New plants can be obtained by dividing the bulbs.

C. Belgian Hybrids—broad leaves, very large
orange-red flowers. Excellent.

C. miniata—strap-shaped dark green leaves to 18 inches, orange flowers. The most popular variety.

C. nobilis—strap-shaped leaves, pendulous red-and-yellow flowers with green tips.

C. Zimmerman Hybrids—salmon, orange, or red flowers.

CLOCK VINE. See THUNBERGIA.

CLUB MOSS. See SELAGINELLA.

COBAEA

cup-and-saucer vine
Polemoniaceae
60°–75°F.

Cobaea is a very handsome vining climber with appealing violet flowers, a fine candidate for the garden room. The plant grows quickly in a well-drained soil. Water it copiously and feed it regularly. This is a greedy plant. Keep it in bright sun for a bountiful harvest of flowers. It is only good for the season but well worth the space you allot it then. Start plants from seed.

C. scandens.

COB CACTUS. See LOBIVIA.

COBWEB HOUSELEEK. See SEMPER-VIVUM.

COCKSCOMB. See CELOSIA.

CODIAEUM

croton
Euphorbiaceae
60°–80°F.

The striking multicolored foliage makes *Codiaeum variegatum pictum* a splendid accent plant. Yours may grow to 36 inches or more. Foliage form varies, and foliage color ranges from pale yellow, to pink, to orange, to red, and to brown, with many shades of green. To grow these well, give them attention. Set them where there is good air circulation and two to three hours of sun each day. Keep soil consistently moist ex-

cept in December and January, at which time decrease watering somewhat. Maintain high humidity (to 70 percent) and watch out for spider mites. Propagate these from cuttings or by air layering. There are countless cultivars:

'America'—oaklike maroon leaves.

'Cameo'—delicate pink leaves.

'Gloriosa'—large, broad, red-purple-maroon leaves.

'Harvest Moon'—broad yellow-and-green leaves.

'Monarch'—brilliant red leaves.

'Spotlight'—narrow green-yellow-red leaves.

'Sunday'—orange-yellow-red leaves.

COELOGYNE

Orchidaceae
50°–60°F.

These epiphytic orchids with pendent scapes of white, beige, or green flowers prefer coolness and perform even better at home than in the greenhouse. Some of them grow all year, others need a month of rest with only occasional watering before blooming and then again afterward. Grow plants in fir bark kept consistently moist except during a rest period. Give them bright light but no sun and provide 40 to 60 percent humidity. Specimen plants sometimes bloom twice a year. These are impressive flowers, sure to please. Buy new plants from specialists.

C. cristata—to 20 inches, 3-inch crystal-white flowers in January and February. Needs a rest period.

C. flaccida—to 16 inches, 1-inch beige flowers in winter or early spring. Needs a rest period.

C. massangeana—to 36 inches; dozens of 1-inch beige flowers in spring, sometimes again in fall. No rest needed.

C. ocellata—to 10 inches, a charmer with pretty 1-inch white-and-orange flowers. Needs a rest period.

C. pandurata—to 30 inches; handsome, green, ribbed leaves; exquisite chartreuse flowers marked with greenish black in the center. Called black orchid.

C. speciosa—to 14 inches; 3-inch beige flowers, usually in winter. No rest needed.

COFFEA
Arabian coffee plant
Rubiaceae
50°–70°F.

This evergreen shrub grows to 15 feet in its native land. Indoors, it makes a superior pot plant, growing to about 36 inches, with glossy green leaves, white flowers, and, in summer, red berries. Give it bright light and keep soil almost wet. Humidity should range between 30 and 50 percent. Propagate coffea from cuttings.

C. arabica.

COLEUS
painted-leaf plant
Labiatae
55°–65°F.

Old-fashioned favorites, these easy-to-grow plants are valued for their colorful foliage: plum, red, pink, green, yellow. Grow them in a bright place, water them every second or third day, and they will grow luxuriantly—to about 16 inches. If you put them outside in summer, you will be rewarded with blue flowers. Watch out for mealy bugs. Grow new plants from seed. New cultivars are frequently announced in garden catalogs. These are good varieties of *C. blumei*, the common coleus:

'Brilliancy'—red-and-gold leaves.
'Candidum'—large, broad, wavy leaves that are yellow, green, and white.
'Christmas Cheer'—wine-red leaves edged with yellow-green.
'Firebird'—orange-red leaves edged with green.
'Forest Park'—red-and-light-green leaves.
'Pink Rainbow'—red-and-moss-green leaves with red veins.
'Sunset'—salmon-rose leaves with moss-green areas.
'The Chief'—ruffled, bright red leaves. Outstanding.

COLLINIA. See CHAMAEDOREA and PALMS.

COLOCASIA
elephant ears, taro
Araceae
60°–80°F.

These have always been among my favorite house plants. The large velvety green leaves on tall stems are very elegant. Keep these plants in a bright place and water them heavily during active growth. In winter, when plants are dormant, keep them almost dry in their pots at 60°F. Grow new plants by division of tubers.

C. antiquorum illustris—to 48 inches, green leaves with purple spots.
C. esculenta—to 40 inches, quilted satiny green leaves.

COLUMNEA
Gesneriaceae
60°–75°F.

Columneas are beautiful trailers, climbers, or upright plants to 36 inches. Foliage varies in size, color, and form, but it is always decorative. Some kinds have tiny button-like leaves, others 1-to-6-inch, elliptical leaves. The 1-to-3-inch, tubular flowers are borne in leaf axils and may be yellow, red, orange, or pink. Since these plants are epiphytic, growing on trees in their native land, put them in a mix of one part fir bark or osmunda to one part soil. Columneas need about the same amount of light as African violets: a rather sunny window in winter and a shaded place in summer. Keep soil consistently moist, and fertilize them every other week during active growth with a 10-10-5 plant food. Keep humidity high, about 70 percent. Propagate columneas from stem tip cuttings.

C. 'Anna C'—a trailer, dark red flowers.
C. arguta—a trailer; dainty, pointed leaves; large salmon-red flowers.
C. 'Butterball'—upright growth, yellow flowers.
C. 'Eagles'—a semierect plant, orange flowers.
C. 'Early Bird'—a trailer, orange-red flowers.
C. microphylla—a trailer, tiny leaves, red-and-yellow flowers.
C. tulae flava—a climber or trailer, soft green leaves, bright yellow flowers.
C. 'Yellow Dragon'—a trailer, yellow flowers.
C. 'Yellow Gold'—a trailer, dark yellow flowers.

COMET ORCHID. See ANGRAECUM and ORCHIDS.

COMMON FIG. See FICUS.

CONOPHYTUM
living stones
Aizoaceae
60°–75°F.

This genus of South African succulents includes many fine indoor plants—different and worth growing. Most have clublike or split leaves that hardly resemble leaves but look rather like colored stones. Their flowers of white, or yellow, or vibrant purple are spectacular when they appear—though indoors this may not occur for many years. These plants require a special potting mix—I use equal parts gravel and sand, then put on a scant top layer of gravel chips. Water conophytums sparingly at all times, as these succulents can be harmed by too much water. Keep them in your warmest and sunniest growing place, and don't fuss the plants. Let them be, and eventually you may find them blooming their heads off. They are very unusual. Purchase new plants from suppliers.

C. intrepidum—to 2 inches, gray-green leaves.
C. lutescens—to 1 inch, gray-green leaves.

CONVALLARIA
lily-of-the-valley
Liliaceae
50°–65°F.

This genus with only one species is grown for the sweet fragrance of its tiny, bell-like white flowers. If you wish to bring these familiar garden plants indoors, buy "forcing pips" in fall and plant these buds with roots in pots or bowls of sphagnum moss or in soil. Keep either medium you choose consistently moist. Grow the pips in a dim place for about ten days, gradually bringing them to light and sun. Flowers open almost exactly in twenty-one days. For Thanksgiving, plant on November 3; for Christmas, on December 3; for Valentine's Day, on January 23. Roots lifted from the garden in October, potted and kept cool and fairly dry, also produce blooms indoors toward spring, but these cannot be so exactly scheduled as can forcing pips. Pips cannot be forced more than once.

C. majalis.

COPPERLEAF. See ACALYPHA.

CORALBERRY. See ARDISIA.

CORDYLINE
dracaena, ti plant
Liliaceae
55°–75°F.

Palmlike growth at the top of a trunk makes these graceful plants most attractive. They are easy to grow in 4- or 5-inch pots in a bright airy spot. Keep soil moderately moist except in winter, when you should grow them cool (55° F.) and quite dry. The miraculous Hawaiian log that comes to life in a dish of water is a member of this family. Check for aphids in the leaf axils. Propagate cordylines from cane cuttings.

C. banksii—to 36 inches; straplike, dark green leaves with a pale yellow midrib; drooping panicles of white flowers.

C. terminalis—to 36 inches; many with brilliant leaves; yellow, white, or reddish flowers. Popular. Called Hawaiian log.

C. terminalis 'Bicolor'—dark metallic-green leaves edged with pink.

C. terminalis 'Firebrand'—a compact rosette of red leaves.

C. terminalis 'Margaret Storey'—green-to-copper-colored leaves splashed with red and pink.

CORNPLANT. See DRACAENA.

CORSAGE FLOWER. See CATTLEYA and ORCHIDS.

CORYPHANTHA
pincushion cactus
Cactaceae
55°–75°F.

Coryphantha comprises a group of rounded or cylindrical desert cactuses, whose flowers open in summer or fall. These plants need bright light. Grow them in sandy soil that drains readily. In winter keep them somewhat drier and cooler than 55°F. Propagate coryphanthas by sowing seed in spring. These grow well under artificial light.

C. palmeri—to 6 inches across; globe-shaped; pale yellow flowers. Pretty.

C. vivipara—to 8 inches across; ovoid; lovely rose-colored flowers.

COSTUS
Zingiberaceae
55°–75°F.

From Central and South America come these charming plants with succulent stems and spectacular, large, paper-thin, open-faced flowers that appear in spring or summer, even in fall. These plants need sun, consistently moist soil, and about 50 percent humidity. Propagate them by dividing root clumps in spring.

C. fappenbackianus—to 10 inches. A lovely dwarf form.

C. igneus—to 36 inches, shiny green leaves, 3-inch orange flowers.

C. malortieanus—to 36 inches, green-banded leaves, orange-and-red flowers. Called stepladder plant.

C. speciosus—to 60 inches, white flowers with yellow centers and red bracts. Called spiral ginger.

COTYLEDON
Crassulaceae
60°–75°F.

These South African succulents of sculptural form have brightly colored leaves and vivid, pendent flowers. (Small species have been placed in the genus Adromischus.) Give them full sun, consistently moist soil, and good air circulation. Don't water from above: moisture on foliage coupled with dark days causes leaf rot. Grow new plants from leaf or stem cuttings in spring.

C. orbiculata—to 36 inches, frosty red leaves, red flowers.

C. orbiculata ausana—to 12 inches, silvery leaves, red flowers.

C. teretifolia—to 36 inches, 10-inch clusters of hairy dark green leaves, yellow flowers.

C. undulata—to 36 inches, waxy white foliage, orange-and-red flowers.

CRAB CACTUS. See ZYGOCACTUS and CACTUSES.

CRASSULA
Crassulaceae
55°–75°F.

Crassulas are ideal house plants. Having fleshy leaves and stems, they tolerate an absence of moisture in air and soil. Some have gray or blue foliage, others are green. Several have branching stems, many produce low rosettes of leaves. Bright light or full sun suits them. Choose a sandy soil and let it dry out between waterings. Grow new plants from seed or from stem or leaf cuttings.

C. argentea—to 60 inches, branching stems of glossy leaves. Called jade plant.

C. cooperi—to 5 inches; small, pointed leaves with dark markings.

C. falcata—to 48 inches; thick, sickle-shaped gray leaves.

C. rupestris—to 16 inches, triangular gray-green leaves.

C. schmidtii—to 6 inches, pointed red-tinted leaves.

CREEPING CHARLIE. See LYSIMACHIA, PILEA.

CREEPING FIG. See FICUS.

CRINUM
angel lily
Amaryllidaceae
50°–65°F.

Forty-inch tropical and semitropical plants with evergreen foliage and lovely fragrant flowers, crinums grow fast and bloom freely in summer. Plant them in March with half the bulb above the soil. Water them heavily *after* growth starts. Shade them lightly from hot sun, and mist foliage frequently. After they flower, move these plants to a shaded location and water them moderately. Repot them only every three or four years. Propagate crinums by separating offset bulbs from the parent bulb when you repot.

C. 'Cecil Houdyshel'—lovely pink flowers. One of the best.
C. 'Ellen Bosanquet'—dark-rose-colored flowers. Striking.
C. moorei—bell-shaped pink flowers.
C. powellii alba—beautiful white flowers.

CROCODILE ALOE. See ALOE.

CROCUS. See Chapter 5.

CROSSANDRA
Acanthaceae
55°–70°F.

This splendid indoor grower to 30 inches is becoming very popular. The shiny-green-leaved plant bears orange flowers on and off throughout the year. Give it sun and an uncrowded place at the window; keep it well watered in spring but give it less moisture the rest of the year. Grow new plants from seed.

C. infundibuliformis.

CROTON. See CODIAEUM.

CROWN CACTUS. See REBUTIA and CACTUSES.

CROWN-OF-THORNS. See EUPHORBIA.

CRYPTANTHUS
star plant
Bromeliaceae
55°–70°F.

Though these small bromeliads have attractive waxy white flowers, it is the rosette of leaves that makes cryptanthuses popular. These leaves are often prickly, always vibrantly colored in shades of copper, gold, silver, or bronze. Undemanding, these plants need only bright light and 3-to-4-inch pots of osmunda and soil kept consistently moist. They make lovely decorative accents for terrariums and dish gardens, and as pot plants they can endure drought for months. Grow new plants from offsets.

C. acaulis—to 10 inches across, apple-green leaves.

C. bahianus—to 10 inches across; curved, lacy-edged dark red leaves.
C. bivittatus—to 8 inches across; salmon-rose, olive-green leaves. A dish-garden favorite.
C. bromeloides tricolor—to 14 inches across, smooth white-rose-and-olive-green leaves. Called rainbow plant.
C. fosterianus—to 14 inches across, dark brown leaves banded with silver.
C. terminalis—to 12 inches across, erect bronze-tinted foliage.
C. zonatus—to 12 inches across, wavy brown-green leaves with silver markings.

CTENANTHE
Marantaceae
55°–75°F.

This genus offers some fine foliage plants with stiff, upright, variegated leaves. Grow them in bright light and keep soil consistently moist. Grow new plants by root division.

C. lubbersiana—to 24 inches, yellow-mottled green leaves.
C. oppenheimiana—to 36 inches, stiff white-and-green leaves.
C. oppenheimiana tricolor—tufted pink-white-and-green leaves.

CUP-AND-SAUCER VINE. See COBAEA.

CYANOTIS
Commelinaceae
55°–70°F.

To 10 inches, with gray-green foliage, these are hardly showy plants; they are desirable, nevertheless, because of their purple-and-orange blooms in spring. Give them full sun and keep soil consistently moist. Propagate plants from cuttings at any time.

C. kewensis—a succulent creeper, hairy velvety brown leaves. Called teddy bear plant.
C. somaliensis—triangular glossy green leaves with white hairs. Called pussy ears.

CYCAS
Cycadaceae
55°–75°F.

Tough, slow-growing plants, these look like a cross between a palm and a fern. Although cycases grow slowly, a well-grown specimen with leathery dark green foliage is indeed handsome. Grow them in bright light in sandy soil kept moist at all times except in winter, when plants are not in active growth. Grow new plants from offsets.

C. circinalis—to 72 inches, shiny dark green leaves. Called fern palm.

C. revoluta—to 60 inches, leaves with rolled edges. Called sago palm.

CYCLAMEN

shooting star
Primulaceae
45°–60°F.

These plants, sometimes called poor-man's orchids, are charming with their shooting-star-like flowers in shades ranging from pure white through rose, pink, salmon, and scarlet. The pretty, mottled dark green leaves are heart-shaped. The single, double, and fringed blooms—some quite dazzling—go on opening for three to four months, from mid-fall to early spring. Mainly gift plants, cyclamens last only if you grow them *cool* and moist and if you shade them from the sun. Mist the tops frequently. Feed these plants every other week and inspect the foliage for cyclamen mites. (Before using an insecticide, try a hard spray of water to eradicate these pests.) When flowers fade in March or April, let the plant rest by gradually withholding water until the foliage dies. Keep it nearly dry, the pot on its side in a shaded place outdoors until August or early September. Then remove dead foliage and repot the tuber in fresh soil (equal parts garden loam, peat moss, and sand). Set the top of the tuber level with the surface of the soil to prevent water from collecting in the depression and causing crown rot. There are many handsome varieties of the most commonly grown species. Grow new plants from seed.

C. persicum (or *C. giganteum).*

CYMBIDIUM

Orchidaceae
50°–75°F.

With grassy leaves and lovely flowers, cymbidiums offer a wealth of orchid beauty for the

The miniature cymbidium orchid has become a favorite house plant—easy to grow and a delight to see. (Photograph by the author)

home. These popular plants—both standard-sized and miniature types—do well in cool temperatures. Pot them in medium-grade fir bark and keep them moist all year. At some season of the year (generally this is done in late summer), give cymbidiums more coolness than usual (50°F.) to force buds to form. Usually putting them outside for a few weeks does the trick. Plants need bright light. Divide plants to make more.

C. 'Doris'—to 30 inches, bronze-red flowers. A well-known hybrid.

C. eburneum—to 30 inches, small whitish yellow flowers.

C. lancifolium—to 40 inches, creamy green flowers.

C. 'Pixie'—to 14 inches, creamy white flowers banded with red. A fine miniature.

C. pumilum—to 24 inches, reddish-brown-and-yellow flowers.

CYPERUS

Cyperaceae
55°–70°F.

Very satisfactory plants, their stems crowned with a fountain of leaves, cyperuses grow best in shade. Set them directly in water or in soil kept quite wet. Look for little green flowers in the leaf crowns in late summer. Grow new plants by root division.

C. *alternifolius*—to 48 inches, tall stems with a green crown of radiating leaves. The familiar umbrella plant.

C. *elegans*—to 36 inches; stiff, narrow leaves.

C. *papyrus*—to 60 inches, flamboyant foliage. Called Egyptian paper plant.

CYPRIPEDIUM ORCHID. See PAPHIO-PEDILUM and ORCHIDS.

DAFFODIL. See Chapter 5.

DANCING LADY ORCHID. See ONCID-IUM and ORCHIDS.

DATE PALM. See PHOENIX and PALMS.

DATURA	angel's trumpet
	Solanaceae
	55°–65°F.

These are large, showy shrubs to 60 inches with attractive green leaves and 3-to-5-inch pendent pink or white trumpet-like flowers. Because of their size and reluctance to bloom indoors, they are rarely seen as house plants. However, if you want to try one, grow it in sun and let soil dry out between waterings. Give it 50 percent humidity. You can grow new plants from cuttings.

D. *mollis*—nodding salmon-pink flowers.

D. *suaveolens*—large green leaves; mammoth, fragrant white flowers.

| **DAVALLIA** | *Polypodiaceae* |
| | 55°–75°F. |

These choice ferns with lacy fronds and brown or gray, hairy rhizomes growing across the surface of the soil are interesting and beautiful for the indoor garden. Grow them in bright light and keep soil consistently moist. Mist foliage frequently and allow them to soak in a pail of water once a month so the full beauty of the pendent, graceful fronds can be appreciated. Propagate davallias by dividing the rhizomes: cut them into sections and partially bury them in sand until they root.

*D. *bullata mariesii*—10-inch fronds, brown rhizomes.

D. *fejeensis plumosa*—15-inch fronds, brown rhizomes. A dainty, fluffy-leaved plant called rabbit's-foot fern.

D. *griffithiana*—similar to D. *fejeensis* but with gray-white rhizomes.

D. *pentaphylla*—to 20 inches, broad leaves, rootstock covered with black fuzz. Unusual.

D. *solida*—24-inch, stiff bright green fronds; brown rhizomes.

D. *tenuifolia*—to 24 inches, leathery fronds, short rhizomes. Also known as carrot fern.

| **DENDROBIUM** | *Orchidaceae* |
| | 55°–75°F. |

A genus of striking epiphytic orchids with 2-to-10-inch cane growth and large flowers of pink, yellow, or white. Leaves are leathery, and some of the prettiest species are deciduous. Grow them at a south or west window with humidity up to 50 percent. Pot them in fir bark and water them heavily when plants are growing. Rest plants with very little water in late October for about four to six weeks at 45°F. to 50°F. to encourage buds. After they flower, rest plants again for about six weeks, then return them to warmth (70°F.). Repot them only if the fir bark has deteriorated. Dendrobiums offer a wealth of color for indoors or out. Buy new plants from specialists.

D. *dalhousieanum*—to 36 inches; evergreen; tawny yellow flowers with crimson markings in spring or early summer.

*D. *jenkinsii*—to 2 inches; evergreen; golden yellow flowers in summer and fall.

*D. *loddigesii*—to 6 inches; evergreen; lavender-pink flowers in late winter or early spring.

*D. *nobile*—to 8 inches; evergreen; fragrant white flowers.

D. *moschatum*—to 36 inches; deciduous; musk-scented, large yellow-rose flowers from spring to August.

A trio of dieffenbachias, all good house plants, particularly suited to shady corners. (Photograph by USDA)

D. pierardii—to 36 inches; deciduous; handsome, 3-inch pink flowers in March or April. Easy to grow.

D. thyrsiflorum—to 36 inches; evergreen; magnificent, 2-inch white-and-gold flowers in April or May.

DICHORISANDRA   *Commelinaceae*
                    60°–75°F.

From South America, these 12-to-20-inch plants bear pretty blue flowers in spring and summer and are good for indoor gardens with north light. Most species need plenty of water while growing. In winter plants are usually dormant, so water them sparingly then. Grow new plants from seed.

D. reginae—small leaves with purple and silver markings.

D. warscewicziana—silver-streaked leaves.

DIEFFENBACHIA   dumbcane
                    Araceae
                    60°–75°F.

Dumbcane is hardly an appropriate name for this easy group of graceful plants with large ornamental leaves marked with yellow, blue, or white. Plants thrive in light shade, and a mature specimen will be with you for years. Give dieffenbachias plenty of water in summer, not so much the rest of the year. They are best grown as tub plants. Propagate them from cane cuttings in spring or by air layering.

D. amoena—to 36 inches, heavy green-and-white leaves. Robust.

D. bowmannii—to 36 inches, mottled chartreuse-green leaves.

D. picta barraquiniana—to 48 inches, bright green leaves spotted with white.

D. splendens—to 36 inches, velvety green leaves with small white dots.

DIONAEA

Venus flytrap
Droseraceae
60°–80°F.

The popular Venus flytrap is a carnivorous perennial with apple-green leaves whose edges have toothlike claws. The plant is miniature, only a few inches high, and makes an unusual addition to the indoor garden. It requires high humidity and is best grown under a glass jar. Use a mucky soil and keep the plant consistently moist. In cultivation, the plant requires no flies, nor does it need to be fed raw meat, as some Hollywood movies suggest. It does just fine in bright light in any type of terrarium. Buy new plants from suppliers.

D. muscipula—to 2 inches, upright leaves. An oddity.

DIPLADENIA
(MANDEVILLA)

Mexican love vine
Apocynaceae
60°–80°F.

These are charming climbing plants, to 7 feet or more, from the jungles of Brazil, with leathery leaves and great displays of pale pink flowers in spring and summer, sometimes into fall. Provide a sunny window and keep soil moist except immediately after flowering, when you should keep them somewhat dry for about six weeks. They like 50 percent humidity. Propagate dipladenias from stem cuttings or by sowing seed in spring.

D. amoena—oblong dark green leaves, 2-inch pink flowers.
D. suaveolens—long light green leaves, deliciously fragrant white flowers. Called Chilean jasmine.

DIZYGOTHECA

false aralia
Araliaceae
55°–75°F.

These graceful, treelike plants with dark green-brown, palmlike leaves make lovely delicate accents. Plants grow to 72 inches but can be kept cut back. Sometimes young plants are difficult to start, so have patience and don't overwater them. Place them in bright light and keep soil consistently moist. Air layer to make new plants or to reduce height, or propagate this handsome foliage plant from cuttings in spring.

D. elegantissima—leathery, notched-ribbon-like, metallic-toned leaves.
D. veitchii—coppery green leaves with light red veins.

DOUBLE-DECKER PLANT. See RECH-STEINERIA and GESNERIADS.

DRACAENA

cornplant
Liliaceae
55°–75°F.

This is a genus of excellent African plants that survive very unfavorable conditions. The lance-shaped or oval leaves are usually dark green banded in white or yellow. Most are large plants—some to 72 inches. *D. marginata* and the cultivar called General Pershing are exceedingly decorative. *D. fragrans massangeana* can be trained to grow like a small tree—most charming. Give these plants good light but no sun, and keep soil consistently moist. Don't let water accumulate on the leaves, as wetness can cause spotting. Grow new plants from stem cuttings.

Some plants in the Cordyline genus are also called dracaena.

D. deremensis—to 30 inches; green-and-white, lance-shaped leaves.
D. deremensis 'Janet Craig'—to 36 inches; dark green, strap-shaped leaves, wavy edges. Popular.
D. deremensis 'Roehrs Gold'—to 36 inches; long canary-yellow leaves bordered with white and green. Stunning.
D. deremensis warneckei—24-inch white leaves, green center stripe.
D. draco—to 60 inches or more; sword-shaped green leaves outlined in red. Called dragon tree.
D. fragrans—to 60 inches or more; green leaves to 36 inches, creamy yellow margins.
D. fragrans 'General Pershing'—creamy pink, almost red, 24-inch leaves.

(continued on page 153)

Cattleya walkeriana. (Photograph by C/D Luckhart)

Cobaea scandens. (Photograph by C/D Luckhart)

Coelogyne pandurata. (Photograph by Joyce Wilson)

145

Columnea hybrid.
(Photograph by C/D Luckhart)

Crinum species.
(Photograph by C/D Luckhart)

Conophytum intrepidum. (Photograph by C/D Luckhart)

Conophytum lutescens.
(Photograph by C/D Luckhart)

Dracaena goldiana. (Photograph by C/D Luckhart)

Epiphylopsis rosea.
(Photograph by C/D Luckhart)

Echinopsis ferox. (Photograph by C/D Luckhart)

Echinocereus luteus. (Photograph by C/D Luckhart)

Epiphyllum hybrid. (Photograph by C/D Luckhart)

Episcia cupreata 'Cygnat.' (Photograph by C/D Luckhart)

Eucharis grandiflora. (Photograph by C/D Luckhart)

Euphorbia globosa. (Photograph by C/D Luckhart)

Euphorbia splendens 'Pixie Red.'
(Photograph by C/D Luckhart)

Gloriosa superba. (Photograph by C/D Luckhart)

Guzmania minor. (Photograph by C/D Luckhart)

Gymnocalycium fleisherianum. (Photograph by C/D Luckhart)

Gymnocalycium venturii. (Photograph by C/D Luckhart)

Haemanthus arabicum. (Photograph by C/D Luckhart)

Heliocereus schrankii. (Photograph by C/D Luckhart)

D. fragrans 'Lindenii'—pendent green-yellow leaves.

D. fragrans massangeana—24-inch, arching yellow-and-green leaves. This is the variety most commonly called cornplant.

D. fragrans 'Victoriae'—pendent silver-gray leaves with a border of creamy yellow.

D. godseffiana—to 30 inches; 6-inch, oval, yellow-and-green leaves. Called gold-dust dracaena.

D. goldiana—to 16 inches, wide gray-and-bright-green leaves with crossbands of darker green.

D. marginata—to 60 inches and more; 18-inch, dark green leaves edged with red.

D. sanderiana—to 50 inches, 9-inch green leaves banded with white.

DRAGON TREE. See DRACAENA.

DROSANTHEMUM
Aizoaceae
50°–70°F.

Small orange-colored spring flowers make this succulent an attractive window plant. Grow it in sun and let soil dry out between waterings. Propagate it from cuttings.

D. floribundum—to 12 inches; thin, drooping branches; pale green, cylindrical leaves.

D. speciosum—to 24 inches; erect bright green leaves.

DUMBCANE. See DIEFFENBACHIA.

DYCKIA
earth star
Bromeliaceae
55°–75°F.

Here are truly carefree bromeliads with 12-to-16-inch rosettes of thick, often spiny, multicolored leaves. In good light, mature plants produce erect spikes of orange flowers. These are excellent terrarium plants. Pot them in osmunda and soil, keep them barely moist, and grow them in bright light. New plants can be started from offsets in spring.

D. brevifolia—dark, glossy green rosette of leaves. Grows for years with little attention.

D. fosteriana—narrow, arching silver leaves. A brilliant accent plant.

D. frigida—large, frosted green leaves. Handsome.

EAGLE-CLAW CACTUS. See ECHINOCACTUS and CACTUSES.

EARTH STAR. See DYCKIA and BROMELIADS.

EASTER CACTUS. See EPIPHYLOPSIS and CACTUSES.

ECHEVERIA
Crassulaceae
55°–75°F.

Beautiful leaf rosettes put these plants from Mexico and central and northern South America high on the list of desirables. Bright and cheery orange, yellow, or red, tubular flowers appear in spring and summer. Grow these 14-to-30-inch plants in a mix of half sand, half ordinary packaged potting soil. Give them sun and keep soil somewhat dry. If you have any difficulties, try watering them from the bottom. Echeverias are easily propagated from seed or offsets.

E. affinis—dark greenish black rosette of leaves, red flowers.

E. amoena—small rosette of leaves, pink flowers.

E. derenbergii—pale green rosette of leaves, orange flowers.

E. elegans—pale blue-white rosette of leaves, coral-pink flowers.

E. glauca pumila—bluish gray rosette of leaves, pinkish yellow flowers.

E. multicaulis—coppery rosette of leaves, orange flowers.

E. pilosa—hairy, red-tipped rosette of leaves; orange flowers.

ECHINOCACTUS
Cactaceae
55°–75°F.

Spiny, attractive desert plants of cylindrical shape, these grow easily at windows. Put them in bright light and let soil dry out between waterings. They need fresh air and coolness in winter, when they rest. Grow new ones from offsets or from cuttings rooted in damp sand. Young plants to 16 inches are best; mature specimens require too much space.

E. grusonii—to 48 inches, yellow flowers. Called golden-barrel cactus.
*E. horizonthalonius—to 10 inches, silver-gray-and-pink leaves with red spines, pink flowers. Called eagle-claw cactus.
E. ingens—to 60 inches; barrel-shaped, brownish blue body; yellow flowers.

ECHINOCEREUS
hedgehog cactus, rainbow cactus
Cactaceae
55°–75°F.

Occasionally bearing bright-colored flowers at the window, these small desert cactuses rarely grow more than 12 inches high, with ribbed, cylindrical or globular, spiny stems. They need little attention. Give them sun and keep their sandy soil somewhat dry. Propagate them from offsets.

*E. baileyi—cylindrical growth to 4 inches, lovely pink flowers.
*E. dasyacanthus—4 to 12 inches, small dense spines, yellow flowers.
*E. delaetii—to 8 inches, long white spines, pink flowers. Known as lesser old-man cactus.
*E. luteus—globular growth to 6 inches, handsome yellowish green flowers in summer.
*E. pentalophus—cylindrical growth to 5 inches, finger-like stems, violet-red flowers.
*E. reichenbachii—globular growth to 8 inches, close ribs, white-to-reddish-brown flowers.
*E. rigidissimus—cylindrical growth to 8 inches; multicolored spines of pink, white, red, and brown.

ECHINOPSIS
sea urchin cactus
Cactaceae
55°–75°F.

These globular desert cactuses from 4 to 16 inches high bear trumpet-shaped spring flowers. Little care is required to coax them into bloom. Place them at a sunny window and keep soil moderately moist except in winter, when you should grow them somewhat dry. Flowers open in the evening and last through the next day. Propagate echinopsis from offsets.

E. calochlora—yellow-and-brown body, white flowers.
E. campylacantha—dark grayish green, globular body, stiff spines; purple-white flowers.
E. eyriesii—brown spines; beautiful, lily-like, pure white flowers.
*E. ferox—globular, spiny, gray-green body to 3 inches; brilliant red flowers.
*E. globosa—unusual contorted body to 3 inches, greenish white flowers.
E. multiplex—barrel-shaped dark green body, brown spines; rose-colored flowers.

EGYPTIAN PAPER PLANT. See CYPERUS.

EGYPTIAN STAR FLOWER. See PENTAS.

ELEPHANT EARS. See COLOCASIA.

EMERALD FEATHER. See ASPARAGUS.

ENGLISH IVY. See HEDERA.

EPIDENDRUM
Orchidaceae
60°–80°F.

These orchids are free-flowering, mostly epiphytic plants; some are cane-stemmed, others grow from pseudobulbs. They bear handsome flowers in shades of pink, red, yellow, or white that last for six weeks. Grow them in fir bark and give them full sun. Keep the cane-stemmed ones moist all year; rest the others for one month both before and after flowering. All require 50 percent humidity. Purchase young plants from suppliers.

E. atropurpureum—to 30 inches, egg-shaped pseudobulbs, dozens of 1-inch brown-and-purple flowers in early spring.
E. cochleatum—to 30 inches, pseudobulbs 2 to 5

Orchids make excellent cut flowers. These epidendrums were colorful for two weeks.
(Photograph by the author)

inches long, shell-shaped dark-maroon-and-chartreuse flowers on and off throughout the year. Plants should rest in November.

E. *fragrans*—to 24 inches, compressed pseudobulbs, fragrant white-and-red flowers in late summer.

E. *lindleyanum*—to 30 inches, cane-stemmed growth, rose-purple flowers with white lips in fall.

E. *nemorale*—to 24 inches, globose pseudobulbs, 3-inch rose-mauve flowers in summer.

E. *obrienianum*—to 7 feet, cane-stemmed growth, tiny flowers in various shades.

E. *pentotis*—to 20 inches, pseudobulbs, fragrant white flowers striped with purple in summer.

*E. *polybulbon*—to 4 inches, tiny yellow-and-brown flowers in summer.

*E. *porpax*—to 2 inches; reddish brown, half-inch flowers in fall.

EPIPHYLLUM
orchid cactus
Cactaceae
55°–75°F.

These plants, mostly epiphytic, will hang to 48 inches or grow upright (if staked). They are famous for their huge blooms: red or pink, purple or white, peaking in July and August. Hybrids have also been developed for day bloom. Keep these plants potbound and in a bright window. Water them heavily in spring and summer, not so much the rest of the year—but never let them dry out. Plants can be staked and will look fine on a windowsill or grown as natural trailers in baskets. Don't miss these plants; they do bloom indoors with little care and always cause comment in my garden room. Take cuttings in spring for new plants.

E. 'Conway Giant'—7 inch, purplish red, daytime flowers. Magnificent.

E. 'Eden'—6-inch, white-and-yellow, daytime flowers.

E. 'Luminosa'—5-inch, white, daytime flowers.

E. 'Nocturne'—6-inch, purple-and-white, night-blooming flowers.

E. oxypetalum—5-inch, night-blooming, white flowers.

E. 'Parade'—6-inch, pink, daytime flowers.

E. 'Royal Rose'—6-inch, rose-buff, daytime flowers.

EPIPHYLOPSIS
(RHIPSALIDOPSIS)

Easter cactus
Cactaceae
55°–70°F.

Somewhat similar to but technically different from Schlumbergera varieties are these 12-to-20-inch epiphytes that begin to bloom when very small with bright flowers—red, pink, or orange-pink. To make them bloom, grow them in sun in fall and winter, with coolness (55°F.) and darkness uninterrupted for twelve hours each night. In spring and summer, water them freely and regularly. They need 60 percent humidity. Propagate them from cuttings.

E. gaertnerii—bright red flowers in spring. The true Easter cactus. Formerly *Schlumbergera gaertnerii.*

E. rosea—short growth, soft pink flowers in spring.

E. 'Orange Spring Beauty'—delicately colored, early spring flowers.

EPISCIA

peacock plant
Gesneriaceae
65°–80°F.

Colorful 14-to-20-inch South American epiphytes, these gesneriads have exotic foliage and brilliant flowers in spring and summer. Mostly trailers, these plants need bright light, copious amounts of water, and 50 percent humidity. If conditions are good, they grow through winter without dormancy. Keep water off their leaves to avoid spotting. Grow plants from seed, cuttings, or offsets.

E. 'Acajou'—bright silver leaves, red flowers.

E. 'Cameo'—glossy, metallic rose-red leaves; orange-red flowers.

Episcias are gesneriads with attractively patterned leaves and flowers of many different colors that appear practically all year long.
(Photograph by Merry Gardens)

E. 'Chocolate Soldier'—dark-brown-and-silver leaves, red flowers.

E. cupreata—copper-colored leaves dusted with white hairs, scarlet flowers.

E. cupreata 'Cygnat'—furry leaves, lovely pale yellow flowers delicately fringed.

E. dianthiflora—velvety green leaves, tufted white flowers.

E. 'Emerald Queen'—green leaves, red flowers.

E. 'Frosty'—white leaves, red flowers.

E. lilacina—coppery leaves, lavender flowers.

E. punctata—toothed green leaves, white flowers spotted with purple.

E. 'Silver Streak'—bronzy-green-and-silver leaves, red flowers.

ERANTHEMUM

blue sage
Acanthaceae
50°–70°F.

Among the nicest true-blue, winter-flowering plants for the window garden, erathemums need full sun and soil kept consistently moist. They also need 40 percent humidity. Overwatering will cause leaf drop. Small plants flower as readily as large ones. Propagate eranthemums from cuttings in spring and summer.

E. nervosum—to 36 inches, pointed green leaves, deep blue flowers.
E. wattii—to 24 inches, green leaves with a metallic sheen, violet-blue flowers.

EUCHARIS

Amazon lily
Amaryllidaceae
55°–75°F.

Most desirable is the Amazon lily, a glossy green, 30-inch, bulbous plant that bears fragrant, starry white flowers once or twice a year. Give it bright light and flood it with water in summer. After it blooms, keep it rather dry for a few weeks, then start the cycle again. To produce bloom, mist foliage frequently, feed moderately. Grow new plants from the small bulbs set off by the mature plants.

E. grandiflora.

EUCOMIS

pineapple lily
Liliaceae
50°–70°F.

This is a genus of interesting bulbous plants to 30 inches with shiny green foliage and handsome crowns of flowers in July or August. Give the growing plants bright light and keep soil moderately wet. In winter, when plants are semidormant, grow them almost dry. To increase your collection, pot the offsets or sow seed in spring.

E. comosa (or *E. punctata*)—dark green leaves, star-shaped greenish-white-and-purple flowers. A lovely curiosity.
E. undulata—bright green leaves, dense head of bright green flowers. Striking.
E. zambexiaca—light green foliage, airy white flowers.

EUGENIA

Myrtaceae
50°–65°F.

These lovely, small trees can be kept to 36 inches indoors. They make a great accent in front of floor-to-ceiling windows. The leaves are attractive, the flowers pretty, and the red berries ornamental. Provide full sun and keep soil consistently moist. Grow new plants from cuttings.

E. jambos—smooth, pointed leaves; greenish yellow flowers. Called rose apple.
E. uniflora—glossy leaves, white flowers. Called Surinam cherry.

EUPHORBIA *Euphorbiaceae*
50°–75°F.

Most of the easy-to-grow plants listed below have small leaves and develop contorted forms; the poinsettia (*E. pulcherrima*) has large leaves (see the special entry following). These plants need full sun and quite sandy soil kept consistently moist, never soggy. Euphorbias resent drafts. Propagate them from cuttings.

E. globosa—ridged, globular body to 8 inches; unusual yellow-green flowers.

E. keysii (a hybrid)—to 30 inches, succulent leaves, coral-pink flowers in winter and spring.

E. lactea cristata—crested, cactus-like, desert species to 24 inches; candelabra form.

E. splendens—a spiny climber to 24 inches, tiny green leaves, red flowers. The familiar crown-of-thorns.

E. splendens 'Bojeri'—a dwarf form, pale green leaves.

E. splendens 'Pixie Red'—to 30 inches, red flowers. An improved form of *E. splendens*, with floriferous habit.

EUPHORBIA PULCHERRIMA poinsettia
Euphorbiaceae
55°–65°F.

The "flowers" of this familiar Christmas-time favorite are actually the highly colored bracts— red, pink, or white—the tiny blooms being hidden in the center of the bracts. The plant grows to 48 inches tall. It usually arrives as a gift, but there is no reason why it should not become a year-round plant for you. When you receive it, put it in a sunny but cool window (65°F.). Water it every other day until the leaves start to fall. Then reduce moisture until the soil is almost dry and move it to a semishaded window (about 55°F.) Water it about once a month. In late March or early April, cut it back to about 6 inches and repot it in fresh soil. Water it well and place it in a sunny window until the weather is warm outdoors. Then put it in the garden in a bright location and keep the soil consistently moist. In September, bring it back into the house, give it more water and sun.

From late September on, this plant must have six weeks of uninterrupted darkness—twelve to fourten hours—to initiate the production of flower buds. If you move plants to a closet at night, you can be sure that no beam from a street light or table lamp will break up the necessarily long period of darkness.

These Mikkelsen varieties hold their foliage and bracts for three to six months:

'Mikkeldawn'—variegated pink-and-cream bracts.

'Mikkelpink'—nice, clear-colored bracts.

'Mikkelwhite'—not so strong as other varieties but very pretty.

'Paul Mikkelsen'—brilliant red bracts.

EXACUM German violet
Gentianaceae
50°–65°F.

With small, fragrant blue flowers and shiny green leaves, this 24-inch plant starts flowering in September and reaches its peak in January. Give it full sun and keep soil consistently moist. Cut it back in August to ensure future bloom. Propagate exacums from seed in spring.

E. affine.

EYELASH BEGONIA. See BEGONIA, Rhizomatous.

FAIRY PRIMROSE. See PRIMULA.

FALSE ARALIA. See DIZYGOTHECA.

FALSE HOLLY. See OSMANTHUS.

FATSHEDERA *Araliaceae*
55°–75°F.

These are shrubby pot plants with green or variegated leaves on a central stem that needs the support of a stake. Accidental hybrids—a cross between an English ivy and a fatsia— fatsheideras are excellent for churches and offices, since they can survive poor light and low humidity. The foliage develops its best color without sun. Soak these plants and allow them to dry out before watering them again. Grow new plants from cuttings or by air layering.

F. lizei—to 36 inches; dark, leathery, lustrous green leaves.

F. lizei variegata—to 36 inches, fresh green leaves edged with white.

FATSIA
Araliaceae
55°–75°F.

A group of undauntable decorative plants with green, ivy-like leaves on graceful stems, fatsias withstand almost any conditions and survive for many years. Give them shade and keep their soil wet but not sodden. Fatsias will grow in a shaded entry or other interior area where most plants would perish. Grow new ones from seed.

F. japonica—to 60 inches; leathery, shiny dark green leaves.

F. variegata—to 60 inches, medium-green leaves edged with white.

FERN PALM. See CYCAS.

FERNS

Ferns were popular house plants years ago and now, once again, their natural grace and handsome fronds are recognized as superb decoration. Grow them at a cool, light window rather than a sunny one (some winter sun is acceptable) and in moist humusy soil (I use one part loam to one part each of sand, peat moss, and leaf mold). Once a week, shower plants in sink or tub, and at least once a month give them a deep soaking so all the roots get moisture. Take care they do not stand in water, as they might in a jardiniere, for this is most harmful to their roots. Summer your ferns outdoors: they love warm, refreshing rains. Though some gardeners feed ferns, I have found mine do very well without additional food. Try not to break or brush against the delicate fronds, for if bruised at the tips, they turn brown. Trim away any dead leaves and train plants so as to emphasize their natural grace. Elevate trailing types on inverted pots or stands, or grow them in baskets for a nice effect. Many ferns can be propagated from their seeds—or spores, as they are properly called. These appear, usually in a pattern, on the underside of the fronds and are not to be confused with the insects called scales, which they resemble. Do check your ferns regularly for scales: a strong spray of water will sometimes eradicate the pests; if not, use the appropriate insecticide. For descriptions of some species and their culture, see:

Adiantum
Asplenium
Blechnum
Davallia
Lygodium
Nephrolepis
Pellaea
Phyllitis
Platycerium
Polypodium
Polystichum
Pteris
Woodwardia

FEROCACTUS
Cactaceae
55°–75°F.

Overlooked but handsome, this spiny desert genus is probably not much grown because of its awesome, often curved spines. Generally these plants are medium-sized, dark green globes with handsome flowers. Pot them in sandy soil that drains readily and keep them just barely moist except in winter, when plants can be somewhat dry and cool. Give them all possible sun. They are different and worth growing. You can start new plants from offsets.

F. acanthoides—globular green body to 14 inches, fearsome spines, lovely orange-yellow flowers.

F. fordii—globular gray-green body to 6 inches, stiff spines, yellow-to-red flowers.

F. latispinus—depressed, globular body to 20 inches; rose-colored flowers. The popular fishhook cactus.

F. orcutti—barrel-shaped body to 8 inches, brownish flowers.

A very versatile plant is the rubber plant *(Ficus elastica)*, a favorite in many homes. Growth is quick and plants are seldom bothered by disease. (Photograph by the author)

FICUS

fig
Moraceae
60°–75°F.

These are almost perfect house plants, with diversified foliage and growth. Some, like *F. elastica decora*, are erect, with broad, leathery, 12-inch leaves. *F. pumila* is a creeping plant with 1-inch leaves. *F. benjamina* forms a small tree, with 2-inch, oval leaves. Grow all varieties in bright light and keep soil consistently moist except in winter, when they can get along with less moisture. Small pots are best even for large plants. Occasionally wipe foliage with a damp cloth to keep it shiny, but avoid clogging leaf pores with oil or any special leaf-polishing preparations. Propagate ficuses from leaf cuttings or by air layering.

F. benjamina—to 60 inches, dense head of gracefully drooping branches. Called weeping or Benjamin fig.

F. benjamina exotica—to 60 inches, arching branches, pendulous glossy green leaves twisted at the tip.

F. benjamina variegata—to 36 inches; small, glossy green, elliptical leaves with white margins.

F. carica—to 48 inches, big green leaves. Plants lose foliage during winter. The common fig.

F. diversifolia—to 36 inches; small, round yellowish fruit. Called mistletoe fig.

F. elastica decora—to 60 inches, thick glossy green leaves. The popular rubber plant.

F. elastica 'Doescheri'—to 60 inches; variegated leaves of green, gray, white, and yellow.

F. lyrata (or *F. pandurata*)—to 60 inches, enormous leaves. Avoid drafts, which cause leaf drop. Called fiddle-leaved fig.

F. nitida—to 60 inches; graceful branching habit; lovely, small glossy green leaves. Easier to grow than *F. benjamina*.

F. pumila (or *F. repens*)—vinelike growth, 1-inch leaves. Often used as a soil cover for big pot plants. Called creeping fig.

F. retusa—to 60 inches, slow-growing; dark green leaves. Called Chinese banyan.

F. roxburghii—to 60 inches; handsome, dark green, scalloped leaves. Nice, branching accent plant.

The fiddle-leaved fig *(Ficus lyrata)* has wonderfully shiny green leaves. (Photograph by the author)

FIDDLE-LEAVED FIG. See FICUS.

FIG. See FICUS.

FISHHOOK CACTUS. See FEROCACTUS and CACTUSES.

FISHTAIL PALM. See CARYOTA and PALMS.

FITTONIA   *Acanthaceae*
                                60°–75°F.

Low, dense creepers to 24 inches from the forests of Peru, fittonias have soft, bright green, 4-inch leaves veined with red or white. These plants need shade. Keep them out of drafts and let soil dry out between waterings. They like 50 percent humidity. Grow several kinds in one container for a colorful display, and try them in dish gardens and planters. Stem cuttings root easily.

F. verschaffeltii—leaves with red veins.
F. verschaffeltii argyroneura—leaves with white veins.

FLAME-OF-THE-WOODS. See IXORA.

FLAMINGO FLOWER. See ANTHURIUM.

FLAMING-SWORD PLANT. See VRIESEA and BROMELIADS.

FLOWERING MAPLE. See ABUTILON.

FLOWERING ONION. See ALLIUM.

FOXTAIL ORCHID. See RHYNCHO-STYLIS and ORCHIDS.

FREESIA   *Iridaceae*
                                50°–60°F.

Tender, bulbous plants to 14 inches with delightfully fragrant flowers, freesias are difficult but not impossible to grow indoors. Put six corms, 1 inch deep and 2 inches apart, in a 5- or 6-inch pot of two parts of sandy loam, one part leaf mold, and one part old manure or compost. Plant from August to November for January to April bloom. Keep plants cool and moist and give them full light. Flowers appear in ten to twelve weeks. After plants bloom, gradually dry out the soil and then shake out the corms and keep them dry for repotting next year. Propagate freesias from offsets.

F. 'Blue Banner'—sky-blue flowers with a white throat.
F. 'Gold Coast'—orange-colored flowers.
F. 'Stockholm'—carmine flowers.

FUCHSIA   lady's eardrops
                                Onagraceae
                                50°–65°F.

Handsome plants—some trailing, others upright to 36 inches—fuchsias have small dark green leaves and dangling red, white, pink, or purple flowers. Their beauty depends on considerable care. Grow them in rich soil, out of the sun but in bright light, and below 65°F. Then they will set flower buds in spring and summer. Feed them biweekly. Flood them with water while they are growing; pinch them at early stages to encourage branching. Mist foliage frequently and provide a buoyant atmosphere. While they are dormant in winter, keep them almost dry in a cold, dim place. Watch out for white flies. Take cuttings in January or February.

F. 'Brigadoon'—a trailer; double, purple-and-pink flowers.
F. 'Carmel Blue'—a trailer; single, blue flowers with white sepals.
F. 'Cascade'—a trailer; single, rose-red flowers with white sepals.
F. 'Dark Eyes'—a trailer; double, violet-blue flowers.
F. 'Marenga'—a trailer; variegated foliage; double, red flowers.
F. 'Mrs. Marshall'—upright growth; single, soft-pink flowers with white sepals.
F. 'Sleigh Bells'—upright growth; large, single, pure white flowers.
F. 'Swingtime'—a trailer; fine, double, white flowers with red sepals.
F. 'Tiffany'—a trailer; double, white flowers.

GARDENIA
Cape jasmine
Rubiaceae
60°–70°F.

Evergreen shrubs with scented, waxy white flowers and shiny dark green leaves, gardenias are difficult to bring to bloom at home but, after adjusting slowly to new conditions, they may well do so. Grow them in equal parts loam, sand, and peat moss. Keep soil consistently moist. Give them bright light in summer, sun in winter, and at least 50 percent humidity. From spring to fall, feed them once a month with an acid fertilizer or a solution of 1 ounce of ammonium sulfate to 2 gallons of water. (A vinegar-and-water solution will acidify soil but not feed the plant.) Mist foliage daily to discourage spider mites. Give plants a deep soaking in the sink or in a pail of water once a week and a refreshing shower at the same time. Buds may drop or fail to open if temperatures fluctuate very much, if there are drafts, if humidity falls below 50 percent, or if night temperatures rise above 70°F. or fall below 60°F. If your plant does not grow or is ailing, try the plastic bag treatment for a few weeks: put the plant in the bag, propping it over the foliage on stakes, and tie it at the base. Propagate gardenias from cuttings in spring.

G. jasminoides—to 48 inches; double flowers.
G. jasminoides stricta nana—to 30 inches, free-flowering. Best for the home.
G. jasminoides veitchii—to 48 inches. Smaller flowers but easier to grow.

GARLAND FLOWER. See HEDYCHIUM.

GAZANIA
Compositae
50°–70°F.

These colorful plants grow to 30 inches and bear large, black-eyed, yellow-to-orange, daisy-like blooms and long, narrow, woolly, gray-green leaves. Flowers open in sunlight and close at night. They are excellent for a cool sun porch, where plants will bloom on and off through spring and summer. They need lots of water but do not require high humidity. Grow new ones from seed or cuttings.

G. rigens—golden yellow flowers with a brown-black center. The typical species.
G. splendens—orange flowers.

GASTERIA
ox-tongue plant
Liliaceae
55°–75°F.

These interesting South American succulents are for windowsills with almost any exposure. The long, flat leaves are usually smooth but sometimes "warted." Long sprays of scarlet bloom appear in spring and summer. Grow them in sun, and water lightly. Propagate gasterias from offsets.

G. carinata—5-to-6-inch, triangular, fleshy leaves; flower spike to 36 inches.
G. lingulata—10-inch dark green leaves with white spots; inflorescence to 36 inches.
G. maculata—8-inch glossy green leaves; inflorescence to 48 inches.
G. verrucosa—6-to-9-inch pink-and-purple leaves; 24-inch flower spikes.

GELSEMIUM
Carolina jasmine
Loganiaceae
55°–75°F.

Choice twining shrubs to 40 inches, gelsemiums bear tiny, fragrant, funnel-shaped, yellow flowers through the winter. Grow them in a sunny place and keep soil consistently moist. Propagate these plants from cuttings or seed.

G. sempervirens.

GERANIUM. See PELARGONIUM.

GERMAN VIOLET. See EXACUM.

GESNERIADS

African violets are well known, and now other gesneriads are enjoying popularity—rightly so, for they offer brilliant color indoors. In baskets achimenes, aeschynanthuses, columneas, episcias, and hypocyrtas are veritable cascades of bloom. Rechsteinerias, sinningias, smithianthas, and streptocarpuses have upright growth and are best grown in ordinary pots and planters. The main requirement for all of them is high humidity: some need as much as 60 percent. While some thrive at 70°F., others require coolness (58°F.). Most gesneriads do not need much sun but rather a place with bright light and plenty of air circulation. Plants do well in a loose soil mixture that holds moisture yet drains readily. In general, gesneriads are healthy and not prone to disease. For descriptions of some species and their culture, see:

Achimenes
Aeschynanthus
Columnea
Episcia
Hypocyrta
Kohleria
Rechsteineria
Saintpaulia
Sinningia
Smithiantha
Streptocarpus

GINGER. See ALPINIA, ZINGIBER.

GINGER LILY. See HEDYCHIUM.

GLORIOSA

glory lily
Liliaceae
55°–75°F.

These splendid climbing plants have narrow green leaves and exquisite lily-like orange-and-yellow flowers in spring and summer. Sure to bloom, they require little attention. Plant one tuber to each 5-inch pot; growth will appear in two weeks. Provide a bamboo stake for the stems to climb on. Give them sun, plenty of water, and 50 percent humidity. After they flower, store them dry in their pots in a paper bag in a dry, cool place. Start them again after a six-to-nine-week rest. Propagate yours from seed or by dividing the tubers in spring.

G. rothschildiana—to 72 inches; orange-and-yellow flowers to 3 inches, edged with crimson.
G. simplex (or *G. virescens*)—to 48 inches,

2-inch orange-and-yellow flowers with broad petals.
G. superba—to about 48 inches, oval dark green leaves, spectacular red flowers with petals handsomely reflex and wavy.

GLORY BOWER. See CLERODENDRUM.

GLORY LILY. See GLORIOSA.

GLOXINIA. See SINNINGIA and GESNERIADS.

GOLD-DUST DRACAENA. See DRACAENA.

GOLD-DUST TREE. See AUCUBA.

GOLDEN BAMBOO. See BAMBUSA.

GOLDEN-BARREL CACTUS. See ECHINOCACTUS and CACTUSES.

GOLDEN CALLA. See ZANTEDESCHIA.

GOLD-SPINED ALOE. See ALOE.

GONGORA

Punch and Judy orchid
Orchidaceae
60°–80°F.

Large, curious epiphytes with pairs of 20-inch green leaves and pendent scapes of tawny yellow flowers, gongoras grow better at a window than in a greenhouse. Give them diffused sun. Pot them in fir bark and keep them moist except in winter, when plants can be grown almost dry. They like 50 percent humidity. Propagate them by division of plant clumps.

G. bufonia—broad pale green leaves, dozens of 1-inch flowers in summer.
G. galata—1-inch flowers from June to September.

GRAPE HYACINTH. See Chapter 5.

GRAPE IVY. See CISSUS.

GRECIAN URN PLANT. See ACANTHUS.

GREVILLEA

silk oak
Proteaceae
55°–75°F.

Fast-growing, with delicate foliage, these make good floor plants, and they almost take care of themselves. Merely place them in sun and give them plenty of water. Propagate grevilleas from seed.

G. *bipinnatifida*—to 48 inches, loose racemes of red flowers.
G. *wilsonii*—to 60 inches, needle-like leaves, curious red-and-yellow flowers.

GROUND IVY. See NEPETA.

GUZMANIA

Bromeliaceae
55°–75°F.

Striking plants, guzmanias have rosettes of leaves and small flowers hidden in vivid bracts that stay colorful for four months. Give these bromeliads bright light, pot them in osmunda and soil, and keep them wet but never soggy. Keep the "vase" formed by the leaves filled with water. They require 50 percent humidity. Try them as a table decoration. Buy new plants from specialists.

G. *berteroniana*—20-inch rosette of wine-red leaves, yellow flowers in spring.
G. *lingulata*—26-inch rosette of apple-green leaves, star-shaped orange inflorescence all summer.
G. *minor*—16-inch rosette of bright green leaves, brilliant orange-red bracts. Very handsome.
G. *monostachia*—26-inch rosette of leaves; red, black, and white flower head in fall.
G. *musaica*—20-inch rosette of dark-green-and-reddish-brown leaves, white flowers in fall.
G. *zahnii*—20-inch rosette of green leaves, red-and-white flowers in summer.

GYMNOCALYCIUM

chin cactus
Cactaceae
55°–75°F.

These interesting desert cactuses grow to 12 inches, with white, or yellow, or chartreuse flowers that usually open in spring and summer. Grow them in sun in sandy, moist soil. Propagate them from offsets.

*G. *fleisherianum*—4-inch, spiny globe with many large pink flowers.
*G. *mihanovichii*—depressed, 2-inch, gray-green globe; yellowish white flowers.
*G. *quehlianum*—6-inch globe, white-and-red flowers.
*G. *schickendantzii*—4-inch globe, white or pinkish flowers.
*G. *venturii*—4-inch, bright green globe, red flowers.

GYNURA

velvet plant
Compositae
65°–75°F.

This popular ornamental with large purple leaves grows rapidly to 30 inches. Give it sun, frequent watering, and humidity between 40 and 60 percent. This is an unusual plant, desirable for planter boxes or where a special accent is needed. The foliage almost glows with color. Propagate gynuras from cuttings.

G. *aurantiaca.*

HAEMANTHUS

blood lily
Amaryllidaceae
55°–70°F.

Blood lilies are ornamental bulbous plants with luxuriant, fleshy leaves and hundreds of tiny flowers in a sphere. Pot one bulb with its tip protruding in a 5- or 7-inch container. Top-dress the pot with fresh soil at the start of each growing season, repotting only once every three or four years in fall or spring. These plants need sun and plenty of water in summer. In winter, keep soil nearly dry. Propagate by individually potting the offset bulbs that grow off the parent.

*H. *arabicum*—to 14 inches, reddish flowers. Beautiful.

H. coccineus—to 10 inches, spectacular red flowers in fall. Plants dormant in summer.

H. katherinae—to 12 inches, salmon-red flowers in spring after foliage develops.

H. multiflorus—to 18 inches, red flowers in spring before foliage develops.

HARDY AMARYLLIS. See LYCORIS.

HARE'S-FOOT FERN. See POLYPODIUM and FERNS.

HARTFORD FERN. See LYGODIUM.

HART'S-TONGUE FERN. See PHYLLITIS and FERNS.

HAWORTHIA

Liliaceae
55°–75°F.

Small foliage plants from South Africa, haworthias resemble aloes, with rosettes of stiff leaves that are brown, or green, or purple-brown. Some are erect, others are low growers. Carefree plants, they thrive in shade. Give them scant water in summer, even less moisture the rest of the year. They prefer a sandy soil and are good for dish gardens. Propagate them from seed.

H. fasciata—small, erect rosette of upcurved dark green leaves banded with white, 1½ inches long.

H. margaritifera—low-growing rosette, 6 inches across; 3-inch, sharply pointed leaves with white tubercles; dense sprays of flowers to 24 inches.

H. retusa—stemless, clustered rosette; flat pale green leaves, 1½ inches long.

H. viscosa—erect rosette to 8 inches wide; 3-inch, rough, dull green leaves.

HEDERA

ivy
Araliaceae
50°–60°F.

These trailing or climbing foliage plants have many leaf forms—all attractive. They make bright decoration for brick walls in a plant room, or in baskets, or trained into topiary forms. They are equally good on a trellis in a pot. But don't try to grow ivy in a warm room: coolness and humidity are the keys to success. Give these plants bright light rather than sun. Soak the soil, then let it dry, then soak it again. Give the foliage a spraying in the sink at least once a week, and an occasional soapy wash is necessary to keep them free of aphids and spider mites. Provide 30 to 50 percent humidity. Propagate ivy from cuttings at any time.

H. canariensis—large, leathery fresh-green leaves, slightly curved. Called Algerian ivy.

H. helix—dark green leaves of various shape and color. Called English ivy.

H. helix 'Goldheart'—gold-centered leaves with green edges.

H. helix 'Green Ripples'—pleated leaves.

H. helix 'Itsy Bitsy'—tiny, pointed leaves.

H. helix 'Jubilee'—green-and-white leaves.

H. helix 'Manda's Crested'—wavy, five-pointed leaves.

H. helix 'Shamrock'—compact, small leaves.

*H. helix 'Star'—fine for a dish garden or terrarium.

HEDGE FERN. See POLYSTICHUM and FERNS.

HEDGEHOG CACTUS. See ECHINO-CEREUS and CACTUSES.

HEDYCHIUM

ginger lily
Zingiberaceae
55°–75°F.

These large plants, to 72 inches, with canes of pale or glossy green leaves and fragrant white or yellow flowers in summer, are excellent for tubs in a sunny corner or outdoors on a terrace. Give them plenty of water and up to 50 percent humidity. Reduce moisture after bloom is over. Increase your supply by dividing rootstocks in spring.

H. coronarium—sweetly scented pure white flowers. Called garland flower.

H. flavum—luxuriant, pointed green leaves; yellow flowers. Called yellow ginger.

H. gardnerianum—18-inch leaves, flamboyant yellow flowers with red stamens. Called Kahili ginger.

HELICONIA

Musaceae
55°–75°F.

The banana family offers some large plants with showy tropical flowers and leathery leaves, and these are good patio or plant-room decoration. Give them sun, rich soil kept consistently moist, and 50 percent humidity. Difficult to make bloom, heliconias are worth the space they require because if flowers do come they are superb. Give plants less water in winter, a time of natural rest. Propagate heliconias by dividing the rootstock when growth starts in spring.

H. angustifolia—to 36 inches; 24-inch, leathery leaves; orange-red bracts.

H. aurantiaca—to 30 inches, smooth leaves, orange-and-green bracts.

H. psittacorum—to 24 inches, rich-green leaves, orange bracts, greenish yellow flowers. The best one for window-growing. Called parrot flower.

HELIOCEREUS

sun cactus
Cactaceae
55°–80°F.

The popular sun cactus blooms by day; its sister genus Selinicereus, by night. Plants sprawl to 8 feet. Their leaves are elongated stems, generally with spines. The flowers are spectacular: large and dramatic. Annual bloom is in later summer. These plants need large tubs and much sun to bloom. Use a sandy soil that drains readily. Once established, plants grow for years in the same container. Splendid for those seeking the dramatic. Grow new plants from stem cuttings.

H. schrankii—to 6 feet, elongated leaves, vivid red flowers.

H. speciosus—to 7 feet, elongated gray-green leaves, red flowers.

HELIOTROPE. See HELIOTROPIUM.

HELIOTROPIUM

heliotrope
Boraginaceae
55°–75°F.

Common heliotrope (*H. arborescens*) is an old-fashioned favorite, with white, lavender, or dark purple flowers—often deliciously fragrant—from January until summer. Growing to 40 inches, this plant makes a good standard. Plants need sun, a rich soil, and constant moisture. Watch out for white flies. Propagate heliotropiums from cuttings or seed.

H. arborescens—vanilla-scented violet flowers.

H. arborescens 'First Snow'—pure white flowers.

H. arborescens 'Marine'—a semidwarf to 20 inches, purple flowers.

HELXINE

baby's tears
Urticaceae
55°–75°F.

Helxine is seldom grown for itself as a house plant but makes a fine ground cover for a bottle garden or terrarium (see Chapter 4). The leaves are tiny, mosslike, and appealing. The plant requires warmth and high humidity.

H. soleiroli.

HEN-AND-CHICKENS. See SEMPERVIVUM.

HIBISCUS

Malvaceae
55°–75°F.

The hibiscus is a large, free-flowering plant to 48 inches, for sun porch or plant room. Single or double blooms in red, yellow, pink, or white open on and off through the year. Grow yours in 10- or 12-inch pots in full sun with plenty of water. These are thirsty plants, requiring 30 to 50 percent humidity. Feed them moderately. Prune them back hard in early spring, as they grow quickly. Watch out for spider-mite attacks. Stand their pots in pail of water once a month for a good soaking. New ones can be grown from cuttings.

H. *chinensis metallica*—to 48 inches; handsome, variegated leaves; large, showy red flowers.

H. *rosa-sinensis*—to 48 inches; long, oval green leaves; flaring, trumpet-like flowers.

H. *rosa-sinensis* 'Agnes Goult'—large, single, rose-colored flowers.

H. *rosa-sinensis* 'California Gold'—large, single, ocher-yellow flowers.

H. *rosa-sinensis cooperi*—variegated leaves, small red flowers.

H. *rosa-sinensis* 'Scarlet'—intensely red flowers.

H. *rosa-sinensis* 'Snow Queen'—variegated leaves, small white flowers.

H. *rosa-sinensis* 'White Wings'—white flowers stained with red.

HIPPEASTRUM

amaryllis
Amaryllidaceae
55°–65°F.

These are striking bulbous plants with straplike foliage and mammoth flowers in white, pink, red, rose, or violet—the throats lighter or darker, the petals sometimes banded, striped, or bordered in a contrasting color. The flower stalks grow to 26 inches. Buy quality bulbs in late fall. Plant them from January to March. Allow one bulb to a 6- or 7-inch pot, always with 1 inch of space between the walls of the pot and the bulb. Don't bury the bulb; let the upper third rise above the soil. Moisten the soil and set the pots in a cool, dark place; grow the plants almost dry until the flower buds are up 6 inches or more. Then move them into sun and water heavily. Three weeks or more elapse from planting to blooming. After your amaryllises bloom, keep them growing so the leaves can manufacture food for next year's flowers. When the foliage turns brown, let the soil stay almost dry for about three months, or until you see a new flower bud emerging; then replant the bulbs in fresh soil but, if possible, in the same containers. If you have a garden, set the plants out when danger of frost is past, plunging them into the soil. When the weather turns cool in fall, bring them indoors to a cool spot (about 55°F.). Water them lightly—only enough to keep the leaves from wilting—until you start them into a new cycle of growth. Propagate this plant from seed or by individually potting the little bulbs that grow next to the mature one.

H. 'Claret'—8-inch flowers, crimson or wine-colored with red-black lines.

H. 'Giant White'—7-inch, glistening flowers.

H. 'Peppermint'—8-inch white-and-red-striped flowers.

H. 'Pink Perfection'—7-inch rose-colored flowers, lighter petal tips, the throat dark carmine.

H. 'Scarlet Admiral'—7-inch glossy red flowers.

H. 'Winter Joy'—5-inch red flowers with a darker throat and orange-red petal tips.

HOFFMANNIA

Rubiaceae
50°–75°F.

Splendid foliage plants from Mexico, hoffmannias have velvety leaves in shades of glowing green and dark red or brown. They grow well at a north window. Keep soil consistently moist. Good for planters or wherever a bright accent is needed, they can be propagated from cuttings.

H. *ghiesbreghtii*—to 48 inches, brown-green leaves.

H. *refulgens*—to 15 inches; almost iridescent, crinkled leaves edged with magenta and rose.

H. *roezlii*—to 30 inches, copper-and-bronze leaves.

HOHENBERGIA

Bromeliaceae
55°–75°F.

Striking plants that need space, these bromeliads have broad golden green leaves in rosettes to 48 inches across and erect spikes of vivid lavender-blue flowers to 40 inches high. Pot them in osmunda and soil. Grow them in full sun and keep the "vase" formed by the leaves filled with water. Thirty to fifty percent humidity is fine for them. They make attractive terrace plants. They are spiny: wear gloves when handling them. Buy new ones from specialists.

H. *ridleyii*—golden yellow rosette of leaves, lavender flower head.

H. stellata—golden green rosette of leaves, violet flower head.

HOLLY FERN. See POLYSTICHUM and FERNS.

HONEYBELLS. See MAHERNIA.

HOUSELEEK. See SEMPERVIVUM.

HOWEIA　　　　　**Kentia palm**
(KENTIA)　　　　*Palmaceae*
　　　　　　　55°–75°F.

Indestructible foliage plants to 60 inches, howeias are decorative, with graceful fronds. Grow them in semishade and keep soil consistently moist. Plants do best when potbound, so provide small containers, even for mature specimens. Soak plants in a pail of water once a month to keep them in good health. Propagate them from offsets.

H. belmoreana—very sharply pointed fronds bending gently away from the main stems. Called sentry palm.

H. forsteriana—dark green fronds, drooping more noticeably from the main stems. Called paradise palm.

HOYA　　　　　**wax plant**
　　　　　　　Asclepiadaceae
　　　　　　　55°–75°F.

The attractive vines in this genus grow to 48 inches or more, with leathery, glossy leaves and charming clusters of very fragrant flowers. Only mature plants, four or five years old, are likely to bloom; young ones rarely do so. These plants need full sun and will not bud at all in shade. Grow them potbound and give them plenty of water in spring, summer, and fall. In winter let soil become almost dry. Don't remove the stem or spur on which the flowers have been produced, as this is the source of next season's bloom. Mist foliage frequently and check for mealy bugs. Best grown on a trellis or support, hoyas can also be handsome hanging from a basket. Propagate them from cuttings in spring.

H. australis—a climber to 60 inches, waxy green leaves, clusters of fragrant white flowers. The most popular species.

H. bandaensis—a climber to 72 inches; large glossy green leaves, dark green veins; greenish white flowers with scarlet centers.

H. bella—a bushy climber to 20 inches, tiny leaves, umbels of purple-centered white flowers. Called miniature wax plant.

H. carnosa—a climber to 48 inches, white flowers with pink centers.

H. 'Compacta'—a short climber to 12 inches, white flowers.

H. engleriana—a climber to 36 inches; thick, round, hairy leaves; tiny, fragrant white flowers.

H. keysii—a climber to 30 inches, gray-green leaves, white flowers.

H. 'Minibel'—a strong climber to 72 inches, green leaves, clusters of scented waxy pink flowers.

H. motoskei—a climber to 48 inches, oval leaves with silver spots, pink flowers.

HUERNIA　　　　**star flower**
　　　　　　　Asclepiadaceae
　　　　　　　55°–75°F.

Resembling stapelias, these are good-looking succulents from South Africa with somewhat gnarled growth (leaves) and gigantic, bizarrely colored flowers more weird than beautiful. They require equal parts sand, gravel, and soil with a thin layer of gravel on top of the mix. Water them carefully—overwatering will kill the plants. Give ample sun and grow them somewhat cool. They are unusual plants that have a certain fascination, but beware: some of the flowers smell awful. Propagate huernias from offsets.

H. barbata—to 20 inches; erect, angled stems with long green teeth; pale yellow flowers spotted red.

H. pillansi—to 20 inches; cylindrical stems covered with tubercles, long spines; pale yellow flowers dotted with crimson.

H. primulina—to 20 inches; short, stout, toothed, angled stems; pale yellow or pinkish yellow flowers.

HYACINTH. See Chapter 5.

HYACINTHUS. See Chapter 5.

HYDRANGEA
Saxifragaceae
55°–70°F.

Familiar Easter pot plants, these large-leaved shrubs have showy clusters of white, blue, or pink flowers. Keep their soil almost wet, sometimes watering more than once a day. Grow them cool—not over 70°F.—in sun with plenty of fresh air and with humidity at about 30 to 50 percent. After plants bloom, cut back the shoots to two joints and repot them in slightly acid soil. Set them outdoors, feed them biweekly, and keep them well watered. After the first frost, store them indoors where it is cool (about 45°F.) and dim. Keep soil barely moist (water about once a month). In January increase warmth, light, and water. When the plants are actively growing, move them to a window where temperatures range between 60°F. and 65°F. The degree of soil acidity determines the coloring of the blossoms. A pink plant can be made blue by changing the soil to an acid 5.0-5.5 pH. These are fine varieties of *H. macrophylla*, the common florists' hydrangea:

  'Merveille'—carmine-rose flowers.
  'Soeur Therese'—pure white flowers.
  'Strafford'—rose-red flowers.

HYLOCEREUS
night-blooming cactus
Cactaceae
55°–75°F.

These huge, vining jungle plants to 7 feet, usually epiphytic, produce slow-opening, mammoth white flowers once a year on a summer night—an occasion for a party because blooms last only 12 to 24 hours. To some, they are hardly worth the trouble of tending them the other 364 days, but to me the annual spectacle makes their care worthwhile. Hylocereuses need sandy soil, sun and lots of water in summer, and bright light in winter with less moisture and a cooler place (about 50°F.). Established plants are really no trouble if you have space for them, and the

yearly blossoming *is* exciting. Grow new plants from cuttings in spring.

H. undatus.

HYPOCYRTA
Gesneriaceae
60°–80°F.

Trailing epiphytes to 24 inches from Central America, hypocyrtas need winter sun, summer shade, and 60 percent humidity. They have tiny leaves and pouchy flowers. Set them on brackets or grow them in hanging baskets in equal parts of shredded osmunda and soil. Flowers bloom in brilliant shades of orange and red. After they fade, prune plants back to encourage branching. After they bloom, some kinds rest for a few months; grow them almost dry then. New blooms appear on new growth the following fall and winter. Propagate hypocyrtas from stem-tip cuttings of new growth.

H. 'Emile'—to 24 inches, leathery dark green leaves, bright orange flowers shaped like goldfish. Floriferous.
H. nummularia—a creeper with vermilion-yellow-violet flowers. May become dormant in summer but leafs out again in fall.
H. strigillosa—spreading, semierect growth; reddish-orange flowers.
H. wettsteinii—a pendent grower with orange-yellow flowers on and off throughout the year.

IMPATIENS
patience plant
Balsaminaceae
50°–65°F.

Excellent window plants, impatiens offer color almost all year with pretty pink, white, orange, or red blooms. These plants need a bright place and consistently moist soil in summer. Keep them barely moist in winter. Grow them in a cool place. Propagate impatiens from cuttings or seed.

I. holstii—to 24 inches, reddish leaves, red flowers.
I. holstii 'Orange Baby'—to 8 inches, deep orange flowers.
I. platypetala aurantiaca—to 26 inches, green leaves, salmon-orange flowers.

I. repens—to 20 inches, red branches, hooded golden yellow flowers with brownish stripes. A delightful trailer.

I. sultani—to 20 inches; green leaves; continuously flowering, red or pink blooms. Called patient Lucy.

INCH PLANT. See TRADESCANTIA.

INDIAN CROCUS. See PLEIONE and ORCHIDS.

INDOOR LINDEN. See SPARMANNIA.

IVY. See HEDERA.

IVY ARUM. See SCINDAPSUS.

IXORA
flame-of-the-woods
Rubiaceae
50°–70°F.

A worthwhile group of robust house plants to 36 inches, ixoras have ornamental foliage and clusters of bright flowers. Some plants bloom twice: in early spring and again in summer. Ixoras need sun and a moist soil except in winter, when they should be kept somewhat dry. Even young plants bloom. Grow new plants from cuttings.

I. chinensis—4-inch leaves, red-to-white flowers.
I. 'Gillette's Yellow'—sunny flowers. Floriferous.
I. javanica—7-inch leaves, willowy branches, orange-red flowers.
I. 'Super King'—compact; 6-inch, ball-shaped flower clusters. Free-flowering, blooms twice.

JACARANDA
Bignoniaceae
50°–75F.

This species of a genus of trees and shrubs grows only to 36 inches, with ferny growth rather like that of the mimosa. Ideal for a sun nook or pedestal table, these plants grow rapidly with little care. Give them a bright location and keep soil consistently moist. Blue-violet panicles may appear in spring or summer, but jacaranda rarely flowers indoors. It is easily grown from seed.

J. acutifolia.

JACOBEAN LILY. See SPREKELIA.

JACOBINIA
king's crown
Acanthaceae
50°–75°F.

From Brazil, these 30-inch plants have downy green leaves and plumes of pink or orange flowers. They offer charming summer color. Grow them at a sunny window with good air circulation and keep soil wet. Insufficient moisture causes leaf drop. Take stem cuttings in spring for new plants, discard old ones.

J. carnea—upright growth, dark green leaves, pink flowers.
J. ghiesbreghtiana—light green leaves, orange flowers.
J. suberecta—spreading growth, hairy leaves, orange flowers.

JADE PLANT. See CRASSULA.

JASMINE. See CESTRUM, JASMINUM.

JASMINE PLANT. See BOUVARDIA.

JASMINUM
jasmine
Oleaceae
55°–65°F.

Every indoor garden with jasmine becomes fragrant. One large vining plant perfumes a whole room from March (sometimes earlier) to November. Some kinds get large, others grow only to 12 inches. With dark green leaves and yellow or white flowers in clusters at the branch tips or in leaf axils, these slow-growing plants are worth their space in gold. Grow them in sun with consistently moist soil and 50 percent humidity. Use an acid fertilizer, mist foliage occasionally, and give pots a deep soaking in the sink once a month. Propagate jasmine from cuttings.

J. humile—bushy growth to 72 inches, yellow flowers.

J. officinale grandiflorum—a shrubby, ferny vine to 72 inches; large white flowers. Called poet's jasmine.

J. parkeri—to 12 inches, tiny yellow flowers.

J. sambac—shrubby growth to 36 inches, white flowers. Called Arabian jasmine.

J. sambac 'Maid of Orleans'—single flowers. Very fine.

J. sambac 'Grand Duke'—double flowers. Less dependable but beautiful.

JATROPHA
Euphorbiaceae
50°–75°F.

These lovely, tropical evergreen shrubs to 48 inches fill my plant room with clusters of brilliant red flowers and broad green leaves. They bloom throughout the year. Place them in sun and keep soil consistently moist. Propagate jatrophas from seed.

J. hastatum—to 30 inches, bright green leaves, vivid red flowers in clusters.

J. pandurifolia 'Dwarf'—a small variety to 14 inches.

J. pandurifolia 'Holly Leaf'—a good scarlet-flowered variety.

JERUSALEM CHERRY. See SOLANUM.

KAEMPFERIA
peacock plant
Zingiberaceae
55°–75°F.

The peacock plant is an exquisite, 12-inch plant with beautiful foliage a ' .ttractive flowers—not to be missed. It bears colorful lavender blooms—a few a day—all summer, and the leaves are almost iridescent. Grow yours in bright light and keep soil fairly moist but not soaked. Let the plant die down in winter and store the rootstock cold in a paper bag. Repot it in March or April in a 6-inch container. Make new plants by dividing the rootstock.

K. roscoeana.

KAFIR LILY. See CLIVIA.

KAHILI GINGER. See HEDYCHIUM.

KALANCHOE
Crassulaceae
60°–70°F.

These plants vary in the type of growth they make and the kind of foliage they have. They can survive in unfavorable environments. They are short-day plants and will only bloom when day-length is less than 12 hours. If the short-day schedule is started in October, flowering will usually commence in about two months. Plants in bloom at Christmas will continue to flower for a month or longer. The fleshy green leaves and clusters of small, showy red or orange blossoms are indeed welcome in winter. Give them bright light and let soil dry out well between waterings. To avoid mildew, take care

Kalanchoes bloom in winter. This variety, called 'Tom Thumb,' has cheerful red flowers. (Photograph by Merry Gardens)

171

Contrary to popular opinion, orchids are not especially delicate plants. This *Laelia purpurata* thrives with ordinary care and brings much beauty to a plant room. (Photograph by C/D Luckhart)

neither to overwater them nor to grow them in a humid atmosphere. If leaves develop a white coating, dust them lightly with Karathane. Use 3- or 4-inch pots, and repot every second year. New plants can be started by sowing seed in spring or by separately potting naturally formed plantlets.

K. blossfeldiana—to 20 inches, waxy leaves. Sometimes blooms twice—in winter and again in spring.

**K. blossfeldiana* 'Tom Thumb'—a dwarf hybrid sold in florists' shops at Christmas.

K. pumila—to 16 inches, dark leathery leaves, vivid pink flowers. Pretty.

K. tomentosa—to 20 inches; fuzzy, brown-spotted gray-green leaves. Grown for its foliage. Called panda plant.

**K. uniflora*—a prostrate species to 14 inches; pink-to-orange, bell-like flowers late in winter, sometimes in spring. Charming.

KANGAROO THORN. See ACACIA.

KANGAROO VINE. See CISSUS.

and attractive foliage. Plants need bright light rather than sun. Water them heavily during active growth, much less the rest of the time—about once a week—but never allow them to become completely dry, or they may die. Use room-temperature water, as cold water spots the soft, furry foliage. Do not mist plants but give adequate humidity, about 60 percent. Take stem-tip cuttings for new plants, or large rhizomes may be divided and replanted singly.

K. amabilis—to 16 inches, green leaves, pink flowers in spring and summer. Basket plants.

K. bogotensis—to 24 inches, brilliant red-and-yellow flowers in summer. Stake and grow upright.

K. eriantha—erect growth to 24 inches, bright red flowers from summer to fall.

K. lindeniana—erect growth to 10 inches, fragrant violet-and-white flowers in late fall.

K. 'Longwood'—upright growth to 24 inches, large spotted pink flowers.

LACE ALOE. See ALOE.

LADY-OF-THE-NIGHT ORCHID. See BRASSAVOLA and ORCHIDS.

LADY PALM. See RHAPIS and PALMS.

LADY'S EARDROPS. See FUCHSIA.

LADY-SLIPPER ORCHID. See PAPHIOPEDILUM and ORCHIDS.

KENTIA, KENTIA PALM. See HOWEIA and PALMS.

KING'S CROWN. See JACOBINIA.

KITE ORCHID. See MASDEVALLIA and ORCHIDS.

KOHLERIA *Gesneriaceae*
60°–80°F.

This gesneriad genus includes fine trailers and upright growers with colorful tubular flowers

LAELIA *Orchidaceae*
50°–75°F.

These showy epiphytic orchids, many to 30 inches, have leathery leaves and pink flowers in fall. Plant them in fir bark, soak it, and then allow it to dry out before watering again. Grow them in sun, with 50 percent humidity. Buy young plants from specialists.

L. anceps—to 30 inches; 4-inch pink flowers, several to a cluster.

L. gouldiana—to 30 inches, many rose-magenta flowers.

*L. *pumila*—a dwarf to 8 inches, 4-inch pale-rose-colored flowers in summer or fall.

L. *purpurata*—to 36 inches; narrow, leathery leaves; fine, large white flowers with a magenta throat.

LANTANA
Verbenaceae
50°–70°F.

These plants have yellow, lavender, or orange blooms. Place them in sun. In summer give them plenty of water. After flowering, cut plants back and grow them somewhat dry. Grow new ones from cuttings or seed. Watch out for white flies. Lantanas can be trained to grow as attractive standards.

L. *camara*—shrubby, spreading growth to 20 inches, orange summer flowers.

L. *montevidensis*—trailing growth to 48 inches, lavender flowers in fall and winter. A good basket plant.

LAPAGERIA
Liliaceae
60°–75°F.

A very showy vine from Chile with leathery dark green leaves and exquisite, bell-shaped rose-colored flowers, lapageria can be grown in a large tub in a plant room. It needs ordinary house-plant soil kept consistently moist. Provide some support, such as a trellis, and keep it in a bright place. Do not put it in sun, however. This new introduction is startlingly beautiful. Buy new plants from suppliers.

L. *rosea*.

LEADWORT. See PLUMBAGO.

LEATHER FERN. See POLYSTICHUM and FERNS.

LEMON TREE. See CITRUS.

LEMON VINE. See PERESKIA and CACTUSES.

LEOPARD PLANT. See LIGULARIA.

LESSER OLD-MAN CACTUS. See ECHINOCEREUS and CACTUSES.

LETTUCE-LEAF BEGONIA. See BEGONIA, Rhizomatous.

LEUCHTENBERGIA
Cactaceae
55°–75°F.

Only one species of this genus is cultivated but it appears frequently in collections and, though not pretty, it has its admirers. These desert cactuses have elongated, fleshy stems with starry spines. The flowers are yellow. Grow them in sun in sandy soil kept barely moist. Water only when soil is dry. Propagate leuchtenbergias from seed.

L. *principis*.

LICUALA
palm
Palmaceae
55°–75°F.

Little known but lovely, this palm, growing slowly to 72 inches with wide fans of foliage, is undemanding and thrives in almost any exposure. It requires 50 percent humidity. Water it several times a week. Here is a good tub plant. Propagate it from seed.

L. *grandis*.

LIGULARIA
Compositae
50°–70°F.

Foliage plants to 24 inches from Japan, they thrive in north light. With round, variegated leaves on graceful stems, they are showy and colorful. Grow them in shade and keep soil quite moist. Grow new plants by root division.

L. *kaempferi argentea*—green leaves with creamy white margins.

L. *kaempferi aureo-maculata*—green leaves with golden flecks. Called leopard plant.

LILY-OF-THE-NILE. See AGAPANTHUS.

LILY-OF-THE-VALLEY. See CONVALLARIA.

LIME TREE. See CITRUS.

LIPSTICK VINE. See AESCHYNANTHUS and GESNERIADS.

LIVING ROCK PLANT. See ARIOCARPUS and CACTUSES.

LIVING STONES. See CONOPHYTUM.

LIVING VASE PLANT. See AECHMEA, BILLBERGIA, NEOREGELIA, and BROMELIADS.

LIVISTONA   Chinese fan palm
Palmaceae
55°–70° F.

This robust palm from China has a solitary trunk and big, fan-shaped leaves—excellent for large rooms. It can grow to 10 feet indoors if given the space. Livistonas need bright light and a consistently moist soil. Buy new plants from specialists.

L. chinensis.

LOBIVIA   cob cactus
Cactaceae
55°–75° F.

This group of small, charming desert cactuses bears lovely paper-thin flowers in summer and early fall. These plants need a sandy soil that drains readily and the sunniest place in your growing area. Water them moderately all year except in winter, when the potting medium should be somewhat dry—cooler temperatures then, too. These pretty plants, which are sure to please, can be propagated from offsets.

L. bruchii—depressed cylindrical globe to 16 inches, small spines, red flowers.
L. cylindrica—deep green, cylindrical plant to 14 inches; brown, needle-like spines; canary-yellow flowers.
L. famatimensis—oval globe to 10 inches, short yellow spines, orange flowers.
L. rubriflora—columnar growth to 10 inches, small spines, red flowers.

L. stienmannii—clustering globes to 6 inches, small spines, red-to-orange flowers.

LOBSTER CLAWS. See VRIESEA and BROMELIADS.

LOPHOPHORA   *Cactaceae*
55°–75° F.

A group of slow-growing, blue-gray, globular cactuses with no spines. Grow them in sun and use equal parts sand and soil as a potting medium. Water them only when the potting mix is dry. Propagate lophophoras from seed in spring.

L. williamsii—pink flowers in summer. The most commonly grown species.

LOVE PLANT. See MEDINILLA.

LYCASTE   *Orchidaceae*
50°–75° F.

These epiphytic or terrestrial orchids grow to about 14 inches, with broad, pleated green leaves and regal flowers in white, green, pink, or vivid yellow. Pot them in fir bark and give them sun and plenty of water when they are growing. Then, to encourage budding, dry them out somewhat for about a month when the leaves mature. After blooming, keep your plants *completely dry* for about six to eight weeks, but maintain 50 to 60 percent humidity. Buy new plants from specialists.

L. aromatica—3 to 10 fragrant yellow flowers in spring.
L. deppei—pale green flowers spotted with red in winter.
L. skinneri—5-inch blush-white winter flowers.

LYCORIS   *Amaryllidaceae*
50°–65° F.

Deciduous bulbous plants from China and Japan, lycoris species have grassy foliage and large, striking flowers in fall or winter. Start the bulbs, with their noses just above the soil, one to a 6- or 7-inch pot, in April or May. Water them moderately until the end of summer, then flood plants and give them sun. As leaf growth develops in late fall, flowers appear. In spring, the leaves turn yellow and die off. Then you should keep them dry for a few months and then start them into growth again. Do not repot your plants frequently. Propagate lycoris by planting the offset bulbs.

L. radiata—to 20 inches; bright orange-red flowers, 4-inches across. Called nerine.
L. squamigera—to 24 inches; fragrant, 4-inch lilac flowers. Called hardy amaryllis.

LYGODIUM
climbing fern
Schizaeaceae (Filices)
50°–70° F.

Vinelike plants to 40 inches with attractive, light, lacy blue-green fronds that survive in almost any situation, lygodiums prefer shade, with a little sun in winter. Grow them in loose, moist, well-drained, acid soil. Start new plants from spores.

L. palmatum—4-to-7-lobed fronds. Called Hartford fern.
L. scandens—2-inch, feathery blue-green fronds.

LYSIMACHIA
creeping Charlie, moneywort
Primulaceae
50°–70°F.

This creeping plant makes a pretty ground cover for large pots and is fine for bottle gardens and terrariums (see Chapter 4). It has trailing stems and round leaves. It will grow in shade or sun but requires a moist soil and humidity to 50 percent. Propagate it from stem cuttings.

*L. nummularia.

MADAGASCAR JASMINE. See STEPHANOTIS.

MAHERNIA
honeybells
Sterculiaceae
50°–60°F.

Fragrant yellow flowers adorn this 20-inch, sprawling plant in winter and spring. It grows best on a sun porch or in a plant room. Soak its soil and let it dry before watering it again. Though not spectacular, it has charm and makes a good basket plant. Propagate mahernias from cuttings.

M. verticillata.

MAIDENHAIR FERN. See ADIANTUM and FERNS.

MALPIGHIA
miniature holly
Malpighiaceae
55°–70°F.

A dwarf evergreen to 20 inches, miniature holly has small, spiny leaves and pale pink flowers that pop out in spring and summer and stay bright and pretty for months. The plant needs sun and a consistently moist soil. Grow new plants from cuttings in spring.

M. coccigera.

MAMMILLARIA
pincushion cactus
Cactaceae
55°–75°F.

This genus includes a number of attractive 12-to-20-inch Mexican globe cactuses with colorful white, red, black, or gray spines and crowns of tiny flowers, usually in late summer and early winter. These desert plants are easily grown at a bright window in sandy soil, with water every other day in summer and about once a week in winter. Propagate them from offsets.

M. applanata—a dark green plant, creamy white flowers.
M. bocasana—clustered, round, dark green stems to 2 inches with white hairs, yellow spines; yellow flowers.
M. fragilis—covered with white spines; cream-colored flowers. Called powder-puff cactus.
M. haageana—spiny globe to 3 inches, circle of small cerise flowers.
M. hahniana—flattened globe to 3 inches, curly white hairs, white spines; red flowers.
M. meyeranii—spiny globe to 4 inches, many small pink flowers.

There are many mammillaria species. This one—
Mammillaria haageana—is perhaps the most popular.
(Photograph by C/D Luckhart)

MANDEVILLA. See DIPLADENIA.

MANETTIA	**Mexican firecracker**
	Rubiaceae
	55°–75°F.

Climbing plants to 24 inches, Mexican fire-crackers bear tubular, yellow-tipped red flowers almost all year at a sunny window. Let the soil dry out between waterings and provide 50 percent humidity. This plant thrives when pot-bound and requires an airy location. Grow new plants from cuttings.

M. inflata.

MARANTA	***Marantaceae***
	60°–80°F.

Ornamental foliage and the will to grow readily at north windows give these plants a top spot on my desirable list. Keep soil moist and give 50 percent humidity. These plants thrive in 4- or 5-inch pots and love good circulation of air. When resting time comes in late fall, cut away the old foliage (leave the more recent foliage) and grow the plants with soil barely moist. In January and February, resume watering. Propagate marantas by root division at repotting time or from leaf cuttings.

M. arundinacea—to 48 inches, zigzag rows of arrow-shaped gray-green leaves. Called arrowroot.

·M. bicolor—to 12 inches; oval, dark gray-green leaves.

M. leuconeura kerchoveana—to 15 inches; 6-inch oval, glaucous, pale grayish green leaves with rows of brown and dark green spots. Leaves fold at night to funnel dew down to the roots. Called prayer plant.

M. leuconeura massangeana—to 15 inches, smaller gray-green leaves with silver markings.

MASDEVALLIA

kite orchid
Orchidaceae
50°–65°F.

Masdevallias are 5-to-15-inch epiphytic or terrestrial orchids with curious triangular flowers that usually appear in winter and leathery, spatulate leaves. They are perfect for a cool north window or a terrarium. These orchids have no pseudobulbs and should be planted in fir bark or osmunda and kept moist all year, with humidity at about 70 percent. Buy new plants from specialists.

M. bella—large yellow-and-red flowers.
M. coccinea—pink-to-magenta flowers. The most popular type.
M. ignea—large cinnabar-red flowers.
M. tovarensis—pure white flowers.

MEDINILLA

love plant
Melastomaceae
55°–75°F.

A lush blue-green plant to 40 inches, medinilla bears stunning pendulous panicles of carmine flowers in pink bracts. Blossoming can occur at any time of year but only on mature plants in 8- or 10-inch tubs. Grow this one in bright light; water it moderately except in winter, and then only twice a week. However, it needs 70 percent humidity. Propagate plants from seed or buy young plants from a specialist.

M. magnifica.

MEXICAN FIRECRACKER. See MANETTIA.

MEXICAN FOXGLOVE. See ALLOPHYTON.

MEXICAN HYDRANGEA. See CLERODENDRUM.

MEXICAN LOVE VINE. See DIPLADENIA.

MEYER LEMON. See CITRUS.

MILTONIA

pansy orchid
Orchidaceae
50°–70°F.

Popular 12-to-20-inch epiphytic orchids, miltonias have large, open-faced flowers that stay fresh on the plant for a month. Pot them in fir bark, keep it moist but not wet, and supply 60 percent humidity. Obtain young plants from a specialist. Many fine species and varieties are listed in catalogs, and new varieties are introduced frequently.

M. candida—fall-blooming chestnut-brown flowers tipped yellow.
M. flavescens—summer-blooming flowers with yellow sepals and petals, yellow lip marked with purple.
M. roezlii—summer-blooming white flowers stained with purple.
M. vexillaria—spring-blooming lilac-rose flowers with yellow lip.
Hybrids—white-and-red flowers with yellow-marked masks: 'Alexandre Dumas,' 'Aramis,' 'Pam Pam,' 'San Roberto.'

MIMULUS

Scrophulariaceae
55°–75°F.

Member of a genus of about sixty annual or perennial herbs, *M. aurantiacus*, from western North America, has simple, toothed green leaves and flowers in a rainbow of colors, with red perhaps being the most popular. These plants are really easy to grow. They need ordinary potting soil that drains readily. Keep them consistently moist all year, and they like sun.

M. aurantiacus.

MINIATURE FLAGPLANT. See ACORUS.

MINIATURE HOLLY. See MALPIGHIA.

MINIATURE ROSE. See ROSA.

MISTLETOE CACTUS. See RHIPSALIS and CACTUSES.

MISTLETOE FIG. See FICUS.

MONEYWORT. See LYSIMACHIA.

MONSTERA
Swiss cheese plant
Araceae
55°–75°F.

Climbing foliage plants to 72 inches or more, with 24-inch perforated green leaves, monsteras are excellent for planters in public rooms. Grow them in bright light and keep soil consistently moist. They like 50 percent humidity. They grow in water almost better than in soil. Plants will adjust to warmth or coolness, but keep them out of drafts. Wash or wipe the foliage about once a month. Older plants bear unusual boat-shaped white flowers. Aerial roots grow from stem nodes; cut these off if you wish. Propagate monsteras from stem cuttings or by air layering.

M. acuminata—14-inch leaves.
M. deliciosa—36-inch leaves with slits.
M. schleichtleinii—20-inch, filigreed leaves.

MOON FLOWER. See PHALAENOPSIS and ORCHIDS.

MOSES-IN-THE-CRADLE. See RHOEO.

MOTHER FERN. See ASPLENIUM and FERNS.

MOTH ORCHID. See PHALAENOPSIS and ORCHIDS.

MUEHLENBECKIA
Polygonaceae
55°–75F.

Small round-leaved vines effective in baskets, muhlenbeckia plants grow rapidly into a tight mat of foliage about 12 inches across. They are sun-lovers and resent overwatering, so keep soil barely moist. Grow new plants from stem-tip cuttings.

M. complexa—small, round green leaves; tiny terminal flowers. Called wire plant.

M. platyclados—soft-jointed green stems, red flowers. Called centipede plant.

MURRAEA
Rutaceae
55°–70°F.

Evergreen shrubs with glossy green, ferny foliage and very fragrant clusters of white flowers in summer and fall followed by red berries, murraeas are charming throughout the year. Give them sun and plenty of water while in active growth, less in winter. Propagate murraeas from cuttings.

M. exotica—smells like orange blossoms. Called orange jasmine.
M. paniculata (perhaps a form of *M. exotica*) —slow-growing to 20 inches, also highly scented. Called satinwood.

MUSA
banana
Musaceae
60°–80°F.

The banana is a good accent plant with a solitary trunk to 60 inches and shiny green, spatulate leaves. This fine porch or terrace decoration needs winter sun and summer shade and consistently moist soil. Propagate it from cuttings.

M. nana.

MUSCARI. See Chapter 5.

NARCISSUS. See Chapter 5.

NATAL PLUM. See CARISSA.

NEOMARICA
walking iris,
apostle plant
Iridaceae
50°–70°F.

These are highly dependable plants with strap-like foliage and fragrant winter flowers on tall stalks. Pot them in sandy soil in shallow, 4- or 5-inch containers. Give them full sun and plenty of water. After they bloom, rest plants for about a month with scant watering. Increase your supply by splitting rhizomes and repotting or by potting the small plantlets that form at the top of the flower stems as you would offsets.

N. caerulea—to 30 inches, blue-and-white flowers. The best one.
N. gracilis—to 18 inches, similar to *N. caerulea*.
N. northiana—to 36 inches; larger, fragrant white-and-violet flowers.

NEOREGELIA

living vase plant
Bromeliaceae
55°–75°F.

These epiphytic bromeliads with 30-to-40-inch rosettes of leaves make planters glow with color for three months. The centers of the plants turn red at blooming time but flowers are insignificant. Pot them in osmunda. Keep the "vase" formed by the leaves filled with water and the compost just damp. Give them good light and wipe leaves with a damp cloth about once a month. Propagate them from the offset suckers that appear after bloom.

N. carolinae—dark-green-and-copper leaves; winter-blooming. An unexcelled house plant.
N. carolinae 'Tricolor'—leaves striped white, pink, and green.
N. cruenta—smaller, upright straw-colored rosette.
N. marmorata—rosette of pale green leaves with reddish brown blotches, to 20 inches across; violet-petaled flowers.
N. spectabilis—pale green leaves tipped with brilliant red; summer-flowering. Called painted-fingernail plant.
N. zonata—rosette of stiff olive-green leaves to 16 inches across, heavily marked and banded with wine-red; pale-blue-petaled flowers.

NEPETA

ground ivy
Labiatae
50°–70°F.

This tiny trailer has prostrate stems and small round leaves with white borders. It occasionally bears minute mauve flowers in summer. It is a fine ground cover for plants in big pots. Grow it in semishade and keep soil consistently moist in summer; in winter, grow it cool and give it less moisture. It makes a nice basket plant. Grow new ones by root division or from runners.

*N. hederacea.

NEPHROLEPIS

Polypodiaceae
60°–80°F.

These ferns will survive in unwelcoming places and still remain beautiful. They are fast-growing natives of the American tropics and subtropics. Most of them form a 30-inch rosette of fronds. Give them winter sun, shade in summer. Keep soil consistently moist but avoid overwatering. In addition, stand large plants up to the pot rim in a sinkful of water for about an hour once a week. These ferns benefit from rains when temperatures outdoors are above 50°F. They are easily propagated from the runners at the base of mature plants.

N. exaltata—stiff fronds to 60 inches, bushy. Called sword fern, often sold as Boston fern.
N. exaltata bostoniensis—36-inch, arching fronds. The true Boston fern.
N. exaltata bostoniensis 'Fluffy Ruffles'—12-inch, lacy fronds.
N. exaltata bostoniensis 'Verona'—an 8-inch dwarf with lacy fronds.
N. exaltata bostoniensis 'Whitmannii'—18-inch fronds. Robust and lovely.

NERINE. See LYCORIS.

NERIUM

oleander
Apocynaceae
55°–75°F.

These summer-flowering plants grow to 60 inches and require little care to produce an abundance of colorful flowers. Although young plants bloom, it is the three-to-four-year-old tub specimens that put on a show, with single or double flowers in shades of pink, white, or red. Growth starts in March or April; it is best to repot them then in fresh soil. Give plants full sun and plenty of water. After they bloom, decrease the amount of water. Prune them in

October or November and store them in a light, cold, but frost-free place through winter with only monthly watering. Neriums can be grown into standards of exceptional beauty. Propagate them from seed or cuttings of stem-tip growth in spring. These are fine varieties of the common oleander, *N. oleander*, which has rose-red, single flowers:

'Comte Barthelemy'—double, red flowers.
'Mrs. Roeding'—double, salmon-pink flowers.
'Peachblossom'—double, apricot-colored flowers.

NEW ZEALAND FLAX. See PHORMIUM.

NIDULARIUM

Bromeliaceae
55°–75°F.

These easy-to-grow epiphytic bromeliads have colorful foliage in 20-to-30-inch rosettes and tiny white or pink flowers in dense clusters. They are excellent for planters and north windows. Pot them in osmunda and soil, and grow them in bright light with 50 percent humidity. Keep the "vase" formed by the leaves filled with water. Wipe foliage with a damp cloth about once a week to bring out the full beauty of the leaves. Propagate nidulariums from offset suckers.

N. billbergioides—to 20 inches, spiny dark green leaves, orange bracts. Flower spike rises high above center of plant.
N. fulgens—yellow-green leaves spotted with dark green.
N. innocentii—glowing purple rosette of leaves.
N. procerum—rosette of broad, leathery light green leaves to 30 inches across tinged with copper; brilliant red bracts.
N. regelioides—rosette of rich-green, leathery leaves to 20 inches across, mottled with dark green; deep orange bracts. Pretty.

NIGHT-BLOOMING CACTUS. See HYLOCEREUS and CACTUSES.

NIGHT-BLOOMING CEREUS. See SELENICEREUS and CACTUSES.

NIGHT JASMINE. See CESTRUM.

NORFOLK ISLAND PINE. See ARAUCARIA.

NOTOCACTUS

ball cactus
Cactaceae
50°–65°F.

These cylindrical, South American desert cactuses with large, showy yellow blooms in spring and summer are dependable and nice for dish gardens. Pot them in sandy soil that drains readily. These plants are easy to grow in sun and with small amounts of water all year. Propagate them from offsets.

N. apricus—a 2-inch globe covered with bristly spines.
N. arachnites—a ridged, 6-inch globe; stellar yellowish green flowers.
N. leninghausi—to 4 inches across, spiny.
N. ottonis—a 2-inch, ribbed globe.
N. rutilans—a 5-inch dark green globe, bright pink flowers. Beautiful.
N. scopa—an 8-inch globe, white hairs.
N. submammulosus—a 3-inch shining green globe.

ODONTOGLOSSUM

Orchidaceae
50°–70°F.

Epiphytes from the cool regions of Colombia and Peru, these orchids are for the unheated, but not freezing, sun porch or plant room. With leathery leaves and generally yellow-and-brown flowers, they stay in bloom for over a month—sometimes for three months—one flower opening as another fades. Grow them in fir bark or osmunda. Give them sun in winter, bright light in summer, and plenty of water except for a four-week rest before and then again after flowering. Mist foliage frequently and try to maintain 50 percent humidity. Obtain seedlings from specialists.

O. bictoniense—15-inch leaves; 24-inch flower spikes; twenty to thirty 2-inch, yellowish-green-and-chestnut flowers in fall.
O. citrosmum—10-inch leaves; 24-to-36-inch

pendent scapes; fifteen to thirty 2-inch, round, fragrant pink flowers in spring or early summer.
O. *grande*—12-inch leaves, erect 10-inch scapes, 5-to-7-inch yellow-and-brown flowers in fall. Called tiger orchid.
*O. *krameri*—to 8 inches, violet flowers.
*O. *pulchellum*—to 10 inches, half-inch fragrant white flowers in spring. Unique in the family.
*O. *rossii*—to 8 inches, 2-to-3-inch pink-and-dark-brown flowers with wavy rose-colored lips, in winter.
O. *uro-skinneri*—14-inch leaves, 24-to-36-inch scapes; ten to fifteen 1-inch greenish flowers marked with brown, in early spring.

OLD-MAN CACTUS. See CEPHALOCEREUS, and CACTUSES.

OLEA. See OSMANTHUS.

OLEANDER. See NERIUM.

ONCIDIUM

dancing lady orchid
Orchidaceae
55°–80°F.

This is a genus of mostly epiphytic, spray-type orchids with either leathery leaves and pseudobulbs or cane-stemmed growth. They produce large solitary flowers, or scapes with hundreds of small flowers. Grow them in fir bark, in sun, with 50 percent humidity, and provide good air circulation. The species that have pseudobulbs need a four-week rest with very little water before and after flowering; the cane-stemmed kinds require constant moisture at the roots. Cut and placed in a vase of water, flowers last a long time. Buy new plants from specialists.

O. *ampliatum*—to 28 inches, leathery leaves, pseudobulbs, 1-inch brown-and-yellow flowers in early spring. Requires a rest.
O. *ceboletta*—to 20 inches; dark green (almost black), leathery leaves; pseudobulbs; charming, tiny, vivid yellow-and-brown flowers in spring. Requires a rest.

O. *lanceanum*—cane-stemmed to 20 inches; spatulate, speckled leaves; fragrant yellow-green flowers in summer. Grows all year.
O. *macranthum*—to 30 inches, leathery leaves, pseudobulbs, wands of pretty yellow flowers. Requires a rest.
O. *papilio*—cane-stemmed to 18 inches; large chestnut-and-yellow flowers, sometimes in summer, at other times in fall. Grows all year. Called butterfly orchid.
O. *splendidum*—to 24 inches; hard, leathery leaves; pseudobulbs; small yellow-and-brown flowers in winter. Requires a rest.
O. *triquetrum*—cane-stemmed to 15 inches, 1-inch purple-green-and-white flowers in fall. Grows all year.
O. *wentworthianum*—to 30 inches, leathery leaves, pseudobulbs, yellow-and-reddish-brown flowers in summer. Requires a rest.

ONION PLANT. See BOWIEA.

OPUNTIA

prickly pear
Cactaceae
55°–75°F.

Some of these desert cactuses are handsome and decorative; others are unsightly and to be avoided. Most have flat, broad joints or pads; others have erect cylindrical growth. Grow all kinds in sun and water them about once a week except in winter, when plants should be moved to a cold place (50°F.). Bloom rarely occurs indoors. Propagate opuntias from offsets.

O. *brasiliensis*—to 48 inches, spineless pads shaped like a beaver's tail, yellow flowers.
*O. *erinacea*—erect cylinder to 12 inches with white spines, pink flowers.
O. *linguiformis*—fleshy, green cylinder to 36 inches; yellow flowers.
O. *microdasys*—to 24 inches, spineless pads with snow-white hairs, yellow flowers.
O. *strobiliformis*—erect cylinder, resembling a pinecone, to 15 inches; yellow flowers.
O. *vestita*—white, woolly cylinder to 20 inches; red flowers.

ORANGE JASMINE. See MURRAEA.

ORANGE TREE. See CITRUS.

ORCHID CACTUS. See EPIPHYLLUM and CACTUSES.

ORCHIDS

The graduation of orchids from greenhouse to home is still a pleasant surprise, but growers now agree that many orchids make splendid house plants, for most of them are easier to tend than some of the familiar foliage plants. The majority of orchids have water-storage vessels (pseudobulbs), and if this type is not watered for a few days, or even a few weeks, they survive. And, of course, few other plants produce such dramatic, colorful flowers. Some orchids are naturally terrestrial (growing in soil), others epiphytic (growing on trees). Pot the terrestrials as you do other plants; for epiphytes, use fir bark or osmunda. Don't smother these beauties with warmth and humidity. Most of them thrive in average home temperatures of 60°F. to 72°F. with 30 to 50 percent humidity. While some need sun to bloom, others bear handsome flowers in bright light. As a rule, orchids need a rest, the potting mixture somewhat dry, for a month before and a month after blooming. Those that grow all year need constant moisture. Insects rarely attack orchids. For descriptions of some species and their culture, see:

Acineta
Aerides
Angraecum
Anguloa
Ansellia
Ascocentrum
Bifrenaria
Brassavola
Broughtonia
Cattleya
Coelogyne
Cymbidium
Dendrobium
Epidendrum
Gongora
Laelia

Lycaste
Masdevallia
Miltonia
Odontoglossum
Oncidium
Paphiopedilum
Phalaenopsis
Pleione
Rhynchostylis
Stanhopea
Vanda
Zygopetalum

ORNAMENTAL PEPPER. See CAPSICUM.

ORNITHOGALUM
Liliaceae
50°–70°F.

These small, bulbous plants bear charming, star-shaped white flowers on leafless stalks in winter. They are good window plants, but their flowers can also be cut and will last for days. Plant six or seven bulbs in a 6-inch pan at any time from September to December. Grow them in full sun and keep soil consistently moist. After plants bloom, let foliage grow until the bulbs dry out naturally. Store them in their pots in a cool, dim place without water until fall. Then repot them in fresh soil. Propagate them from the small offset bulbs by the parent bulb when repotting.

O. arabicum—to 24 inches, clusters of fragrant white flowers with black centers.

O. thyrsoides—to 18 inches, white or yellow flowers in dense racemes. Called chincherinchee.

O. umbellatum—to 12 inches, satiny white flowers with green stripes. Called star-of-Bethlehem.

OSMANTHUS
(OLEA)
Oleaceae
60°–70°F.

These are evergreen shrubs that make excellent house plants, and one species is prized for its fragrance. Give them sun, keep soil consistently moist, and assure good circulation of air. Keep plants potbound to stimulate flower production.

The flowers of *Osmanthus fragrans* are small— but their scent is unforgettable. (Photograph by Merry Gardens)

Propagate osmanthus species from cuttings in summer.

O. fragrans—to 24 inches; plain green leaves; heavily scented, tiny white flowers on and off throughout the year. Called sweet olive.

O. ilicifolius variegatus—to 20 inches, white-edged green leaves; slightly scented, tiny white flowers. Called false holly.

OTAHEITE ORANGE. See CITRUS.

OXALIS   **wood sorrel**
Oxalidaceae
55°–75°F.

With dainty flowers and shamrock-shaped leaves, these 6-to-12-inch bulbous plants are ideal for baskets or pots. Some varieties are everblooming, others flower in winter, spring, summer, or fall. The delicate blooms, like buttercups, are yellow, pink, red, violet, or white. Put four to six tubers about one-half inch deep in a 6-inch pot of soil; keep them fairly moist but do not water them heavily until growth starts. Then feed them biweekly with a liquid fertilizer and give full sun to produce abundant bloom. Flowers close at night and on dull days. Summer- and fall-flowering types require a rest in winter; store them in their pots without water at 50°F. Grow new plants by dividing the tubers.

O. bowieana—rose-red flowers in summer. Rest in winter.

O. cernua—yellow flowers in summer. Rest in winter. Called Bermuda buttercup.

O. lasiandra—purple flowers in summer and fall. Rest in winter and spring.

O. melanosticta—yellow flowers in fall. Rest in spring and summer.

O. ortgiesii—yellow flowers on and off throughout the year. No resting time necessary.

O. rosea—pink flowers in spring. No resting time necessary.

O. rubra alba—pink flowers in summer. Rest in winter.

OX-TONGUE PLANT. See GASTERIA.

184

Hibiscus chinensis metallica.
(Photograph by C/D Luckhart)

Hoya 'Minibel.' (Photograph by C/D Luckhart)

Hypocyrta 'Emile.'
(Photograph by C/D
Luckhart)

Jatropha hastatum. (Photograph by C/D Luckhart)

Lapageria rosea. (Photograph by C/D Luckhart)

Mammillaria meyeranii. (Photograph by C/D Luckhart)

Notocactus arachnites. (Photograph by C/D Luckhart)

Notocactus leninghausi. (Photograph by C/D Luckhart)

Oncidium macranthum. (Photograph by C/D Luckhart)

Ornithogalum species. (Photograph by C/D Luckhart)

Paphiopedilum sedeni. (Photograph by C/D Luckhart)

Parodia rubriflora. (Photograph by C/D Luckhart)

Passiflora coriacea.
(Photograph by C/D Luckhart)

189

Pentas lanceolata. (Photograph by C/D Luckhart)

Rechsteineria cardinalis. (Photograph by C/D Luckhart)

Spathiphyllum hybrid. (Photograph by C/D Luckhart)

Streptocarpus hybrid. (Photograph by C/D Luckhart)

Tillandsia caulescens. (Photograph by C/D Luckhart)

PACHYPODIUM
Apocynaceae
55°–75°F.

With fifteen species, this is a genus from South Africa and Madagascar. The roots are thick and fleshy, and the plants have a single trunk. The leaves are shiny green and the plant bears handsome orange flowers. Grow pachypodiums in equal parts sand, gravel, and soil. Water them carefully because too much moisture can hurt them. Give them ample light. They are highly prized plants—different and worthwhile. Grow new ones from cuttings in spring.

P. baroni windsori.

PAINTED-FINGERNAIL PLANT. See NEO-REGELIA and BROMELIADS.

PAINTED-LEAF PLANT. See COLEUS.

PALM. See CHAMAEDOREA and PALMS.

PALMS

With single or multiple trunks and fan-shaped leaves or feathery foliage, these are long-lived plants that need little care. They thrive if firmly potted in rich soil with some peat moss and sand. My palm in a 6-inch pot grows better than two others in large containers. Peak growth is in spring and summer, so water heavily then but not so much at other times; however, never let soil get really dry. Give bright light and keep foliage clean by wiping leaves with a damp cloth once a week. Feed moderately, not more than once a month in spring and summer, not at all the rest of the year. Palms benefit from a summer outdoors where they can enjoy warm showers. Pests rarely bother these plants. For descriptions of some plants in this family and their culture, see:

Caryota
Chamaedorea (Collinia)
Howeia (Kentia)
Licuala
Livistona
Phoenix
Rhapis

PANDANUS
screw pine
Pandanaceae
60°–75°F.

Years ago, almost every barber shop in the Midwest had one of these plants in the window. With spiny, lance-shaped leaves arranged in a spiral (hence the common name), some reach to 60 inches indoors; the ones listed below rarely grow above 40 inches. They prefer a bright light and a warm place with soil somewhat dry. These plants dislike fluctuating temperatures. Propagate them from offsets.

P. baptistii—stiff bluish-green-and-yellow leaves.
P. utilis—long, curving olive-green leaves.
P. veitchii—variegated, curved leaves. The best one for indoors.

Pachypodium baroni, a stately, treelike plant, is unusual and attractive.
(Photograph by C/D Luckhart)

193

Vanda rothschildiana.
(Photograph by C/D Luckhart)

PANDA PLANT. See KALANCHOE.

PANSY ORCHID. See MILTONIA and ORCHIDS.

PAPER FLOWER. See BOUGAINVILLEA.

PAPHIOPEDILUM cypripedium orchid, lady-slipper orchid
Orchidaceae
50°–80°F.

These terrestrial 10-to-16-inch orchids readily make the move from forest floor to indoor garden and produce flowers in glowing colors. Some are warm-growers (60°F. to 80°F.), some like it cool (50°F. to 70°F.). All are desirable. Give them a shaded place and keep the potting mixture (equal parts soil and shredded osmunda) moist. Give them 50 percent humidity. Buy new plants from suppliers. They are fine as cut flowers or for corsages.

P. *callosum*—marbled leaves, 2-inch pale-green-to-rose-colored flowers from winter to summer. Cool-growing.
*P. *concolor*—2-inch yellow flowers spotted with red, early summer bloom. Warm-growing.
*P. *fairieanum*—soft green leaves, 1-inch yellow-and-purple flowers in late summer and winter. Cool-growing.
P. *hirsutissimum*—2-to-3-inch apple-green flowers with rose-colored spots, in spring. Warm-growing.
P. *sedeni*—dark green leaves; lady-slipper-shaped flowers, red with a tinge of white in the center, in summer.
*P. *spicerianum*—2-inch pale green leaves, purple-and-white flowers in winter. Cool-growing.
P. *venustum*—mottled leaves, 2-inch purple-and-green flowers in spring. Cool-growing.

PARADISE PALM. See HOWEIA and PALMS.

PARLOR PALM. See CHAMAEDOREA and PALMS.

PARODIA ball cactus
Cactaceae
55°–75°F.

The genus includes a large group of beautiful desert cactuses, most of which are small globes that bear large, colorful flowers in summer. They are popular with indoor gardeners because most of them bloom readily indoors, given sufficient sun. Plants need a soil of equal parts sand and potting mix; put a thin layer of gravel on top of the soil. Give them as much sun as possible. In winter, allow them to rest at 55°F. Keep soil just barely moist—never too wet. They are highly recommended. Propagate them from offsets.

*P. *mutabilis*—olive-green globe to 9 inches, golden-yellow flowers.
*P. *rubriflora*—3-inch, spiny ball; large scarlet flowers.
*P. *sanguiniflora*—soft green globe to 3 inches, red flowers.

PARROT FLOWER. See HELICONIA.

PARTRIDGE-BREAST ALOE. See ALOE.

PASSIFLORA passion vine
Passifloraceae
55°–75°F.

Handsome Brazilian vines to 72 inches, passion vines require space but reward you with exquisite, large, summer or fall flowers. These plants, preferably potted in 10-inch tubs, are for sun porch or plant room; they are too large for a window. They need sun, plenty of water, and fertilizer when they are actively growing. Rest them for about three months after they bloom, and prune them then. Cuttings taken in summer root readily for spring plants, or you can sow seed.

P. *alata*—lobed leaves, blue-and-white flowers.
P. *caerulea*—dark-blue-and-pink flowers.
P. *racemosa*—breathtaking red flowers.
P. *coriacea*—yellowish green flowers.
P. *trifasciata*—glowing purple-and-green leaves, blue flowers.

The zonal geranium (*Pelargonium hortorum*), is one of the most widely and easily grown house plants. (Photograph by Merry Gardens)

PASSION VINE. See PASSIFLORA.

PATIENCE PLANT. See IMPATIENS.

PATIENT LUCY. See IMPATIENS.

PEACOCK PLANT. See EPISCIA and GESNERIADS; KAEMPFERIA.

PEANUT CACTUS. See CHAMACEREUS and CACTUSES.

PELARGONIUM geranium *Geraniaceae* 50°–70°F.

Geraniums offer almost constant color if given full sun and grown rather cool, with frequent airing and no crowding at the window. Plant them in a rather firm soil mixture of three parts loam to one part sand, plus a little peat moss to increase acidity slightly to, say, pH 6.0–6.5, with some leeway in either direction acceptable. Water them freely, then let them dry out a little before watering again. Geraniums bloom best when potbound, so grow them in pots as small as possible. Martha Washington's and the ivy-leaved kinds rest somewhat in winter; water them moderately then and do not feed them. Feed the others every other week when they are in active growth, which is most of the time in sunny weather. Geraniums are sometimes troubled by edema: water-soaked spots appear on the leaves when moisture collects in the plants faster than it can be transpired and leaf cells burst. Avoid overwatering and high humidity; don't mist the foliage. Be sure to investigate the new so-called Carefree geraniums that grow true to type and color from seed. Vining geraniums in mixed colors can also be grown from seed. Propagate most other geraniums from cuttings taken either in spring for winter bloom or in August or early September for spring and summer flowering. Geraniums are usually classified in this way:

Zonal Geraniums (P. hortorum)

These are the familiar, old-fashioned type, with scalloped leaves and brilliant single and double flowers.

Standard types

'Apple Blossom Rosebud'—single, rose-edged white flowers. Fine for winter.
'Better Times'—single, red flowers.
'Dreams'—double, salmon-pink flowers.
'Flare'—single, salmon-pink flowers.
'Harvest Moon'—single, orange flowers.
'Holiday'—single, red flowers with white centers.
'Patricia Andrea'—brilliant rose-colored, single flowers.
'Princess Fiat'—double, shrimp-pink flowers.
'Salmon Irene'—double flowers. One of five 'Irenes.'
'Snowball'—double, white flowers.
'Starlight'—single, white flowers.
'Summer Cloud'—double, white flowers.

Carefrees

This new kind grows true to type and color from seed. Do not pinch them back to make them bushy, as these plants grow thick on their own. Seeds sown in mid-February will produce blooming plants in early July in the Midwest. Colors include: three pinks, five light-to-dark salmons, four white-edged rose-pinks, two reds, and one white.

Fancy-leaved types

'Crystal Palace Gem'—yellow and bright green leaves.
* 'Filigree'—tricolored silver leaves; single, dark salmon-pink flowers.
'Jubilee'—yellow-green and red-brown leaves.
'Skies of Italy'—tricolored golden leaves, red flowers.

Free-blooming, large dwarfs

These are particularly good window plants for 4-inch pots because of their restricted growth habit and their almost constant bloom.
* 'Brooks Barnes'—dark-zoned leaves; single, pink flowers.
* 'Dancer'—single, salmon-colored flowers. One of the largest "dwarfs."
* 'Emma Hossler'—double, white-centered rose-pink flowers.
* 'Mr. Evaarts'—large, fast-growing; double, pink flowers.
* 'Prince Valiant'—single, crimson flowers.
* 'Red Riding Hood'—bushy growth; double, red flowers.
* 'Tu-Tone'—double, pink flowers shaded from light to dark.

Dwarfs

These grow somewhat shorter than the above.
* 'Capella'—forest-green leaves; double, salmon-pink flowers.
* 'Epsilon'—soft pink flowers.
* 'Goblin'—large, double, scarlet flowers.
* 'Lyric'—double, orchid-pink flowers with white centers.
* 'Minx'—double, crimson-purple flowers.
* 'Perky'—single, white-centered bright red flowers.
* 'Pigmy'—scalloped leaves; semidouble, bright red flowers.

Miniatures

* 'Black Vesuvius'—dark leaves; single, orange-scarlet flowers.

* 'Fairy Tale'—white flowers with lavender centers.
* 'Imp'—dark leaves; single, pink flowers.
* 'Saturn'—dark leaves, red flowers.
* 'Venus'—strongly zoned leaves; double, light pink flowers.

Scented-leaved Geraniums

With delightful scent and variegated foliage, these plants are charming. Some have leaves resembling maple leaves, others have foliage like the gooseberry's or even like that of some ferns.

P. crispum—lemon-scented.
P. graveolens—rose-scented.
P. odoratissimum—apple-scented.
P. tomentosum—peppermint-scented.

Ivy-leaved Geraniums (P. peltatum)

Trailing stems and glossy, ivy-like foliage make these plants good for hanging baskets. They are also a colorful sight in summer with cascades of flowers. Pinch plants in late winter or early spring to encourage many shoots to grow.

'Charles Turner'—double, pink flowers. A fine variety.
'Comtesse de Grey'—single, light pink flowers.
'New Dawn'—double, rose-cerise flowers.
'Santa Paula'—double, lavender-purple flowers.
'Victorville'—double, dark red flowers.

Martha Washington or Lady Washington Geraniums (P. domesticum)

For a colorful spring display, choose these. The flowers are two- or three-color blends—whites tinged with lavender or pink, vibrant reds, and deep purples. There are also some small, free-blooming, pansy types. Cut back plants after flowering and always grow them cool (45°F. to 55°F.).

'Dubonnet'—ruffled wine-red flowers.
'Easter Greetings'—cerise flowers.
'Gardener's Joy'—blush-white flowers with rose markings and stripes.
'Holiday'—ruffled white flowers with crimson markings.

'Lavender Grand Slam'—a compact grower, deep-toned flowers.
'Madame Layal'—purple-and-white flowers. The pansy type.
'Springtime'—ruffled white flowers with a rose-colored throat.

PELLAEA
cliff-brake fern, button fern
Polypodiaceae
50°–65°F.

These New Zealand and West Indian ferns with fronds of heart-shaped segments bear little resemblance to most other ferns. Fronds are either erect or low and spreading, and the plants grow to 30 inches. They make satisfactory house plants that need little care. Pot them in soil with good drainage in 5- or 6-inch containers that will accommodate the fast-growing rhizomes. In a natural state they prefer limestone rock, but I have not found it necessary to add lime to their potting soil. Keep soil moist but avoid overwatering. Watch out for scales on both sides of the foliage but do not confuse the spores under the fronds with scales. Propagate pellaeas from spores.

P. rotundifolia—low and spreading growth; small, round, dark leaves. Nice for baskets.
P. viridis—larger green leaflets. Will climb if supported.

PENNYWORT BEGONIA. See BEGONIA, Rhizomatous.

PENTAS
Egyptian star flower
Rubiaceae
55°–75°F.

With showy umbels of pink, rose, or white, this plant, which grows to 30 inches, flowers almost continuously and has attractive pointed leaves, besides. Pentas make fine house plants if humidity can be kept to 50 percent or more. Grow yours in sun with plenty of water while they are in active growth. Old plants get leggy, so every year start new ones from seed (which will produce flowers in a medley of colors), or take stem cuttings. The flowers last a long time in a vase of water.

P. lanceolata—small, rose-colored flowers.
P. lanceolata 'Orchid Star'—large lavender flowers.

PEPEROMIA
Piperaceae
55°–75°F.

Outstanding small foliage plants for window, table, planter, or terrarium, peperomias have smooth-edged leaves and insignificant flowers. Many have vining growth, others make upright bushes. Place them in bright light, and water them sparingly. They prefer a sandy soil. Propagate them from stem cuttings.

P. cubensis—upright growth to 12 inches; waxy fresh-green leaves.
P. gardneriana 'Minima'—dwarf, bushy growth to 12 inches; glossy green, crinkled leaves.
P. glabella variegata—vining growth to 12 inches, yellow-and-pale-green leaves.
P. gracilis—to 10 inches; crinkled leaves, red underneath, with silver veins. Rare beauty.
P. hederaefolia—vining growth to 14 inches, bright silvery leaves with purple hues.
P. maculosa—upright growth to 12 inches, narrow gray-green leaves.
P. metallica—upright growth to 12 inches; small, waxy brown leaves with pale green stripes.
P. nivalis—to 14 inches; unusual, keel-shaped, succulent leaves.
P. obtusifolia—vining growth to 16 inches; large, fleshy, oval leaves.
P. ornata—upright growth to 12 inches, dark green leaves with maroon lines.
P. pericattii—to 12 inches, thick green leaves with red edges.
P. prostrata—creeping stems to 18 inches; gray-green, succulent leaves. Unusual.
P. resedaeflora—to 8 inches, rosette of green leaves.

PEPPER. See CAPSICUM.

PERESKIA
lemon vine
Cactaceae
55°–75°F.

These unusual desert cactuses hardly appear as such. They have long, narrow leaves and spiny stems—and mine occasionally bear greenish white or pink flowers in late summer. They need full sun and an airy place. Water them moderately all year. Propagate them from offsets or cuttings.

P. aculeata—to 8 feet; thick, oval leaves; white, yellow, or pink flowers.
P. godseffiana—similar to *P. aculeata* but with somewhat smaller green leaves marked with crimson and yellow.

PETREA
queen's wreath
Verbenaceae
55°–70°F.

True-blue flowers open in spring and summer on this twining, 6-to-8-foot vine with brittle dark green leaves. This is a big plant that grows rapidly and makes a fine accent for a garden room. Give it full sun and let soil dry out between waterings. Plants must be three or four years old before they will reward you with a real harvest of flowers, so have patience. Propagate petreas from cuttings.

P. volubilis.

PHALAENOPSIS
moon flower,
moth orchid
Orchidaceae
60°–80°F.

Here is a popular group of orchids with large, exquisite, paper-thin, white or pink flowers, dozens to a stem. The leaves are leathery, spatulate, and attractive. Pot your plants in medium-grade fir bark. These are epiphytes and require an area with good air circulation. Keep the potting mix uniformly moist all year. Provide relatively high humidity (50 percent) and be sure water does not accumulate in the crowns of plants. These orchids are fall- or winter-blooming. Buy new plants from specialists.

P. amabilis—leaves to 26 inches across, large white flowers. The granddaddy of the genus, used extensively for hybridizing.
P. amabilis 'Doris'—to 30 inches, one of the finest white-flowering forms. Outstanding.
P. leuddemmanniana—leaves to 26 inches across, fine pale pink flowers.

PHILODENDRON

Araceae
55°–75°F.

This has been a popular house plant for many years and is still a favorite for locations with little light, especially in apartments. Some species have medium-sized leaves, others large ones. Many are vining plants, and several have rosette (self-heading) growth. The majority thrive with soil kept consistently moist and an occasional misting of leaves. Philodendrons are favorite planter subjects for public places. Propagate them from stem or cane cuttings or by air layering.

P. andreanum—vining growth to 36 inches, 10-inch dark green leaves.
P. bipinnatifidum—vining growth to 30 inches; 8-inch, scalloped dark green leaves.
P. cannifolium—20-inch rosette of lance-shaped leaves on short stems.
P. cruentum—vining growth to 20 inches, 8-inch leaves.
P. erubescens—vining growth to 24 inches, 10-inch dark green leaves.
P. hastatum—vining growth to 36 inches; 10-inch, arrow-shaped leaves.
P. imbe—vining growth to 24 inches; 10-inch, leathery maroon leaves.
P. 'Multicolor'—to 36 inches, lance-shaped green-yellow leaves.
P. oxycardium—vining growth to 36 inches, 10-inch leaves.
P. selloum—to 30 inches; rosette of 15-inch, notched leaves.
P. verrucosum—vining growth to 24 inches; 8-inch, multicolored, heart-shaped leaves.
P. wendlandii—36-inch rosette of 15-inch lush green leaves.

PHOENIX

Palmaceae
55°–75°F.

Impressive palms with crowns of feathery leaves, these need little care. Grow them in bright light, soak the soil, and then let it dry out before watering again. From Africa and Asia, where they reach 100 feet, date palms indoors seldom grow above 72 inches. They like small pots—a 10-inch container is fine for a mature specimen—and, though they are difficult to move, occasionally they do need a deep soaking in a tub. Propagate these palms from seed, or buy young plants.

P. canariensis—shiny green, feathery leaves.
P. dactylifera—fine blue-green leaves. Called date palm.
P. roebelenii—a dwarf to about 40 inches, thick crown of dark green leaves. Familiar. Often called pygmy date palm.

PHORMIUM

New Zealand flax
Liliaceae
50°–70°F.

Lovely, lance-shaped leaves margined in red or orange make these excellent plants for a corner. In time, they grow tall, to 7 or 8 feet, but young ones do not exceed 4 feet. Give them sun and let soil dry out between waterings. The species naturally have dark red flowers, but these blooms rarely appear indoors. They make attractive terrace plants against a brick wall or redwood fence. Grow new plants from offsets.

P. atropurpureum—green leaves delicately marked with bronze.
P. tenax—dark brownish green leaves edged in red. The most popular kind.

PHYLLITIS

hart's-tongue fern
Polypodiaceae
50°–65°F.

This 20-inch fern with dark green, crinkly fronds thrives indoors if kept cool. It makes a nice, shapely plant. Grow it in shade and give it plenty of water. It will even tolerate the dim light of an entry hall for many months. Set it in a decorative container to show off the flamboyant fronds. Propagate it by root division.

P. scolopendrium cristatum.

PIGGYBACK PLANT. See TOLMIEA.

PILEA

Urticaceae
50°–75°F

Small foliage plants with plain or variegated leaves and clusters of tiny flowers, pileas make good ground cover for planters or large pots. Keep soil moist. Propagate them from cuttings.

P. cadierei—to 12 inches or more, silver-and-green leaves, rose-red flowers. Called aluminum plant or watermelon pilea.

P. grandis—to 16 inches; glossy green leaves deeply serrated along the edges, copper-colored underneath.

P. involucrata—to 12 inches or more, bushy brown leaves, rose-red flowers.

P. microphylla—a tiny ground cover. Called artillery plant.

P. mollis—to 12 inches, puckered bright green leaves with a deep maroon center.

P. nummulariaefolia—to 8 inches, green leaves, rose-red flowers. Fine for baskets. Called creeping Charlie.

P. repens—to 8 inches; quilted, round coppery-brown leaves; greenish-white flowers.

PINCUSHION CACTUS. See CORYPHANTHA, MAMMILLARIA, and CACTUSES.

PINEAPPLE. See ANANAS and BROMELIADS.

PINEAPPLE LILY. See EUCOMIS.

PINK AGAPANTHUS. See TULBAGHIA.

PINK CALLA. See ZANTEDESCHIA.

PITTOSPORUM

Pittosporaceae
50°–70°F

Decorative evergreens to 40 inches with thick glossy green leaves, pittosporums like slightly acid soil. Grow them in bright light or in shade and keep soil almost dry all year. They are good tub plants, but yours could also be trained to become a miniature tree. Propagate them from cuttings or by air layering.

P. eugenioides—to 24 inches; large shiny green leaves, honey-scented flowers.

P. speciatum—to 24 inches; small, glossy gray-green leaves, satiny black branches. A nice miniature tree.

P. tobira—to 36 inches; thick, leathery green leaves; white or greenish yellow flowers with orange-blossom scent.

P. tobira variegatum—green-and-yellow leaves.

PLATYCERIUM

staghorn fern
Polypodiaceae
60°–80°F.

Extraordinary epiphytes with forked fronds, these ferns do surprisingly well indoors. However, they must be grown in osmunda on slabs of decay-resistant wood (cedar or cork) and soaked daily in a tub of water. The fertile fronds are pendent and give the plant its common name; the sterile ones are flat and rest against the shield of wood. Give these plants strong light or semishade and mist them frequently; otherwise, they will not survive. Propagate plateceriums by potting individually the little plants that grow between the sterile fronds.

P. bifurcatum—grayish green fronds to 36 inches.

P. grande—spreading glossy green fronds to 72 inches. For a plant room.

P. stemmaria—curious, thick gray-green fronds to 36 inches.

P. veitchii—vigorous, rounded, basal fronds to 24 inches.

P. wilhelminae-reginae—glossy silvery green fronds to 36 inches. Superb.

PLECTRANTHUS

prostrate coleus,
Swedish ivy
Labiatae
60°–75°F.

Foolproof plants related to coleus, with scalloped waxy green leaves on trailing stems and pretty little flowers on and off throughout the year, these plants are seldom seen but certainly are worth space at a window. Grow them in light or shade and keep soil consistently moist. Propagate them from seed sown in spring or from cuttings at any time.

P. australis—to 20 inches; waxy, saw-toothed leaves; pink flowers. For a basket.
P. australis variegatum—irregular white-edged leaves.
P. behril—to 30 inches; leaves slightly hairy and green above, rose-pink underneath.
P. coleoides—to 20 inches; small, crinkled leaves; white-and-purple flowers.
P. oertendahlii—to 20 inches, apple-green leaves veined with silver, pale pink flowers.
P. saccatus—to 20 inches, matted dark green leaves, spreading branches.

PLEIONE

Indian crocus
Orchidaceae
55°–75°F.

This group of mostly deciduous orchids makes any window sing with color. Beautiful plants from China, Taiwan, and Southeast Asia, they produce large, solitary, showy flowers, many to a plant. Pleiones have compressed, cormlike pseudobulbs tipped with a few light green leaves that generally fall after the bulb matures. Flower scapes are produced from the base of the bulb before or along with the new growth. Most species bear autumn flowers that last more than a week on the plant. Grow pleiones in a potting mix of equal parts fine-grade fir bark and soil. Keep the mix consistently moist except in late summer, when it should be somewhat dry to encourage bloom. Keep them in bright light. Purchase new plants from suppliers.

P. hookeriana—to 5 inches, paper-thin leaves, rose-colored flowers with a purple splotch on the lip.
P. maculata—to about 12 inches, 4-inch white flowers with the lip streaked purple.
P. pricei—to 5 inches; lovely pale rose flowers with a white, fringed lip.

PLEOMELE

Liliaceae
65°–75°F.

Similar to dracaenas, pleomeles have a somewhat denser and bushier habit. The foliage is narrow and leathery, edged with pale yellow stripes. These plants do fine in a north exposure, although brighter light makes a healthier specimen. Use a freely draining house-plant potting mix and keep soil consistently moist all year. Wipe the foliage occasionally with a damp cloth and disturb the plants only when absolutely necessary; instead of repotting, top-dress the soil. Pleomeles can tolerate coolness (55°F.) if necessary. Grow new plants from cuttings in spring.

P. angustifolia—willowy stems to 30 inches, leathery green leaves with yellow borders. Handsome.
P. reflexa—to 40 inches, sword-shaped green leaves lined with yellow.
P. reflexa 'Variegata'—to 40 inches. Richer leaf color than *P. reflexa*.

PLUMBAGO

leadwort
Plumbaginaceae
50°–70°F.

Though most are large, bushy, 36-inch shrubs, with small leaves and cheerful flowers in summer, some plumbagos are sprawling climbers (if supported) or trailers. A mature specimen in bloom is a breathtaking sight. Give yours full sun and plenty of water during growth. Feed it moderately. In winter keep it almost dry. Mist foliage in summer. Propagate plumbagos from seed or cuttings.

P. capensis—bushy growth; 2-inch, phloxlike, azure flowers.
P. indica coccinea—sprawling or climbing habit, smaller than *P. capensis*; 1-inch scarlet flowers. Rare.

POCKETBOOK PLANT. See CALCEOLARIA.

PODOCARPUS
southern yew
Podocarpaceae
55°–75°F.

Evergreen shrubs and trees, these make superb tub plants. They are long-lived, with narrow, fluffy leaves. Grow them in shade and let soil dry out between waterings. Grow new plants from seed.

P. macrophyllus maki—erect, slender, branching growth to 72 inches; waxy black-and-green leaves.

P. nagi—spreading growth, shiny green foliage.

POET'S JASMINE. See JASMINUM.

POINSETTIA. See EUPHORBIA PULCHERRIMA.

POISON PRIMROSE. See PRIMULA.

POLYPODIUM
polypody fern
Polypodiaceae
55°–75°F.

Easy tropicals for an indoor planter or a sunroom, these ferns are robust, growing to 30 inches, with bold-textured blue-gray fronds and colorful, usually orange-brown or white, scaly rhizomes. The latter are irregular, sometimes an inch in diameter. Grow polypodiums in shallow tubs or hanging baskets in a mixture of humus, sphagnum moss, and sand. Keep them moist and mist them often. Give them winter sun and shade in summer. Propagate them by rhizome division in spring.

P. aureum glaucum—wavy-edged blue-gray fronds to 24 inches. Called hare's-foot fern.

P. aureum mandaianum—similar to *P. aureum glaucum*, but with crested or fringed fronds.

P. formosum—to 24 inches, creeping bright green rhizomes, lacy fronds. Highly desirable.

P. lepidopteris—to 30 inches; striking silver-green fronds, deeply pinnate. Handsome.

P. polycarpon—yellow-green fronds.

P. subauriculatum—long, pendent fronds. Good for baskets.

POLYPODY FERN. See POLYPODIUM.

POLYSCIAS
aralia
Araliaceae
55°–75°F.

Comprising a handsome genus of treelike plants, polyscias species have either finely cut, somewhat fernlike leaves or simple, shiny dark green leaves. These plants like a bright location and a quickly drying soil that drains readily—they will not tolerate stagnant soil. Allow them to dry out between waterings. Provide good air circulation. Repot them at most every third year; they resent being disturbed. When well-grown, all polyscias species make fine specimen plants for a decorative accent. Propagate them from stem cuttings or by air layering.

P. balfouriana—to 40 inches; round, shiny dark green leaves.

P. balfouriana marginata—dark green leaves edged with white.

P. balfouriana variegata—to 48 inches; handsome, white-striped green leaves.

P. fruticosa—to 40 inches; finely cut, fernlike leaves. Very pretty.

P. guilfoylei—to 40 inches, saw-toothed leaflets. Especially good-looking.

POLYSTICHUM
holly fern
Polypodiaceae
55°–70°F.

Here is a charming group of ferns, some large, some small. Many have feathery fronds, some have stiff foliage. The leaves grow from a dark, partly underground, scale-covered crown. Keep soil moist and slightly acid. In warm weather, set plants outside in protected places for refreshing showers. Propagate them by root division in spring.

P. acrostichoides—attractive, feathery fronds to 24 inches. Called Christmas fern.

P. aculeatum—heavy, 24-inch fronds. Called hedge fern.

P. adiantiforme—24-inch bright green fronds. Called leather fern.

P. tsus-simense—low and compact growth; triangular fronds to 12 inches, with a bright metallic sheen. Good for terrariums.

POMEGRANATE. See PUNICA.

PONY PLANT. See BEAUCARNEA.

POOR-MAN'S ORCHID. See CYCLAMEN.

PORTEA   *Bromeliaceae*
                             55°–75°F.

Thirty-six-inch rosettes of dark green leaves and spectacular green-and-pink flower heads in summer or fall make this a valued plant. It will grow in shade but does best in sun, potted in osmunda that is kept well moistened. Grow new plants from offsets.

P. petropolitana extensa.

POTHOS. See SCINDAPSUS.

POWDER-PUFF CACTUS. See MAMMIL-LARIA and CACTUSES.

PRAYER PLANT. See MARANTA.

PRICKLY PEAR. See OPUNTIA and CAC-TUSES.

PRIMROSE. See PRIMULA.

PRIMULA   **primrose**
                             Primulaceae
                             45°–55°F.

January-to-April-blooming gift plants for cool locations, primroses offer color during the darker months. Pick off some flower buds to keep new flowers coming. Give them filtered morning or afternoon sun and keep soil consistently moist, as these plants need a lot of water. If the soil dries out, leaves turn yellow at the edges. A mixture of a pinch of iron vitriol (obtainable at nurseries) and two drops of ammonia in a quart of water usually turns them green again. Pot up young plants that grow at the side of the parent plant or sow seed.

P. malacoides—to 26 inches. Tiny flowers, white through rose to red, encircle tall stems and look like a mist. Called fairy primrose or baby primrose.

P. obconica—to 24 inches; big clusters of white, red, or purple flowers. Called poison primrose because the large leaves irritate some sensitive skins.

P. sinensis—to 24 inches, lobed leaves, flowers of many shades. Called Chinese primrose.

PROSTRATE COLEUS. See PLECTRAN-THUS.

PTERIS   **brake fern, table fern**
                             Polypodiaceae
                             55°–75°F.

Large and small ferns from the tropics, with feathery growth, pteris species are fine for table decoration or for the window garden. Give them sun in winter, shade in summer. Keep soil consistently moist and the humidity at 50 percent. Mist foliage frequently. Rapid growers under good conditions, pteris can be propagated easily by crown division.

P. cretica wilsonii—slender 12-inch fronds.
P. ensiformis victoriae—charming, variegated, 12-inch fronds. Called sword brake fern.
P. quadriaurita argyraea—24-inch white-and-green fronds.
P. tremula—fast-growing, yellow-green, 24-inch fronds. Called Australian bracken.

PUNCH AND JUDY ORCHID. See GON-GORA and ORCHIDS.

PUNICA   **pomegranate**
                             Punicaceae
                             55°–70°F.

Versatile, treelike plants to 12 inches, pomegranates have shiny little green leaves and orange or red flowers; in autumn they produce brownish red fruits. They are suitable for the window garden or for bonsai training. Give them full sun and let soil dry out between waterings. They like 50 percent humidity. The leaves fall off naturally in winter. Propagate them from seed.

P. granatum nana—red flowers.
P. granatum nana 'Chico'—orange flowers. Does not bear fruit.

PURPLE PASSION. See BROWALLIA.

PUSSY EARS. See CYANOTIS.

QUEEN-OF-THE-NIGHT. See SELENI-CEREUS and CACTUSES.

QUEENSLAND UMBRELLA PLANT. See SCHEFFLERA.

QUEEN'S TEARS. See BILLBERGIA.

QUEEN'S WREATH. See PETREA.

RABBIT'S-FOOT FERN. See DAVALLIA and FERNS.

RAINBOW CACTUS. See ECHINOCE-REUS and CACTUSES.

RAINBOW FLOWER. See ACHIMENES and GESNERIADS.

RAINBOW PLANT. See CRYPTANTHUS.

RAIN LILY. See ZEPHYRANTHES.

RATTAIL CACTUS. See APOROCACTUS and CACTUSES.

REBUTIA
crown cactus
Cactaceae
55°–75°F.

Diminutive, 1-to-5-inch, barrel-shaped plants with bright flowers in spring, rebutias like sun. These desert species require more water than most cactuses except in winter, when they can be grown cool (55°F.) and somewhat dry. Propagate them by division of clumps.

R. calliantha—gray-green globe, showy red flowers.
R. cristata—small globe with white spines, carmine-rose flowers.
R. deminuta—clustering small globes with rigid spines, beautiful orange flowers.
R. kupperiana—tiny globe, scarlet flowers.
R. minuscula—flattened globe with white spines, scarlet flowers.
R. pseudodeminuta—little globe, golden yellow flowers.
R. violaciflora—depressed olive-green globe, purple flowers.

RECHSTEINERIA
Gesneriaceae
60°–80°F.

Handsome South American gesneriads with velvety green leaves and red, pink, or orange-red tubular flowers in summer, rechsteinerias need more light than African violets. Don't grow them in strong sun, however. A west window is usually ideal. Water them moderately and feed them biweekly during active growth. Give them 50 percent humidity. After they bloom, leave the tubers in their pots and store them dry in a dim place (55°F.). After a three- or four-month rest, fresh growth will show; at that point, repot the plants for the next season. Grow new plants from seed or cuttings or by tuber division.

R. cardinalis—to 16 inches, heart-shaped dark green leaves, 2-inch brilliant red flowers. Called cardinal flower.
R. leucotricha—to 14 inches, green leaves covered with hairs, 1-inch rose-coral flowers. Called Brazilian edelweiss.
R. lineata—to 14 inches; hairy dark green leaves; small, nodding dark red flowers in clusters of a dozen or more.
R. macropoda—to 9 inches; soft, heart-shaped dark green leaves; brick-red flowers. Often confused with *R. cyclophylla*.
R. verticillata (or *R. purpurea*)—to 24 inches; pointed dark green leaves with serrated edges; hundreds of small, wine-spotted pink flowers. Called double-decker plant.

Easily grown at home is rebutia. This cactus has brilliantly colored flowers.
(Photograph by Johnson)

RED PEPPER PLANT. See CAPSICUM.

RESURRECTION PLANT. See SELAGI-
NELLA.

RHAPHIDOPHORA

shingle plant
Araceae
60°–80°F.

A climber to 24 inches, the shingle plant has
dark, leathery foliage similar to that of monsteras. Grow it in sun or shade and keep soil
consistently moist. Sponge the leaves occasionally to keep them shiny. Grow new plants from
cuttings.

R. celatocaulis.

RHAPIS

lady palm
Palmaceae
55°–75°F.

These tough, robust palms have fanlike fronds
on tall cane stems. Grow them at a north or west
window and soak the soil well, allowing it to
dry out before watering again. Provide an 8- or
10-inch container and repot only every three or
four years. Propagate these plants from offsets.

R. excelsa—to 60 inches, leathery glossy green
leaves with three to ten segments.
R. humilis—slender, more graceful, slightly
smaller in size than *R. excelsa.*

RHIPSALIDOPSIS. See EPIPHYLOPSIS
and CACTUSES.

RHIPSALIS

chain cactus,
mistletoe cactus
Cactaceae
55°–80°F.

This fine group of spineless, generally epiphytic
cactuses grows in a pendent fashion to 36 inches and has handsome, colorful berries in winter. It is attractive for baskets. Pot all species in
osmunda, fir bark, or an osmunda-and-soil mix
and grow them moist in summer, somewhat
dry in winter. Give them bright light. Grow
new ones from cuttings.

R. burchelli—cream-colored flowers, pink
berries.
R. capilliformis—cream-colored flowers, white
berries.
R. paradoxa—three-angled stems, white flowers, red berries.

RHODODENDRON. See AZALEA.

RHOEO

Moses-in-the-cradle
Commelinaceae
55°–75°F.

These easy-to-grow plants have fleshy, olive-
green, lance-shaped leaves and little white flowers in dense umbels almost hidden by two
boat-shaped bracts. Give them bright light and
constant moisture. Grow new plants from seed.

R. discolor—12-inch rosette of stiff, dark green,
almost black leaves with purple underneath.
R. discolor variegata—leaves with a white
border.

RHYNCHOSTYLIS

foxtail orchid
Orchidaceae
60°–80°F.

Large, 30-inch epiphytes, these orchids have
pendent scapes of small, highly scented summer flowers—dozens to a scape—and long,
leathery dark green leaves in fountain-like
growth. Pot them in fir bark kept moist at all
times—these plants do not rest. Grow them in
full sun. Buy new plants from specialists.

R. gigantea—great plumes of pink-and-white
flowers.
R. retusa—long stems with 1-inch rose-colored
flowers.

RIVINA

rouge plant
Phytolaccaceae
55°–70°F.

One of the handful of species in this genus, the
rouge plant has oval leaves, drooping clusters
of white flowers, and lustrous red berries on
and off throughout the year. This 24-inch plant
is very pretty at the window. Grow it in sun

with consistently moist soil. Propagate the rouge plant from cuttings.

R. humilis.

ROHDEA
Liliaceae
55°–75°F.

A favorite ornamental house plant in China and Japan, *Rohdea japonica* has white flowers and stiff, dark, handsome leaves that form a pleasing rosette. Place it in bright light and keep soil consistently moist. Slow-growing to 24 inches, it lives for years without much attention. Wipe foliage with a damp cloth once a month or so to bring out the glowing color. Decorative red berries are usually produced in fall. Propagate rohdeas from cuttings.

R. japonica—thick, leathery, dull green leaves.

R. japonica marginata—leaves with a white border.

ROSA
miniature rose
Rosaceae
50°–60°F.

The miniature rose, *R. chinensis minima*, makes a delightful house plant, becoming a perfect replica of the ordinary garden rose. Grow it in a sunny, well-ventilated place with the soil kept consistently moist. Give it biweekly feedings except in late fall and early winter. At that time, cut back the plants a little and store them in a cool but frost-free place (about 40°F.). In January start forcing bloom with some warmth and plenty of water. Mist plant tops daily and watch the foliage for spider mites. Propagate these miniatures from seed or stem cuttings. These are excellent varieties:

* 'Bo-Peep'—6 to 8 inches; double, star-shaped pink flowers in clusters.
* 'Cinderella'—to 10 inches; single, shell-pink-to-white flowers.
* 'Lilac Time'—4 to 10 inches; clusters of lavender flowers. Floriferous.
* 'Lollipop'—6 to 15 inches, clusters of brilliant red flowers.
* 'Pixie'—3 to 9 inches; single, pure white flowers.
* 'Tinker Bell'—5 to 10 inches, clusters of purple-red flowers.

ROSARY VINE. See CEROPEGIA.

ROSE. See ROSA.

ROSE APPLE. See EUGENIA.

ROSE-OF-CHINA. See HIBISCUS.

ROUGE PLANT. See RIVINA.

RUBBER PLANT. See FICUS.

RUELLIA
Acanthaceae
60°–70°F.

Graceful, with dark green leaves and pale pink, red, or white flowers from fall through spring, ruellias prefer full sun and soil kept barely moist. They react poorly to too much water. Good for basket or bracket, they are also dependable and colorful in the window garden. Grow new plants from cuttings.

R. amoena—to 24 inches; wavy, oval leaves; red flowers.

R. macrantha—to 40 inches, dark green leaves, rose-colored flowers.

R. makoyana—to 18 inches, silver-veined leaves, carmine flowers.

SAGO PALM. See CYCAS.

SAINTPAULIA
African violet
Gesneriaceae
65°–80°F.

Out of the original few African species of this gesneriad genus, hybridists have created thousands of cultivars, free-flowering and sturdy, much easier to grow. Foliage may be somewhat velvety or smooth, scalloped or wavy, lance- or heart-shaped, green or variegated. Flowers are single, double, or semidouble in shades of pink, blue, lavender, purple, or white. Be sure to sterilize the soil you pot them in or use mixes packaged specifically for these plants. Set them so that the crown is slightly above the soil line.

Give them bright light in spring and summer, some sun in fall and winter, and always good air circulation. Water soil moderately to keep it slightly moist, never wet. Apply only tepid water to soil and leaves, as cold water spots foliage. Bottom watering (filling the saucer under the pot with water) is often advised to ensure that the roots receive adequate moisture, but you can water from the top, too, and alternating the two methods is a good idea. In any case, arrange perfect drainage when you pot the plants and don't let them stand in water. Humidity of 40 to 60 percent is essential, and you can ensure it by setting plants on pebble-filled trays of water. Dry air causes leaf curl and bud drop. Propagate African violets from leaf cuttings or seed. There are countless hybrids. Here are some I enjoy:

'Alakazam'—double, lavender flowers.
'Big Boy Blue'—double, blue flowers.
'Bloom Burst'—semidouble, pink flowers.
'Chateaugay'—double, blue-purple flowers.
'Cochise'—semidouble, star-shaped, red flowers.
'Flash'—double, rose-pink flowers.
'Happy Time'—double, pink flowers.
* 'Honeyette'—red-and-lavender bicolor.
'Lady Wilson'—double, lavender-blue flowers edged with white.
* 'Miniature White Girl'—single, white flowers.
* 'Pink Rook'—double, pink flowers.
'Purple Knight'—single, dark purple flowers.
'Red Honey'—double, red flowers.
'Spitfire'—single, deep pink flowers fringed with white.
* 'Tinkle'—double, lavender flowers.
* 'White Doll'.
'White Perfection'—immense double flowers.
'Zorro'—double, lavender flowers.

SANSEVIERIA

snake plant
Liliaceae
55°–75°F.

These are indestructible, old-fashioned favorites with sharp-pointed, thick, fleshy leaves,

variously mottled and marked. Some kinds are upright, others form a ground-hugging rosette. They thrive in sun or shade. Tolerant of moisture, the plants remain attractive but hardly change in size if kept dry. Mature plants produce tall sprays of pretty, fragrant pink-white flowers. Propagate them from offsets.

S. *cylindrica*—to 60 inches; arching dark green leaves, several to a shoot.
S. *ehrenbergii*—slow-growing to 18 inches, blue leaves edged with white.
S. *parva*—dense rosette of green leaves to 18 inches, dark crossbands.
S. *trifasciata laurentii*—to 30 inches, lance-shaped leaves with yellow bands.

SATINWOOD. See MURRAEA.

SAXIFRAGA

strawberry geranium
Saxifragaceae
55°–75°F.

With geranium-like strawberry-pink-and-green leaves, these are charming trailing plants for dish gardens, terrariums, or window sills. Grow them in 3- or 4-inch pots or in baskets. Give them bright light with less moisture and warmth in winter. Watch out for mealy bugs. Grow new plants by potting the runners.

S. *sarmentosa*—to 20 inches, coarsely toothed reddish leaves veined in white, white flowers. The most common species.
S. *sarmentosa* 'Tricolor'—to 18 inches, dark-green-and-white leaves with rosy red edges and undersides. A veritable rainbow.

SCARBOROUGH LILY. See VALLOTA.

SCHEFFLERA
(BRASSAIA)

Queensland umbrella plant
Araliaceae
55°–75°F.

Tough tub plants to 60 inches with large decorative fronds and flowers in panicles, scheffleras like bright light and need water only once or twice a week. Neglect them and they still seem to thrive. They are good choices for public rooms; well-grown specimens become handsome trees. Grow new plants from seed or cuttings of half-ripened stems.

S. *actinophylla*—fast-growing, large, palmate leaves; greenish flowers.

S. *digitata*—hairy yellow leaves, 7 to 10 leaflets; greenish-yellow flowers. Needs a cooler location than S. *actinophylla*.

SCHIZOCENTRON Spanish shawl plant
Melastomaceae
55°–75°F.

For a sunny window, here is a fine, creeping basket plant with dark green, hairy leaves and pretty, vivid purple flowers starting in late winter and remaining colorful into summer. Keep soil consistently moist. Schizocentrons prefer partial shade. Propagate them from cuttings.

S. *elegans*.

SCHLUMBERGERA Christmas cactus
Cactaceae
55°–70°F.

Appealing jungle cactuses to 24 inches with scalloped, margined branches that distinguish them from Zygocactus varieties, schlumbergeras have cascades of flowers in pink, red, or salmon. They are an example of nature at her best. Give these epiphytes sun in fall and winter; keep soil barely moist then. In spring and summer, water the plants freely. In mid-October or November, give them sun during the day and twelve hours of uninterrupted darkness and cool nights (55°F.) so they will set buds. Humidity should be kept at 60 percent. They prefer a potting mix of leaf mold, sand, and shredded osmunda. A mature specimen is an impressive sight. Propagate schlumbergeras from cuttings.

S. *bridgesii*—red flowers. The old-fashioned Christmas cactus.

S. *bridgesii* 'Pink Perfection'—large flowers, bright clear red.

S. *bridgesii* 'Parna'—small bright red flowers.

S. *bridgesii* 'Salmonea'—scarlet flowers.

SCILLA. See Chapter 5.

SCINDAPSUS ivy arum
(POTHOS)
Araceae
55°–75°F.

Climbers to 36 inches with smooth dark green leaves splashed with yellow, white, or silver, these are vines amenable even to apartment conditions. Grow them in a light, well-ventilated place but avoid drafts. Keep soil consistently moist. They are nice for a basket or bracket. Propagate them from cuttings.

S. *aureus*—12-inch dark green leaves laced with yellow.

S. *aureus* 'Marble Queen'—green leaves richly streaked with white.

S. *aureus* 'Orange Queen'—apricot-and-yellow leaves.

S. *aureus* 'Silver Moon'—creamy yellow leaves.

S. *pictus argyraeus*—6-inch satiny green leaves edged with silver.

SCREW PINE. See PANDANUS.

SEA URCHIN CACTUS. See ECHINOPSIS and CACTUSES.

SEDUM stonecrop
Crassulaceae
50°–70°F.

Most of these succulents are low-growing, with thick or needle-like blue or green leaves. They have many uses in indoor gardens. Some have bushy growth, others form low mats, and some trail. All prefer full sun with soil dried out between waterings. Try them in dish gardens. Grow new plants from seed sown in spring.

*S. *adolphii*—bushy growth to 6 inches, yellow-green leaves, white flowers in spring.

*S. *dasyphyllum*—matted growth to 2 inches, blue-green leaves, pink flowers in summer.

*S. *lineare*—trailing growth to 6 inches, needle-like leaves, yellow flowers in summer.

S. *morganianum*—trailing growth to 36 inches, blue-green leaves, yellow flowers in summer. Called burro's tail.

*S. *multiceps*—shrubby growth to 4 inches, yellow flowers in summer.

SELAGINELLA
club moss
Selaginellaceae
55°–75°F.

Selaginella is a genus of small, ferny plants, excellent for terrariums and dish gardens. Some are attractive hanging plants, others are creepers good for covering the soil in the pots of larger plants. Grow them in shade. Soak soil and let it dry out between waterings. Give them 50 percent humidity. Avoid spilling water on the foliage: it causes rot. Propagate selaginellas from cuttings.

S. kraussiana—a 12-inch creeper with tiny bright green leaves.

S. lepidophylla—a 6-inch ball of foliage. Called resurrection plant, because, a dense mat when dry, it only needs soaking to live again.

S. martensii variegata—upright growth to 12 inches; lacy silver-tipped leaves.

S. uncinata—a creeper to 24 inches, blue-green leaves.

S. willdenovii—a nice climber to 10 inches, blue-green leaves.

SELENICEREUS
night-blooming cereus
Cactaceae
55°–75°F.

Climbing to 7 feet, generally epiphytic, and bearing exquisitely fragrant summer flowers, the night-blooming cereus can be tied to a bark support to grow tall or can be allowed to hang. It is too large for a window but is suitable for a plant room or sun porch. Provide a sandy soil and 5- or 6-inch pots; I use one-pound coffee cans, painted. These plants need sun in winter, shade in summer. Water them moderately in fall and winter, flood them the rest of the year. Give them 30 to 50 percent humidity. Get your camera ready when they bloom; no one will believe the dinner-plate size of these beauties. Propagate them from cuttings or buy young plants from a specialist.

S. donkelaari—7-inch white flowers.

S. grandiflorus—7-inch white or salmon-pink flowers. Called queen-of-the-night.

S. macdonaldiae—12-inch gold-and-white flowers.

S. pteranthus—12-inch white flowers.

SEMPERVIVUM
houseleek
Crassulaceae
50°–70°F.

These plants, composed of stemless, many-leaved rosettes growing from a half-inch to 12 inches across, soon become decorative, colorful mats. Starry white, yellow, or pink flowers in dense heads open in summer. The flowering rosettes die but are replaced by new ones. Easy to grow, these plants need morning or afternoon sun and moderately moist soil. They are nice for dish gardens. Grow new plants from the offsets in leaf axils.

S. arachnoideum—to 4 inches, white hairs, red flowers. Called cobweb houseleek.

S. montanum—to 6 inches; pointed, fleshy green leaves; purple flowers.

S. tectorum calcareum—to 12 inches, leathery light green leaves, pink flowers. Called hen-and-chickens.

SENECIO
cineraria
Compositae
50°–70°F.

These plants bloom for two to three weeks at Easter, with round heads of daisy-like flowers in vivid colors. Place them in a bright spot, not a sunny one, keep them as cool as possible, and water them heavily. They are best treated as annuals, grown each year from seed or purchased.

S. confusus—vining growth, orange or orange-red flowers.

S. cruentus—upright growth to 20 inches; white, pink, or purple flowers. The typical florists' cineraria.

SENNA. See CASSIA.

SENTRY PALM. See HOWEIA and PALMS.

SEVEN STARS. See ARIOCARPUS and CACTUSES.

SHINGLE PLANT. See RHAPHIDO-PHORA.

SHOOTING STAR. See CYCLAMEN.

SHOWER TREE. See CASSIA.

SHRIMP PLANT. See BELOPERONE.

SILK OAK. See GREVILLEA.

SINNINGIA
gloxinia
Gesneriaceae
60°–75°F.

Glamorous plants from tropical Brazilian forests, these gesneriads have single or double, tubular or slipper-shaped flowers in bright colors. Though some species are dormant in winter, today's hybrids bloom at intervals throughout the year. Tubers from mail-order suppliers can be started in spring or fall. Put one tuber in equal parts sand, loam, and peat moss in a 5-inch pot. Set the tuber hollow side up and cover it with soil. Keep the pot consistently moist in a warm place (about 60°F.) and maintain 40 to 50 percent humidity. When flowers fade, gradually decrease watering. Remove tops and store tubers in pots in a cool dark place. Keep soil barely moist. Rest the plants from six to ten weeks (no more, or tubers will lose vitality). Repot them in fresh soil in larger pots. Propagate these plants from cuttings or by root division.

S. barbata—4-to-6-inch bluish green leaves, white flowers streaked with red.

S. concinna—to about 2 inches; small, tubular lavender flowers with white throats.

S. pusilla—to 2 inches across; single, pale lavender, tubular flowers. Perhaps the tiniest house plant.

S. regina—to 10 inches across; velvety dark green leaves with white veins; 2-inch, dark purple, tubular flowers.

S. speciosa—to 12 inches across; ovate green leaves; nodding, pink or blue, slipper-shaped flowers.

S. speciosa 'Cinderella'—to 6 inches across; single, red flowers with white edges.

S. speciosa 'Dollbaby'—to 3 inches across; single, tubular lavender flowers.

S. speciosa 'Miss America'—double, red flowers with a variegated throat.

S. speciosa 'Wyoming Glory'—double, bright red flowers with white edges.

SMITHIANTHA
temple bells
Gesneriaceae
65°–80°F.

Handsome, richly colored foliage plants, these gesneriads have splendid, bell-shaped flowers from November through May. In March or April, start each rhizome in a 4- or 5-inch pot, 1 inch deep in soil. Grow the plants at an east or south window. Keep soil consistently moist. Humidity should range between 60 and 70 percent. After the plants bloom, store the rhizomes dry in the pots in a cool, shaded place for about three months. Then repot them and return them to a bright window. Propagate smithianthas from seed or by dividing the rhizomes.

S. cinnabarina—to 16 inches, serrated leaves with red hairs, orange-red flowers.

Cornell Series Hybrids—flowers of various colors: peach-colored ('Abbey'); red ('Carmel'); apricot-colored ('Cloisters'); straw-yellow ('San Gabriel').

S. multiflora—to 20 inches, deep green leaves, creamy unspotted flowers.

S. zebrina—to 30 inches, rounded dark green leaves marked with brown or purple and covered with silvery hairs, bright red flowers with darker spots.

SNAKE PLANT. See SANSEVIERIA.

SOLANUM
Solanaceae
50°–60°F.

These are dark-leaved shrubs from Brazil and Uruguay. The one with red or yellow fruit in winter is known as the Jerusalem cherry, a favorite Christmas gift plant. The other is prized for its fragrant, star-shaped flowers. These plants need bright light and soil kept barely moist. In winter, grow them cool, at about 50°F., with little moisture. If you want to hold them over from year to year, set them out in the garden in late spring and prune them back to about 10 inches. Propagate them from seed.

S. jasminoides—a shrubby climber to 72 inches, scented white flowers in fall or winter.

S. pseudo-capsicum—upright growth to 36 inches, white flowers, red or yellow fruit in fall and winter. Called Jerusalem cherry.

SOUTHERN YEW. See PODOCARPUS.

SPANISH SHAWL PLANT. See SCHIZO-CENTRON.

SPARAXIS
wand flower
Iridaceae
50°–70°F.

These bulbs with narrow leaves and arching flower stems make lovely, 20-inch pot plants. The 2-inch flowers appear in April and May. In fall, set five or six bulbs 1 inch deep in a 6-inch pot. At first, water them moderately. As growth develops, water them freely. Place them in sun, with night temperatures not exceeding 55°F., or flowers will wither. When bloom is over, allow foliage to dry off gradually; then store the plants in their pots absolutely dry. Repot them in fresh soil in fall. Propagate sparaxis by bulb division or from offsets.

S. grandiflora—yellow or purple flowers.

S. tricolor—multicolored flowers.

SPARMANNIA
indoor linden
Tiliaceae
55°–70°F.

Evergreen, with pale hairy leaves and charming white flowers in winter and spring, sparmannias are good window plants. They need bright light, plenty of water, and 40 percent humidity. Set them outside in summer. They can grow to 10 feet, so prune them occasionally to keep them in bounds. New plants can be started from stem-tip cuttings in spring.

S. africana—umbels of single flowers.

S. africana florepleno—double flowers.

SPATHIPHYLLUM
Araceae
55°–75°F.

Twenty-inch aroids from South America, spathiphyllums have shiny leaves and white flowers carried in bracts called spathes, resembling anthuriums. Bloom usually appears in winter, sometimes in summer or fall. Give plants a bright location and keep soil consistently moist except in winter; then grow them on the dry side. Propagate them from seed or by root division.

S. cannaefolium—to 24 inches, leathery black-green leaves.

S. clevelandii—to 20 inches, long leaves, white flowers.

S. commutatum—to 30 inches; broad, elliptical green leaves.

°S. floribundum—a dwarf to 14 inches, green leaves, white flowers.

S. floribundum 'Marion Wagner'—to 30 inches, quilted rich green leaves.

S. floribundum 'Mauna Loa'—to 30 inches, satiny dark green leaves.

SPIDER ORCHID. See ANSELLIA and ORCHIDS.

SPIDER PLANT. See CHLOROPHYTUM.

SPIDERWORT. See TRADESCANTIA.

SPIRAL GINGER. See COSTUS.

SPREKELIA
Aztec lily, Jacobean lily
Amaryllidaceae
55°–70°F.

The Aztec or Jacobean lily is a fine, 20-inch, bulbous pot plant with spectacular red flowers in spring before its foliage develops. Pot one bulb in a 6-inch container in late winter or spring. Set it in a sunny place and keep soil consistently moist from the time growth starts until September; then keep soil somewhat dry until December. They like 70 percent humidity. Propagate sprekelias at repotting time from the small offset bulbs by the parent bulb.

S. formosissima.

SQUILL. See Chapter 5.

STAGHORN FERN. See PLATYCERIUM and FERNS.

STANHOPEA   *Orchidaceae*
                                 60°–80°F.

These orchids with 30-inch leaves and large, late-summer spikes borne from the base of the bulb prefer warmth. The flowers, in scapes, are very fragrant and of vibrant color, but last only a few days. Grow these epiphytes in osmunda in slatted redwood baskets. Give them plenty of water all year, sun in winter and spring, some shade in summer and fall. They like 70 percent humidity. Buy new plants from a specialist.

S. insignis—one to four 4-inch, pale yellow flowers spotted with purple.

S. oculata—three to seven 6-inch flowers, usually yellow and orange.

S. wardii—three to seven 8-inch flowers, usually white with purple spots.

STAPELIA   carrion flower
                                 Asclepiadaceae
                                 55°–75°F.

Succulents from South Africa, stapelias bear star-shaped, five-petaled, usually evil-smelling flowers. These plants grow well in a sunny window. Soak the soil and then let it dry a little between waterings. Grow them almost dry in winter. They are not my idea of a good house plant but children are fascinated by the unusual shape. Grow new ones by dividing the root clumps.

S. hirsuta—to 12 inches, hairy brownish white flowers.

*S. variegata—to 6 inches, greenish yellow flowers with brown spots. Called star-flower.

STAR BEGONIA. See BEGONIA, Rhizomatous.

STAR CACTUS. See ASTROPHYTUM and CACTUSES.

STAR FLOWER. See HUERNIA, STAPELIA.

STAR JASMINE. See TRACHELOSPERMUM.

STAR-OF-BETHLEHEM. See CAMPANULA, ORNITHOGALUM.

STAR PLANT. See CRYPTANTHUS and BROMELIADS.

STEPHANOTIS   Madagascar jasmine
                                 Asclepiadaceae
                                 50°–70°F.

Scented waxy-white flowers cover stephanotis in June, July, and August, making a handsome foil for the dark green, leathery leaves. These vines thrive in an east or south window with 30 to 50 percent humidity. Mist them frequently to keep them in health. Water the soil about three times a week except in winter, when once a week is enough. Stephanotis can reach 15 feet, but my plant grown in a pot against a trellis has never exceeded 30 inches. Propagate stephanotis from cuttings in spring.

S. floribunda.

STEPLADDER PLANT. See COSTUS.

STONECROP. See SEDUM.

STRAWBERRY GERANIUM. See SAXIFRAGA.

STRELITZIA   bird-of-paradise
                                 Musaceae
                                 55°–75°F.

Large tropical plants with banana-like leaves and exotic flowers that resemble birds, these are a favorite of flower arrangers. Give the plants a sunny place and plenty of water except in winter, when they can be grown somewhat dry and cooler (60°F.). Only mature specimens

Streptocarpuses are charming gesneriads
that many indoor gardeners overlook.
(Photograph by C/D Luckhart)

with seven to ten leaves bloom. They are essentially terrace plants grown for their summer flowers, but I have also seen them in glorious color indoors in late spring. Propagate them by dividing the rootstocks or sowing seed.

S. nicolai—to 48 inches or more, white-and-purple flowers. Less showy than *S. reginae*.

S. reginae—slow-growing to 72 inches, orange-and-purple flowers. The more popular species.

STREPTOCARPUS
Cape primrose
Gesneriaceae
50–75°F.

These underrated gesneriads have rich green leaves and funnel-shaped flowers ranging in color from pure white, through pink, salmon, and blue, to deep violet. Place them in bright light or sun and keep soil consistently moist. Feed them moderately while they are in active growth. Different species rest at different times, so watch for signs of dormancy and don't try to force plants then. Stop fertilizing them and water them only to prevent wilting. After a few months, fresh leaves will appear. Then repot your plants. Propagate streptocarpuses from seed or cuttings.

S. dunnii—generally one large leaf, red flowers.

S. grandis—a curious, stemless plant with but one large leaf to 36 inches long; small blue flowers.

S. rexii—leaves to 8 inches long, blue or white flowers.

S. saxorum—a trailer to 16 inches, succulent leaves, 1½-inch lavender flowers.

STRING-OF-HEARTS. See CEROPEGIA.

STROBILANTHES
Acanthaceae
50°–70°F.

These attractive house plants grow to about 24 inches. They are not often seen but are quite decorative for a sunny place. One species bears pale purple flowers that look like foxgloves, another is valued both for its handsome blue foliage tinged with silver and for its blooms. Keep soil wet but not soggy and provide 30 to

50 percent humidity. These plants are only good for one season, so take cuttings in spring for new plants.

S. dyerianus—8-inch purple-green leaves, violet flowers.

S. isophyllus—4-inch, willowy, toothed leaves; pinkish or blue-and-white flowers.

SUN CACTUS. See HELIOCEREUS and CACTUSES.

SURINAM CHERRY. See EUGENIA.

SWAINSONA
Leguminosae
50°–60°F.

This 36-to-48-inch semiclimber has white or red flowers like sweet peas and lacy light green foliage. Grow it in sun. Water it heavily until September and then keep soil only fairly moist. Prune it after blooming. Stake your plants. Provide 30 to 50 percent humidity and pinch young shoots when they are a few inches tall. Mist foliage frequently. Grow new plants from seed.

S. galegifolia—red flowers.

S. galegifolia albiflora—pure white flowers.

S. galegifolia violaceae—rose-colored flowers.

SWEDISH IVY. See PLECTRANTHUS.

SWEET OLIVE. See OSMANTHUS.

SWISS CHEESE PLANT. See MONSTERA.

SWORD BRAKE FERN. See PTERIS and FERNS.

SWORD FERN. See NEPHROLEPIS and FERNS.

SYNGONIUM
arrowhead
Araceae
55°–75°F.

Desirable, old-fashioned pot plants, syngoniums grow to 30 inches, with green or variegated leaves that may be small or large, lance- or arrow-shaped. They are fast-growing and easy to maintain in bright light or shade, in soil or in water. Propagate them from cuttings.

S. *podophyllum*—a trailer, 6-inch leaves.

S. *podophyllum* 'Emerald Gem'—smaller rich-green leaves.

S. *podophyllum* 'Imperial White'—greenish white leaves.

S. *wendlendii*—a dainty creeper, dark green leaves with white veins.

TABLE FERN. See PTERIS and FERNS.

TARO. See COLOCASIA.

TEDDY BEAR PLANT. See CYANOTIS.

TEMPLE BELLS. See SMITHIANTHA and GESNERIADS.

TETRANEMA. See ALLOPHYTON.

THANKSGIVING CACTUS. See ZYGO-CACTUS and CACTUSES.

THUNBERGIA

black-eyed-Susan vine
Acanthaceae
50°–70°F.

Uncommonly beautiful plants, thunbergias bear cheerful flowers and have attractive foliage. Grow them in full sun, the soil kept consistently moist except in winter, when plants can remain almost dry. Train most of them to a trellis. They stay quite small indoors. *T. erecta* is best as a tub plant for the terrace. Propagate them from seed.

T. *alata*—a vine to 72 inches, dark-centered yellow-orange or white summer flowers.

T. *erecta*—shrubby growth to 72 inches, dark green foliage, blue summer flowers.

T. *grandiflora*—a vine to 60 inches, large pale blue flowers in fall. Called clock vine.

TIGER ORCHID. See ODONTOGLOSSUM and ORCHIDS.

TILLANDSIA

Bromeliaceae
55°F–75°F.

With tufted growth or palmlike foliage, tillandsias require full sun. Some of these bromeliads are small, attractive for dish gardens or terrariums; others are large, for the window. Pot them in osmunda and soil and keep them moist. Grow new plants from offsets.

T. argentea—to 4 inches; narrow, soft gray leaves; rose-colored inflorescence.

T. bulbosa—to 6 inches, bulbous base; contorted bright green leaves; erect and short red flower spike.

T. caulescens—to 10 inches, bright green leaves, handsome red flower bracts.

T. circinnata—to 8 inches; thick, strongly contorted grayish leaves coiling around an ovoid bulb; pink flower spike.

T. *cyanea*—to 30 inches, palmlike dark green leaves, pink flower spike with butterfly-like purple flowers in fall.

T. *fasciculata*—to 30 inches; tapering gray-green leaves, multicolored, tall flower spikes with violet petals.

T. ionanthe—to 3 inches. A tufted beauty with red-and-violet flowers in summer.

T. juncea—to 12 inches, yellow-and-red inflorescence in summer.

T. kegeliana—to 4 inches, silvery green leaves, bright red bracts.

T. stricta—to 6 inches; recurved, leathery, usually silvery leaves; flower crown yellow-white to rose-colored.

TI PLANT. See CORDYLINE.

TOLMIEA

piggyback plant
Saxifragaceae
55°–70°F.

The piggyback plant is a creeper that bears new plants on the back of old leaves. With fresh green, toothed foliage, it spreads to about 30 inches. Give it sun or full light and keep soil moist. It grows almost untended. Propagate by cutting the leaves bearing new plants and potting them in sand until they form roots.

T. *menziesii*.

TRACHELOSPERMUM   star jasmine
Apocynaceae
50°–60°F.

A twining woody vine, star jasmine has glossy green foliage and bears fragrant white or yellow, star-shaped flowers from early spring into fall. Prune your plants to the size you prefer. Star jasmine grows easily on a trellis. Give it sun and keep soil moist. It will stop growing at temperatures below 50°F., but in this semidormant state, budding is often initiated. Propagate it from cuttings in spring.

T. jasminoides.

TRADESCANTIA   inch plant, spiderwort
Commelinaceae
55°–75°F.

Fast-growing, small, trailing plants to 24 inches, tradescantias have oval, fleshy leaves in shades of cream, pink, red, mauve, gold, and dark green. Grow them in shade or sun and in soil that is allowed to dry out a little between waterings. They are decorative in a vase, basket, or pot. Grow new plants from cuttings.

T. blossfeldiana—green leaves with silver hairs, pale purple flowers.
T. blossfeldiana variegata—green-and-cream leaves.
T. fluminensis—green leaves, white flowers. Called wandering jew.
T. fluminensis albo-vittata—bluish-green-and-white leaves, white flowers.
T. laekenensis—green-and-pink leaves, white flowers.
T. multiflora—dark green leaves, white flowers.
T. navicularis—boat-shaped coppery green leaves, clusters of rosy purple flowers. Called chain plant.

TREE FERN. See BLECHNUM and FERNS.

TRICHOCEREUS   *Cactaceae*
55°–75°F.

This is a group of large, slow-growing columnar cactuses. Most have gray-green stems and only occasionally bear their lovely, night-blooming flowers indoors. Grow them in a sandy soil that drains readily. Give them full sun and allow them to dry out between waterings. In winter keep them dry and cool (45°F.). They make good tub plants where space permits. Grow new plants from seed.

T. johnsonii—deeply ribbed column to 60 inches, greenish white flowers.
T. spachianus—close-ribbed, torchlike growth to 24 inches; white flowers.

TRICHOSPORUM. See AESCHYNAN-THUS.

TULBAGHIA   *Liliaceae*
45°–60F.

These lilies on 20-inch stems are wonderful for growing indoors. They have pale-pink-to-lavender flowers and evergreen, strap-shaped leaves. Arrange several bulbs 1 inch apart and one half-inch deep in a 6-inch pot of sandy soil mixed with a little peat moss. Give them plenty of water and feed them bimonthly. In summer keep them in shade, but give them full sun the rest of the year. Blooms appear on and off from March to November. Propagate tulbaghias by dividing and repotting bulbs or from seed.

T. cepacea (or *T. fragrans*)—umbels of pink, scented flowers. Leaves without garlicky odor. Called pink agapanthus.
T. violacea—taller than *T. cepacea*, pale lilac-colored flowers. Leaves with garlicky odor.

TULIP. See Chapter 5.

TULIPA. See Chapter 5.

TULIP ORCHID. See ANGULOA and ORCHIDS.

UMBRELLA PLANT. See CYPERUS.

VALLOTA

Scarborough lily
Amaryllidaceae
50°–65°F.

The Scarborough lily is a large, bulbous plant to 24 inches with clusters of startling, funnel-shaped red flowers in summer and autumn, the perfect accent for a cool place. In spring or fall, place a bulb in a rather small (4- or 5-inch) pot; crowded roots induce good bloom. Be sure the point of the bulb is just below the surface of the soil. Grow it in an east or south window. Keep soil moderately moist except after flowering; then grow it not quite so wet for about a month, but never let it dry out completely. Feed it every three to four weeks during growth. Make new plants by potting offset bulbs when you repot the mature one.

V. speciosa.

VANDA

Orchidaceae
60°–80°F.

The orchids that made Hawaii famous are not native there but come from the Far East, the East Indies, and various other warm areas. Durable plants with succulent, strap-shaped leaves, they produce tall wands of flat flowers, some 5 inches across. Plant these epiphytes in fir bark in 6- or 7-inch pots and do not disturb them for several years. Keep the bark constantly wet, give plants full sun and up to 80 percent humidity. Grow new plants from offsets (called kikis).

V. caerulea—to 30 inches, blue flowers in fall. Called blue orchid.

V. rothschildiana—to 40 inches, 3-inch blue flowers in winter. Most desirable.

V. roxburghii—to 26 inches; pale-green-purple-and-brown flowers in summer and sometimes in spring, too.

V. tricolor—to 30 inches, generally yellow-to-pink flowers at various times of year.

VELTHEIMIA

Liliaceae
50°–70°F.

A prettier house plant than veltheimia is hard to find. It usually blooms at Christmas, producing yellow-green, rose-tinged flowers on 20-inch stalks. The leaves are large, glossy green, and wavy-margined. Place two or three bulbs in a 6-inch container with their tips above the soil line. Grow them in sun. Keep soil moist except in summer, when a dry rest of three to five weeks is needed. Make new plants by dividing the bulbs.

V. viridifolia.

VELVET PLANT. See GYNURA.

VENUS FLYTRAP. See DIONAEA.

VIOLET-STEMMED TARA. See XAN-THOSOMA.

VITIS. See CISSUS.

VOLCANO PLANT. See BROMELIA and BROMELIADS.

VRIESEA

flaming-sword plant
Bromeliaceae
55°–75°F.

Feathery, colorful plumes that last for several months make these bromeliads ideal north-window plants. Some kinds have pale green leaves, others dark green foliage marked and banded in brown; all have rosette growth. Pot them in equal parts osmunda and soil (these are terrestrials), and keep the "vase" formed by the leaves filled with water. Do not fertilize them or spray them with insecticides. They are good plants for room dividers. Buy new plants from specialists.

V. carinata—to 18 inches, smooth pale green leaves, yellow-and-crimson "sword." Called lobster claws.

V. hieroglyphica—to 30 inches, banded green rosette of leaves with darker markings.

V. malzinei—to 12 inches, plain green leaves, cylindrical orange spike.

V. splendens—to 20 inches, green leaves with mahogany stripes, orange "swords" on erect stems. Does not produce offsets, but new plants push up from center of mature growth.

WALKING IRIS. See NEOMARICA.

WANDERING JEW. See TRADESCANTIA, ZEBRINA.

WAND FLOWER. See SPARAXIS.

WATERMELON PILEA. See PILEA.

WATTLE. See ACACIA.

WAX PLANT. See HOYA.

WEDELIA   *Compositae*
50°–70°F.

This fast-growing, yellow, annual daisy brings summer to the window. It makes a good trailing basket plant with 3-inch, oblong, fresh green leaves. Grow it in sun and keep soil moist. Propagate it from cuttings in spring or summer or from seed.
W. trilobata.

WEEPING FIG. See FICUS.

WILLOW-LEAVED JASMINE. See CESTRUM

WIRE PLANT. See MUEHLENBECKIA.

WOOD SORREL. See OXALIS.

WOODWARDIA   chain fern
Polypodiaceae
55°–75°F.

Not usually thought of for indoor growing, these stiff and leathery, broad-fronded ferns make a pleasing contrast to more delicate and airy types. Grow them in bright light and keep soil barely moist, not wet. They like 30 to 50 percent humidity. Give them a deep soaking in the sink once a week. In summer set plants outdoors, where they will benefit from warm rains. They are usually large, to 30 inches across. Make new plants by rootstock division.
W. fimbriata—leathery, broad, massive fronds.
W. orientalis—long, drooping but stiff fronds.
    A good basket plant.

XANTHOSOMA   *Araceae*
65°–85°F.

Jungle plants from South America to 36 inches and with exquisite foliage, xanthosomas are handsome for accent. They need bright light, a consistently moist soil, and 70 percent humidity. Make new plants by dividing the tubers in summer.
X. lindenii 'Magnificum'—12-inch green-and-white leaves.
X. violaceum—deep green foliage with purple edges. Called violet-stemmed tara.

YELLOW GINGER. See HEDYCHIUM.

YESTERDAY-TODAY-AND-TOMORROW. See BRUNFELSIA.

YUCCA   bayonet plant
Liliaceae
50°–75°F.

Most species of yucca make handsome indoor plants, with white flowers and rich green, attractive leaves growing in rosette fashion. Yuccas like a sandy soil that drains readily and must be kept very moist almost all year except for a short time in winter. Keep them in bright light. Wipe the leaves with a damp cloth occasionally. Plants are easily shaped to a treelike appearance and thus are ideal for accents in rooms. Obtain new plants by air layering. Don't miss these—they are better than you think for indoor decoration.
Y. aloifolia—rosette of stiff, pointed, bluish-green leaves to 48 inches.
Y. aloifolia marginata—leaves variegated with yellow-cream coloring.
Y. filamentosa—nearly stemless rosette of bluish green leaves to 40 inches.
Y. whipplei—stemless rosette of stiff green leaves to 60 inches.

ZANTEDESCHIA   calla lily
Araceae
50°–70°F.

With stunning, funnel-shaped spathes on erect stalks, these make colorful additions to the winter indoor garden. Plant one rootstock to a 4- or 5-inch pot in a mixture of peat moss and sand in spring. Supply larger containers when plants become potbound, not before. Place the pots in a sunny window. Water them moderately at first, but when growth appears, keep soil fairly wet. Give them liquid plant food once a month. After they flower, allow the plants to ripen off naturally by gradually decreasing their water. Then rest them in pots in a shaded, cool spot and withhold water entirely. About August, take up the rootstocks and clean them; repot them in fresh soil. You can also start rootstocks in fall for summer bloom. Watch plants for spider mites. Propagate zantedeschias by separating and planting offset rootstocks.

Z. aethiopica—to 30 inches, white spathes. The common calla.
Z. albo-maculata—to 20 inches, spotted leaves, creamy white spathes.
Z. elliottiana—to 30 inches, vivid yellow spathes. Called golden calla.
Z. rehmannii—to 18 inches, rose-red spathes. The best kind for indoors. Called pink calla.

ZEBRA PLANT. See APHELANDRA.

ZEBRINA
wandering jew
Commelinaceae
55°–75°F.

From Mexico, these pretty, trailing silver-and-purple-leaved plants bear tiny purple flowers in spring and summer. Fast-growing, a basket specimen is a mass of color in sun or bright light. Keep soil consistently moist, or grow plants in a vase of water. They resemble tradescantias. Propagate zebrinas by rooting cuttings.

Z. pendula—to 16 inches, purple leaves with silver bands.
Z. pendula discolor—to 16 inches, brown leaves with purple and silver stripes.
*Z. pendula minima—to 12 inches; hairy, purple-red leaves with silver bands.
Z. pendula quadricolor—to 16 inches, purple-green leaves banded with white and striped with pink and purple.

ZEPHRANTHES
rain lily
Amaryllidaceae
50°–70°F.

These small, 8-to-14-inch, summer-through-fall-blooming bulbs have grassy foliage and pretty flowers—pink, white, or orange. Some bloom at night, others in the day. In spring, pot four or five bulbs in a 6-inch pot. Grow them in a sunny window and let soil dry out between waterings. In winter, store the bulbs dry in pots in a cool, shaded place. Propagate zephranthes by potting separately the small bulbs that grow next to the mature ones.

*Z. atamasco—day-blooming, 3-inch white flowers.
*Z. grandiflora—day-blooming, rose-pink flowers.
*Z. pedunculata—white evening flowers, partly open through the day.

ZINGIBER
ginger
Zingiberaceae
60°–80°F.

Commercial ginger requires little care. A reed-like plant to 30 inches, it has glossy, dark, grassy leaves and white flowers in summer. Grow it in sun or shade with soil kept moderately moist. Make new plants by dividing a mature specimen.

Z. officinale.

ZYGOCACTUS
Thanksgiving or crab cactus
Cactaceae
50°–70°F.

The many varieties of Z. truncatus, a popular plant from Brazil, bring color to the fall indoor garden. With toothed branches that distinguish them from Schlumbergera cactus varieties, they bear exquisite, dainty blossoms from late October into December. In general epiphytic, these 24-to-30-inch plants need sun in fall and winter and bright light in spring and summer. Keep soil (a mix of leaf mold, sand, and shredded osmunda) moderately moist except in fall, when roots should be somewhat dry and plants grown quite cold (50°F.) with twelve hours daily of uninterrupted darkness for a month to encourage bud formation. Fifty percent humidity is required. Pieces of stem root easily. These are fine varieties:

‘Amelia Manda’—large crimson flowers.
‘Gertrude W. Beahm’—bright red flowers.
‘Llewellyn’—orange flowers.
‘Orange Glory’—pale orange flowers with a white throat.
‘Symphony’—flowers in a delicate shade of orange, petals white at the base.

ZYGOPETALUM
Orchidaceae
50°–75°F.

Mostly epiphytic, from different parts of the world, these orchids have glossy green leaves and spikes of vivid, fragrant flowers in shades of green, blue, and purple. The majority are winter-blooming. Plant them singly in 6-to-8-inch pots of osmunda and keep them moderately moist in an airy, bright location. When growth stops in fall (as leaves are fully expanded), rest the plants without water and with only an occasional misting. They prefer 50 percent humidity. Sometimes the leaves get black streaks and are unsightly, yet the plants are not unhealthy. No remedy for this discoloration has as yet been discovered. Purchase new plants from specialists.

Z. *crinitum*—to 26 inches; 2-to-3-inch green-and-violet flowers in winter, several to a scape.
Z. *mackayi*—to 36 inches; 3-to-4-inch green-and-violet flowers spotted purple-brown, in winter, many to a scape.

Appendix 1
WHERE TO BUY PLANTS, SEED, AND EQUIPMENT

Alberts & Merkel Bros.
Boynton Beach, FL 33435

Orchids, anthuriums, and other tropical plants.

Buell's
Box 218
Weeks Rd.
Eastford, CT 06242

Gesneriad specialist.
Catalog.

W. Atlee Burpee
Philadelphia, PA 19132

Full range of seed;
fruit trees and
berry bushes; some
nursery stock.
Catalog.

L. Easterbrook
10 Craig St.
Butler, OH 44822

African violets.
Catalogs.

HHH Horticultural
68 Brooktree Rd.
Hightstown, NJ 08520

Specializes in alliums.

House Plant Corner
Box 810
Oxford, MD 21654

Plants and equipment.
Catalog.

International Growers Exchange
Box 397U
Farmington, MI 48024

Extensive selection of house plants.
Catalog ($2, deductible
from order).

Jones & Scully
2200 N.W. 33rd Ave.
Miami, FL 33142

Wide variety of orchids
suitable for growing indoors.

Logee's Greenhouses
55 North St.
Danielson, CT 06239

All kinds of house plants.
Catalog ($1).

Philodendron 'Multicolor.' (Photograph by C/D Luckhart)

McComb Greenhouses Rte. 1 New Straitsville, OH 43766	Unusual variety of exotic house plants. Catalog (35¢).
Oak Hill Nursery Binnie Rd. Box 25 Dundee, IL 60118	Exotic plants. List.
George W. Park Seed Co. Greenwood, SC 29649	Full range of seed—annuals, perennials, vegetables, tropicals, etc. Catalog.
Seaborn Del Dios Nursery Rte. 3, Box 455 Escondido, CA 92925	Wide variety of bromeliads.
Stokes Seeds Box 548 Buffalo, NY 14240	Vegetable and flower seed. Catalog.
Wilson Bros. Roachdale, IN 46172	Specialist in geraniums, including dwarfs and miniatures.

Artificial-light-growing equipment can be purchased at plant stores, some nurseries, and some hardware stores.

Appendix 2
PLANT SOCIETIES

African Violet Society of America
    Box 1326
    Knoxville, TN 37901

American Begonia Society
    10934 East Flory St.
    Whittier, CA 90696

American Boxwood Society
    Box 85
    Boyce, VA 22620

American Camellia Society
    P.O. Box 212
    Fort Valley, GA 31030

American Daffodil Society
89 Chichester Rd.
New Canaan, CT 06840

American Fern Society
The Field Museum
Chicago, IL 60605

American Fuchsia Society
Hall of Flowers
Garden Center of San Francisco
San Francisco, CA 94122

American Gesneria Society
P.O. Box 549
Knoxville, TN 37901

American Gloxinia & Gesneriad
Society, Inc.
Eastford, CT 06242

American Hibiscus Society
P.O. Box 98
Eagle Lake, FL 33839

American Ivy Society
128 West 58th St.
New York, NY 10019

American Lily Society
North Ferrisburg, VT 05473

American Orchid Society
c/o The Botanical Museum of
Harvard University
Cambridge, MA 02138

American Primrose Society
14015 84th Ave. NE
Bothell, WA 98011

American Rhododendron Society
24450 S.W. Graham's Ferry Rd.
Sherwood, OR 97140

Bromeliad Society, Inc.
Box 3279
Santa Monica, CA 90403

Cactus and Succulent Society
of America
Box 167
Reseda, CA 91335

International Geranium Society
11960 Pascal Ave.
Colton, CA 92324

Los Angeles International Fern Society
c/o Wilbur W. Olson
2423 Burrett Ave.
Redondo Beach, CA 90278

National Chrysanthemum Society, Inc.
8504 Laverne Dr.
Adelphi, MD 20783

National Oleander Society
315 Tremont
Galveston, TX 77550

Palm Society
7229 S.W. 54th Ave.
Miami, FL 33145

Saintpaulia International
Box 10604
Knoxville, TN 37919

GLOSSARY

Annual   A plant that grows from seed, flowers, and dies in one year.

Anther   The top part of the stamen of a flower, containing pollen.

Apex   The tip of a shoot or root.

Areole   The hairy cushion of a cactus from which arise spines, leaves (when present), lateral branches, and flowers.

Axil   The upper angle between a stalk and a stem arising from that stalk. *Adj.:* axillary.

Bedding plant   A plant used for seasonal display in a bed or tub.

Berry   A fleshy fruit with one or several seeds enclosed.

Bicolor   A flower that has more than one distinct color.

Bisexual   Two-sexed; of flowers possessing both stamens and pistils.

Bloom   *1:* A flower or a collective term for flowers. *2:* A waxy, powdery substance on the leaves of some succulents.

Bottom heat   In plant propagation, heat applied from below, usually via electric cables, to encourage rooting.

Bract   A leaf or leaflike structure, often scalelike, which usually has a flower in its axil.

Bud   A small lateral or terminal growth containing the developing parts of a leaf or flower.

Bulb   A swollen, underground, budlike structure with a shortened stem enclosed by fleshy inner and scalelike outer leaves. An organ of food storage and vegetative propagation.

Bulbil   A small bulb formed among flowers, in the axil of a leaf, or beside another bulb.

Bulbous   Having, bearing, or growing from a bulb.

Cactus   A member of *Cactaceae*, the cactus family. *Pl.:* cactuses, cacti.

Calyx   The outer part of a flower, composed of sepals, which may be separate or fused.

Canes   The jointed, erect stems of some orchids.

Chlorophyll   A green pigment found in the cells of algae and higher plants that is fundamental in the use of light energy in photosynthesis.

Column   The central body of a flower formed by the union of the stamens and pistil.

Corm   A swollen, underground stem surrounded by scales, serving as an organ of food storage and vegetative propagation.

Corolla   The part of a flower within the calyx, consisting of a group of petals, which may be separate or fused.

Cotyledon   *1:* The first leaves that emerge from a seed. *2:* A group of succulent plants of the *Crassulaceae* family.

Crocks Broken pieces of clay pot, also called shards, used in plant containers to improve drainage.

Crown The part of a plant between stem and roots.

Cultivars Cultivated plant varieties that are not propagated from seeds but by grafting or from cuttings.

Cutting A piece of stem, leaf, or root severed from a plant and used to grow a new plant.

Desiccation The drying-out of a plant through exposure to heat, usually scorching sunlight.

Division One means by which a single plant may be made into two or more plants.

Dormancy Resting period. *Adj.:* dormant.

Double Of a flower with more (usually many more) than the usual number of petals. Flowers with a few more than the usual number of petals are described as being semidouble.

Epiphyte A plant growing above ground level, usually relying upon another plant for support. Epiphytic plants gain nourishment from rain and debris, not from their host. *Adj.:* epiphytic. (Cf. *Terrestrial.*)

Eye *1:* An undeveloped bud. *2:* The differently colored center of a flower.

Family A taxonomic group made up of related plant genera. (See *Genus.*)

Fertilization Fusion of the male and female gametes (contained in the pollen and ovule of plants) to form an embryo. (See *Seed.*)

Fibrous (of roots) Thin and wiry.

Floret A single flower of a dense flower head.

Flower A specialized reproductive shoot, usually consisting of sepals, petals, stamens, and pistil.

Forcing The encouragement of plants into bloom earlier than their normal flowering season.

Genus A subdivision of a plant family, consisting of one or more species that show similar characteristics and that appear to have a common ancestry. *Adj.:* generic. *Pl.:* genera.

Germination The first stirrings of life in a seed as it grows into a plant.

Grafting The joining of a bud or stem of one plant to the root or stem of another, so forming a single plant.

Heel A piece of the main stem or old wood left on a side shoot taken as a cutting. It may assist rooting.

Hormones Chemical messengers that control such physiological processes as growth. As a component of rooting powder, they stimulate rooting in cuttings.

Hybrid A plant produced from the crossbreeding of two different species and possessing characteristics of both parents.

Inflorescence A general term for the flowering part of a plant, whether containing one flower or many, typically consisting of bracts, flower stalks, and flowers.

Inorganic Describing a chemical compound that does not contain carbon.

Internode The part of a stem between two nodes.

Lateral shoot A side shoot.

Layering The establishment of a new plant

when a shoot makes contact with the ground and roots into it.

Leaf mold   *1:* A mildew or mold on foliage. *2:* A partly or completely decayed compost of leaves; added to soil, it improves porosity and drainage.

Leggy (of growth)   Thin and elongated.

Long-day plant   A plant that flowers only in response to increasing day length. (Cf. *Short-day plant.*)

Midrib   The central vein of a leaf.

Mist   To spray a plant with a very fine jet of a liquid (usually water).

Monopodial   Growing only from the apex of a plant.

Node   The point on a stem where one or more leaves arise.

Offset (Offshoot)   A young plant growing at the base of its parent.

Old wood   Any growth made before the current season and hence more mature.

Organic   Containing carbon. Of substances formed from the decay of living material.

Osmunda   *1:* A genus of ferns. *2:* The chopped fibrous roots of such ferns, widely used for potting such epiphytic plants as bromeliads and orchids.

Ovary   The basal part of the female reproductive unit of a flower, containing the ovules and later the seeds.

Panicle   See *Raceme.*

Peat moss   Partially decayed bog moss fiber, widely used to improve porosity and drainage of soil and to increase its acidity. If not desirable, this acidity may be countered by the addition of lime to soil.

Pedicel   The stalk of an individual flower.

Peduncle   The secondary axis of an inflorescence, bearing the pedicels. *Adj.:* pedunculate.

Pendulous (Pendent)   Hanging or inclined downward.

Perennial   A plant that lives for more than two years, usually flowering each year.

Perianth   A collective term for the sepals and petals that together form the asexual part of the flower.

Petal   A segment of the corolla surrounding the sexual parts of the flower. Petals are usually brightly colored or marked.

Petiole   A leaf stalk.

pH   Mathematical notation expressing the degree of acidity or alkalinity of a soil or fertilizer; pH 7 is neutral, pH 8 is alkaline, pH 4 is very acid.

Photoperiodism   The response of plants, especially flowering and fruiting plants, to relative lengths of light and darkness.

Photosynthesis   In the tissues of green plants, a series of chemical reactions that synthesize organic compounds from water and carbon dioxide using the energy absorbed by chlorophyll from light.

Pinching out (Pinching back)   The removal or "stopping" of growing points to produce lateral shoots.

Pistil   The female organ of a flower, composed of ovary, stigma, and style.

Plunge   To bury potted plants in a bed of soil or ashes to prevent them from drying out outdoors in the summer.

Pollen   Dustlike grains produced by the anthers of flowering plants and carrying the male gamete in fertilization. (See *Pollination*.)

Pollination   The process by which pollen is transferred from an anther to a stigma.

Potbound (Rootbound)   Of a plant whose roots are crowded in a pot. This condition is easily observed when the pot is removed.

Pricking out (Pricking off)   The first transplantation of seedlings.

Pseudobulb   A structure formed from thickened stem internodes, typically a food- and water-storage organ of orchids.

Raceme   A type of pendulous inflorescence bearing its youngest flowers at the tip.

Receptacle   The apex of a flower stalk, bearing the flower parts.

Rhizome   A root-bearing horizontal stem, which often lies on or just beneath the ground surface. A rootstock.

Rootbound   See *Potbound*.

Rootstock   *1:* A rhizome. *2:* The lower half of a graft, supplying the root system.

Runner   A prostrate, above-ground stem that produces a daughter plant at its tip.

Scale   *1:* A small leaf or bract. The word is loosely applied to many structures, as, for example, in the terms *bud scale* and *bulb scale*. *2:* An insect pest.

Scape   A flower stalk, usually without leaves, arising directly from the ground, as seen in cyclamen.

Seed   A structure within a flower ovary produced by fertilization of an ovule and consisting of a seed coat, food reserves, and an embryo capable of germination.

Seedling   A very young plant arising from a germinating seed.

Semidouble   See *Double*.

Sepal   One of the segments of a flower calyx. Sepals are usually green and serve to protect the flower bud.

Shards   See *Crocks*.

Short-day plant   A plant that flowers only in response to shortening day length. (Cf. *Long-day plant*.)

Single   Of a flower with the normal number of petals.

Spadix   A flower spike, usually fleshy, surrounded by a spathe.

Spathe   A large bract, sometimes colored, surrounding a spadix.

Species   A group of plants sharing one or more common characteristics that make it distinct from any other group. (Cf. *Genus*.)

Spike   A single elongated inflorescence with sessile flowers occurring up the stem, the youngest at the top.

Stagnant (of atmosphere)   Unmoving.

Stamen   One of the male sexual parts of a flower, consisting of a filament (usually) and an anther that contains pollen.

Stigma   The part of the style that receives the pollen.

Stolon   A creeping, usually underground stem that roots at the nodes and produces plantlets.

Strain   A selection of a species raised from seed.

Style   The often elongated part of the female sexual organ of a flower, located between stigma and ovary.

Succulent   Storing water in specially enlarged spongy tissue of the roots, stems, or leaves; a plant of this type.

Sympodial   Of the kind of plant growth in which each new shoot, arising from the rhizome of the previous growth, is a complete plant in itself.

Systemic   A pesticide that is absorbed by a plant and poisons sucking insects.

Tender   Not capable of surviving frost.

Terrestrial   Growing at ground level and gaining nourishment from the soil. (Cf. *Epiphyte*.)

Top-dressing   The replacement of the surface layer of soil in a pot by fresh compost.

Transpiration   The loss of water from a plant by evaporation, mainly through the leaves.

Tuber   The swollen part of a stem, often formed beneath the ground each year, serving as an organ of food storage and vegetative propagation.

Umbel   An inflorescence in which three or more pedicels arise from the same level.

Variegation   Markings on leaves or petals resulting from localized failure in the development of pigment. *Adj.:* variegated.

Vegetative propagation   Asexual reproduction in which part of a plant is detached and subsequently becomes a new plant.

Vein   A strand of strengthening and conductive tissue running through a leaf or modified leaf.

Virus   A disease-causing agent that invades living cells.

Whorl   A type of inflorescence in which the flowers all arise from one point.

BIBLIOGRAPHY

Abraham, George. *The Green Thumb Book of Indoor Gardening.* Englewood Cliffs, NJ: Prentice-Hall, 1967.

Bailey, Liberty H. *The Standard Cyclopedia of Horticulture.* 3d rev. ed. 3 vols. London and New York: Macmillan, 1942.

Bailey, Liberty H. and Ethel Zoe. *Hortus Third.* New York: Macmillan, 1976.

Ballard, Ernesta D. *Garden in Your House.* New York: Harper & Row, 1971.

Brooklyn Botanic Garden. *Handbook on Biological Control of Plant Pests.* Brooklyn: Brooklyn Botanic Garden, 1960.

———. *A House Plant Primer.* Brooklyn: Brooklyn Botanic Garden, 1972.

———. *House Plants.* Brooklyn: Brooklyn Botanic Garden, 1965.

———. *Plants and Gardens: Gardening under Artificial Light.* Brooklyn: Brooklyn Botanic Garden, 1970.

Cherry, Elaine C. *Fluorescent Light Gardening.* Princeton: Van Nostrand, 1965.

Chidamian, Claude. *The Book of Cacti and Other Succulents.* New York: American Garden Guild and Doubleday, 1958.

Elbert, George and Virginia. *Plants That Really Bloom Indoors.* New York: Simon & Schuster, 1974.

Evans, Charles M., and Pliner, Roberta Lee. *Rx for Ailing House Plants.* New York: Random House, 1974.

Fitch, Charles Marden. *The Complete Book of Houseplants.* New York: Hawthorn Books, 1972.

Free, Montague. *Plant Propagation in Pictures.* New York: American Garden Guild and Doubleday, 1957.

Graf, Alfred B. *Exotica. Series Three.* 9th rev. ed. E. Rutherford, NJ: Julius Roehrs, 1978.

———. *Tropica.* 2d ed. E. Rutherford, NJ: Julius Roehrs (distrib. Charles Scribner's Sons), 1981.

Haring, Elda. *The Seedling Handbook.* New York: Literary Guild of America, 1968.

Hay, Roy, and Synge, Patrick M. *The Color Dictionary of Flowers and Plants for Home and Garden.* New York: Crown, 1969.

Kramer, Jack. *Cacti As Decorative Plants.* New York: Charles Scribner's Sons, 1974.

———. *Ferns and Palms for Interior Decoration.* New York: Charles Scribner's Sons, 1972.

———. *Grow Your Own Plants.* New York: Charles Scribner's Sons, 1971.

———. *Hanging Gardens.* New York: Charles Scribner's Sons, 1971.

———. *Your Homemade Greenhouse.* New York: Walker, 1975. (Paperback ed.: Cornerstone Library.)

Kranz, Frederick H. and Jacqueline L. *Gardening Indoors under Lights.* New York: Viking, 1976.

Lamb, Edgar and Brian. *Pocket Encyclopedia of Cacti.* New York: Macmillan, 1969.

Loewer, Peter. *The Indoor Water Gardener's How-To Handbook.* New York: Walker, 1973.

Nicolaisen, Age. *The Pocket Encyclopedia of Plants and Flowers.* New York: Macmillan, 1974.

Perry, Frances. *Flowers of the World.* London: Hamlyn, 1972.

Royal Horticultural Society. *Dictionary of Gardening.* Ed. Frank Chittenden. 2d ed. 4 vols. London and New York: Oxford University Press, 1965. *Supplement.* Ed. Patrick M. Synge. 2d ed. 1969.

Westcott, Cynthia. *The Gardener's Bug Book.* New York: Doubleday, 1964.

Wilson, Helen Van Pelt. *African Violet Book.* New York: Hawthorn, 1970.

————. *The Joy of Geraniums.* 2d ed. New York: Morrow, 1972.

Wyman, Donald. *Wyman's Gardening Encyclopedia.* London and New York: Macmillan, 1972.

INDEX

Italicized page numbers in this index indicate the location of illustrations.

Plants *not* included in the index may be found in Chapter Eight, pages 103 through 221, by both genus and common name.